✷ *Highlights* ✷
of this
Study Guide

❋ Each Chapter of this **Study Guide** includes—

✷ Chapter **Introduction**

✷ Easy to Read & Understand, Comprehensive **Outline**

✷ **True-False** Questions

✷ **Fill-In** Questions

✷ **Multiple-Choice** Questions

✷ **Short Essay** Questions

✷ **Issue Spotters**—hypothetical fact problems & black letter law questions on key issues

❋ This **Study Guide** also contains an **Answer Appendix** with answers to all of the Questions & explanations of the Answers

Study Guide

to Accompany

Business Law Today: The Essentials

Text and Summarized Cases—E-Commerce, Legal, Ethical, and International Environment

Seventh Edition

ROGER LeROY MILLER
Institute for University Studies
Arlington, Texas

GAYLORD A. JENTZ
Herbert D. Kelleher
Emeritus Professor of Business Law
MSIS Department
University of Texas at Austin

Prepared by

William Eric Hollowell
Member of
  U.S. Supreme Court Bar
  Minnesota State Bar
  Florida State Bar

Roger LeRoy Miller
Institute for University Studies
Arlington, Texas

THOMSON
WEST

Australia · Canada · Mexico · Singapore · Spain · United Kingdom · United States

THOMSON

WEST

Study Guide to Accompany *Business Law Today: The Essentials*, Seventh Edition

By Roger LeRoy Miller and Gaylord A. Jentz

Vice President/Editorial Director:
Jack W. Calhoun

Publisher for Business Law & Accounting:
Rob Dewey

Acquisitions Editor:
Steven Silverstein

Senior Developmental Editor:
Jan Lamar

Executive Marketing Manager:
Lisa Lysne

Production Editors:
Bill Stryker and Anne Sheroff

Manufacturing Coordinator:
Charlene Taylor

Printer:
West Printing Company

Table of Contents

To the Student

This **Study Guide** is designed to help you read and understand **Business Law Today: The Essentials,** Seventh Edition.

How the *Study Guide* Can Help You

This *Study Guide* can help you maximize your learning, subject to the constraints and the amount of time you can allot to this course. There are at least six specific ways in which you can benefit from using this guide.

1. The *Study Guide* can help you decide which topics are the most important. Because there are so many topics analyzed in each chapter (and in *all* textbooks), many students become confused about what is essential and what is not. You cannot, of course, learn everything; this *Study Guide* can help you concentrate on the crucial topics in each chapter.

2. If you are forced to miss a class, you can use this *Study Guide* to help you learn the material discussed in your absence.

3. There is a possibility that the questions that you are required to answer in this *Study Guide* are representative of the types of questions that you will be asked during examinations.

4. You can use this *Study Guide* to help you review for examinations.

5. This *Study Guide* can help you decide whether you really understand the material. Don't wait until examination time to find out!

6. Finally, the questions in this *Study Guide* will help you develop critical thinking skills that you can use in other classes and throughout your career.

The Contents of the *Study Guide*

Business law sometimes is considered a difficult subject because it uses a specialized vocabulary and also takes most people much time and effort to learn. Those who work with and teach business law believe that the subject matter is exciting and definitely worthy of your efforts. Your text, **Business Law Today: The Essentials,** Seventh Edition, and this student learning guide have been written for the precise purpose of helping you learn the most important aspects of business law. We always try to keep you, the student, in mind.

Every chapter includes the following sections:

1. What This Chapter Is About: You are introduced to the main subject matter of each chapter in this section.

2. Chapter Outline: Using an outline format, the salient points in each chapter are presented.

3. True-False Questions: Ten true-false questions are included for each chapter. Generally, these questions test knowledge of terminology and principles. The answers are given at the back of the book. Whenever an answer is false, the reasons why it is false are presented at the back of the book also.

4. Fill-in Questions: Here you are asked to choose between two alternatives for each space that needs to be filled in. Answers are included at the back of the book.

5. Multiple-Choice Questions: Ten multiple-choice questions are given for each chapter. The answers, along with an explanation, are included at the back of this book.

6. Short Essay Questions: Two essay questions are presented for each chapter.

7. Issue Spotters: These questions alert you to certain principles within the chapter. Brief answers to these questions are included at the end of this text.

How to Use this Study Guide

     What follows is a recommended strategy for improving your grade in your business law class. It may seem like a lot of work, but the payoffs will be high. Try the entire program for the first three or four chapters. If you then feel you can skip some steps safely, try doing so and see what happens.

     For each chapter we recommend you follow the sequence of steps below:

1. Read the What This Chapter Is About and Chapter Outline.

2. Read any of the Concept Summaries that may be included in the chapter you are studying in *Business Law Today: The Essentials,* **Seventh Edition**.

3. Read about half the textbook chapter (unless it is very long), being sure to underline only the most important topics (which you should be able to recognize after having read no more than two chapter outlines in this *Study Guide*). Put a check mark by the material that you do not understand.

4. If you find the textbook's chapter easy to understand, you might want to finish reading it. Otherwise, rest for a sufficient period before you read the second half of the chapter. Again, be sure to underline only the most important points and to put a check mark by the material you find difficult to understand.

5. After you have completed the entire textbook chapter, take a break. Then read only what you have underlined throughout the entire chapter.

6. Now concentrate on the difficult material, for which you have left check marks. Reread this material and *think about it*; you will find that it is very exciting to figure out difficult material on your own.

7. Now do the True-False Questions, Fill-In Questions, and Multiple-Choice Questions. Compare your answers with those at the back of this book. Make a note of the questions you have missed and find the pages in your textbook upon which these questions are based. If you still don't understand, ask your instructor.

8. If you still have time, do one or both of the essay questions.

9. Before your examination, study your class notes. Then review the chapter outline in the text. Reread the Chapter Outline in this *Study Guide*, then redo all of the questions within each chapter. Compare your answers with the answers at the back of this *Study Guide*. Identify your problem areas and reread the relevant pages in ***Business Law Today: The Essentials,*** **Seventh Edition**. Think through the answers on your own.

If you have followed the strategy outlined above, you should feel sufficiently confident and be relaxed enough to do well on your exam.

Study Skills for *Business Law Today: The Essentials,* Seventh Edition

Every student has a different way to study. We give several study hints below that we think will help any student to master the textbook ***Business Law Today: The Essentials,*** **Seventh Edition**. These skills involve outlining, marking, taking notes, and summarizing. You may not need to use all these skills. Nonetheless, if you do improve your ability to use them, you will be able to understand more easily the information in ***Business Law Today: The Essentials,*** **Seventh Edition**.

MAKING AN OUTLINE

An outline is simply a method for organizing information. The reason an outline can be helpful is that it shows how concepts relate to each other. Outlining can be done as part of your reading or at the end of your reading, or as a rereading of each section within a chapter before you go on to the next section. Even if you do not believe that you need to outline, our experience has been that the act of *physically* writing an outline for a chapter helps most students to improve greatly their ability to retain the material in ***Business Law Today: The Essentials,*** **Seventh Edition** and master it, thereby obtaining a higher grade in the class, with less effort.

To make an effective outline you have to be selective. Outlines that contain all the information in the text are not very useful. Your objective in outlining is to identify main concepts and to subordinate details to those main concepts. Therefore, your first goal is to *identify the main concepts in each section*. Often the large, first-level headings within your textbook are sufficient as identifiers of the major concepts within each section. You may decide, however, that you want to phrase an identifier in a way that is more meaningful to you. In any event, your outline should consist of several levels written in a standard outline format. The most important concepts are assigned a roman numeral; the second most important a capital letter; the third most important, numbers; and the fourth most important, lower-case letters. Even if you make an outline that is no more than the headings in the text, you will be studying more efficiently than you would be otherwise. As we stated above, the process of physically writing the words will help you master the material.

MARKING A TEXT

From kindergarten through high school you typically did not own your own text-books. They were made available by the school system. You were told not to mark in them. Now that you own your own text for a course, your learning can be greatly improved by marking your text. There is a trade-off here. The more you mark up your text-book, the less you will receive from your bookstore when you sell it back at the end of the semester. The benefit is a better understanding of the subject matter, and the cost is the reduction in the price you receive for the resale of the text. Additionally, if you want a text that you can mark with your own notations, you necessarily have to buy a new one or a used one that has no markings. Both carry a higher price tag than a used textbook with markings. Again there is a trade-off.

Different Ways of Marking The most commonly used form of marking is to underline important points. The second most commonly used method is to use a felt-tipped highlighter, or marker, in yellow or some other transparent color. Marking also includes circling, numbering, using arrows, brief notes, or any other method that allows you to remember things when you go back to skim the pages in your textbook prior to an exam.

Why Marking Is Important Marking is important for the same reason that outlining is—it helps you to organize the information in the text. It allows you to become an *active* participant in the mastery of the material. Researchers have shown that the physical act of marking, just like the physical act of outlining, helps you better retain the material. The better the material is organized in your mind, the more you will remember. There are two types of readers—passive and active. The active reader outlines or marks. Active readers typically do better on exams. Perhaps one of the reasons that active readers retain more is because the physical act of outlining and/or marking requires greater concentration. It is through greater concentration that more is remembered.

Points to Remember When Marking

1. Read one section at a time before you do any extensive marking. You can't mark a section until you know what is important and you can't know what is important until you read the whole section.

2. Don't over mark. Just as an outline cannot contain everything that is in a text (or in a lecture), marking can't be of the whole book. Don't fool yourself into thinking you've done a good job just because each page is filled up with arrows, asterisks, circles, and underlines. When you go back to review the material you won't remember what was important. The key is *selective* activity. Mark each page in a way that allows you to see the most important points at a glance. You can follow up your marking by writing out more in your subject outline.

SUMMARIZING THE MATERIAL

Even if a certain chapter has a concept summary, it is still worthwhile for you to make your own summary points. The reason is that the more active you are as a reader, the better you will understand the material.

Summarization helps you in your reading comprehension. It is the final step in reviewing the book. There is probably nothing else you can do that works as well to help you remember what your textbook has to say.

The importance of summarization is that the notes you make are in your own words, not in the words of the author. Writing down a summary in your own words is the most effective use of your time. This allows you to process the information into your own memory by being required to think about it. You also have to make it part of your vocabulary. Whenever you cannot state important legal concepts in your own words, you probably haven't understood the concepts necessary to master the material. Indeed, summary notes are a good way to determine whether you have actually understood something. Don't simply make a mechanical listing of quotes taken right out of the textbook. Rather, you should make summary notes using complete sentences with correct grammar. This forces you to develop your ideas logically and clearly. Also, summary notes written in this matter can be more easily remembered.

Be Brief. Your notes should condense the information in the text into statements that summarize the concepts. It is when you force yourself to make the statements brief that you best learn the material. By making only brief summary notes, you have to think about the essence of each concept and present it in a form that is compact enough to remember. You should typically have no more than a one-paragraph summary for each important topic in the chapter.

What Format to Use? The authors find that using 5" x 8" cards is the best way to take summary notes. Don't fill up each note card. You need to leave room to make additional notes later on when you are reviewing for the final exam. That is to say, leave margins for further notes and study markings. Additionally, if you leave enough room, you can integrate the notes that you take during lectures onto these summary note cards.

Another reason to place your summary notes on 5" x 8" cards is because in so doing you have a set of flash cards that you can use in studying for a final exam.

HOW TO STUDY AND TAKE EXAMS

There is basically one reason why you have purchased the *Study Guide*—to improve your exam grade. By using this *Study Guide* assiduously, you will have the confidence to take your mid-terms and final examinations and to do well. The *Study Guide*, however, should not just be used a day before each exam. Rather, the guide is most helpful if you use it at the time that you read the chapter. That is to say, after you read a chapter in *Business Law Today: The Essentials,* **Seventh Edition** you should directly go to the appropriate chapter in the *Study Guide*. This systematic review technique is the most effective study technique you can use.

Besides learning the concepts in each chapter as well as possible, there are additional strategies for taking exams. You need to know in advance what type of exam you are going to take—essay or objective or both. You need to know which reading materials and lectures will be covered. For both objective and essay exams (but more importantly for the former) you need to know if there is a penalty for guessing incorrectly. If there is, your strategy will be different: you will usually only mark what you are certain of. Finally, you need to know how much time will be allowed for the exam.

FOLLOWING DIRECTIONS

Students are often in a hurry to start an exam so they take little time to read the instructions. The instructions can be critical, however. In a multiple-choice exam, for example, if there is no indication that there is a penalty for guessing, then you should never leave a question unanswered. Even if there only remains a few minutes at the end of the exam, you should guess for those questions about which you are uncertain.

Additionally, you need to know the weight given to each section of an exam. In a typical multiple-choice exam, all questions have equal weight. In some exams, particularly those involving essay questions, different parts of the exam carry different weights. You should use these weights to apportion your time accordingly. If an essay part of an exam accounts for only 20 percent of the total points on the exam, you should not spend 60 percent of your time on the essay.

You need to make sure you are answering the question correctly. Some exams require a No. 2 lead pencil to fill in the dots on a machine-graded answer sheet. Other exams require underlining or circling. In short, you have to look at the instructions carefully.

Lastly, check to make sure that you have all the pages of the examination. If you are uncertain, ask the instructor or the exam proctor. It is hard to justify not having done your exam correctly because you failed to answer all the questions. Simply stating that you did not have them will pose a problem for both you and your instructor. Don't take a chance. Double check to make sure.

TAKING OBJECTIVE EXAMINATIONS

The most important point to discover initially with any objective test is if there is a penalty for guessing. If there is none, you have nothing to lose by guessing. In contrast, if a half-point is subtracted for each incorrect answer, then you probably should not answer any question for which you are purely guessing.

Students usually commit one of two errors when they read objective-exam questions: (1) they read things into the questions that don't exist, or (2) they skip over words or phrases.

Most test questions include key words such as:

- all
- always
- never
- only

If you miss these key words you will be missing the "trick" part of the question. Also, you must look for questions that are only *partly* correct, particularly if you are answering true/false questions.

Never answer a question without reading all of the alternatives. More than one of them may be correct. If more than one of them seems correct, make sure you select the answer that seems the most correct.

Whenever the answer to an objective question is not obvious, start with the process of elimination. Throw out the answers that are clearly incorrect. Even with objective exams in which there is a penalty for guessing, if you can throw out several obviously incorrect answers, then you may wish to guess among the remaining ones because your probability of choosing the correct answer is high.

Typically, the easiest way to eliminate incorrect answers is to look for those that are meaningless, illogical, or inconsistent. Often test authors put in choices that make perfect sense and are indeed true, but they are not the answer to the question under study.

WRITING ESSAY EXAMS

To write an essay exam, you should be prepared. One way of being prepared is to practice writing timed essays. In other words, find out in advance how much time you will have for each essay question, say fifteen minutes, and then practice writing an answer to a sample essay question during a fifteen-minute time period. This is the only way you will develop the skills needed to pace yourself for an essay exam. Do your timed essay practice without using the book, because most essay exams are closed book.

Usually you can anticipate certain essay exam questions. You do this by going over the major concept headings, either in your lecture notes or in your text; search for the themes that tie the materials together and then think about questions that your instructor might ask you. You might even list possible essay questions as a review device; then write a short outline for each of those most likely questions.

As with objective exams, you need to read the directions to the essay questions carefully. It's best to write out a brief outline *before* you start writing. The outline should present your conclusion in one or two sentences, then your supporting argument. It is important to stay on the subject. We can tell you from first hand experience that no instructor likes to read answers to unasked questions.

Finally, make a strong attempt to write legibly. Again speaking from experience, we can tell you that it's easier to be favorably inclined to a student's essay if we don't have to reread it five times to decipher the handwriting.

Acknowledgments

We wish to thank Suzanne Jasin of K & M Consulting for her expert design and composition of this guide.

We welcome comments and criticisms to help us make this guide even more useful. All errors are our sole responsibility.

Roger LeRoy Miller
Eric Hollowell

Chapter 1:
The Historical and Constitutional Foundations

WHAT THIS CHAPTER IS ABOUT

The first chapters provide the background for the entire course. Chapter 1 sets the stage. From this chapter, you must understand that (1) the **law** consists of enforceable rules governing relationships among individuals and between individuals and their society, (2) in applying these rules, a judge cannot fit a case to suit a rule, but must fit (or find) a rule to suit the case, and (3) in fitting (or finding) a rule, a judge must also supply reasons for the decision. This chapter also emphasizes that the Constitution is the supreme law in the United States and discusses some of the constitutional limits on the law.

CHAPTER OUTLINE

I. **SOURCES OF AMERICAN LAW**

    A. **CONSTITUTIONAL LAW**
The U.S. Constitution distributes power among the branches of government. It is the supreme law of the land. Any law that conflicts with it is invalid. The states also have constitutions, but the federal constitution prevails if their provisions conflict.

    B. **STATUTORY LAW**
Statutes and ordinances are enacted by Congress and by state and local legislative bodies. Uniform laws and model codes are created by panels of experts and scholars and adopted at the option of each state's legislature.

    C. **ADMINISTRATIVE LAW**
Administrative law consists of the rules and regulations issued by administrative agencies, which derive their authority from the legislative and executive branches of government.

        1. **Agency Creation**
Congress passes enabling legislation to set out the powers of an agency. These include powers of the legislature (rulemaking), the executive branch (investigation and enforcement), and the courts (adjudication).

        2. **Rulemaking**
Begins with publication of a notice of proposed rulemaking in the *Federal Register.* A public hearing is held. Proponents of the rule and its opponents present evidence and question witnesses. After the hearing, the agency drafts a final rule and publishes it in the *Federal Register.*

        3. **Investigation and Enforcement**
Agencies can compel individuals or organizations to hand over specified books, papers, records, or documents. Through on-site inspections and testing, agencies also gather information.

        4. **Adjudication**
If a rule violation is suspected, an agency may order a hearing. An administrative law judge (ALJ) presides and may order a party to pay a fine or stop doing some activity. The order may be appealed to the board or commission that runs the agency or to a federal appeals court.

D. CASE LAW AND COMMON LAW DOCTRINES
Case law includes courts' interpretations of constitutional provisions, statutes, and administrative rules. Because statutes often codify common law rules, courts often rely on the common law as a guide to the intent and purpose of a statute. Case law governs all areas not covered by statutes or other rules.

II. THE COMMON LAW TRADITION

A. COMMON LAW
The American legal system, based on the decisions judges make in cases, is a **common law** system, which involves the application of principles applied in earlier cases with similar facts.

B. *STARE DECISIS*
The use of precedent in a common law system is known as the doctrine of ***stare decisis***. *Stare decisis* makes the legal system more efficient, just, uniform, stable, and predictable. When there is no precedent, a court may look at other legal principles and policies, social values, or scientific data.

C. EQUITABLE REMEDIES
As a rule, courts grant an equitable remedy only when the remedy at law is inadequate.

1. Remedies at Law
Remedies at law include awards of land, money, and items of value. A jury trial is available only in an action at law.

2. Remedies in Equity
Remedies in equity include decrees of specific performance, injunctions, and rescission. Decisions to award equitable remedies are guided by equitable maxims.

III. CLASSIFICATIONS OF LAW

A. SUBSTANTIVE AND PROCEDURAL LAW
Substantive law includes laws that define, describe, regulate, and create rights and duties. *Procedural law* includes rules for enforcing those rights.

B. CYBERLAW
Cyberlaw is the emerging body of law (court decisions, new and amended statutes, etc.) that governs Internet transactions.

C. CIVIL LAW AND CRIMINAL LAW
Civil law regulates relationships between individuals. *Criminal law* regulates relationships between individuals and society.

D. NATIONAL AND INTERNATIONAL LAW

1. National Law
National law is the law of a particular nation. Laws vary from country to country, but there are broad similarities.

2. International Law
International law consists of written and unwritten laws observed by independent nations and governing the acts of individuals and governments. Sources include treaties and international organizations.

IV. THE CONSTITUTIONAL POWERS OF GOVERNMENT
In a federal form of government (the United States), the states form a union and sovereign power is divided between a central authority and the states.

A. THE COMMERCE CLAUSE
The Constitution (Article I, Section 8) gives Congress the power to regulate commerce among the states.

1. The Commerce Power Today

The national government can regulate every commercial enterprise in the United States. The United States Supreme Court has held, however, that this does not justify regulation of areas that have "nothing to do with commerce."

2. The Regulatory Powers of the States

States possess police powers (the right to regulate private activities to protect or promote the public order, health, safety, morals, and general welfare). Statutes covering almost every aspect of life have been enacted under the police powers.

3. The "Dormant" Commerce Clause

When state laws impinge on interstate commerce, courts balance the state's interest in regulating a certain matter against the burden on interstate commerce. State laws that *substantially* interfere with interstate commerce violate the commerce clause.

B. THE SUPREMACY CLAUSE

The Constitution (Article IV) provides that the Constitution, laws, and treaties of the United States are the supreme law of the land.

1. When Federal and State Laws Are in Direct Conflict

The state law is rendered invalid.

2. Federal Preemption

If Congress chooses to act exclusively in an area in which states have concurrent power, Congress preempts the area (the federal law takes precedence over a state law on the same subject).

V. BUSINESS AND THE BILL OF RIGHTS

The first ten amendments to the Constitution protect individuals and businesses against some interference by the federal government. Under the due process clause of the Fourteenth Amendment, many rights also apply to the states.

A. THE FIRST AMENDMENT—FREEDOM OF SPEECH

The First Amendment guaranty of freedom of speech applies to the federal and state governments.

1. Speech with Limited Protection

a. Corporate Political Speech

States can prohibit corporations from using corporate funds for independent expressions of opinion about political candidates.

b. Commercial Speech

A state restriction on commercial speech (advertising) is valid as long as it (1) seeks to implement a substantial government interest, (2) directly advances that interest, and (3) goes no further than necessary to accomplish its objective.

2. Unprotected Speech

a. Defamatory Speech

Speech that harms the good reputation of another can take the form of libel (if it is in writing) or slander (if it is oral).

b. Lewd and Obscene Speech

States can ban child pornography. One court has banned lewd speech and pornographic pinups in the workplace.

c. "Fighting Words"

Words likely to incite others to violence.

3. **Online Obscenity**
   Attempts to regulate obscene materials on the Internet have been challenged, and some have been struck, as unconstitutional.

B. **THE FIRST AMENDMENT—FREEDOM OF RELIGION**
Under the First Amendment, the government may not establish a religion (the establishment clause) nor prohibit the exercise of religion (the free exercise clause).

   1. **"Sunday Closing Laws"**
      Restrictions on commercial acts on Sunday have been upheld on the ground it is a legitimate government function to provide a day of rest.

   2. **Government Accommodation**
      This amendment mandates government accommodation of all religions and forbids hostility toward any.

   3. **Business Accommodation**
      Statutes prohibit employers and unions from discriminating against persons because of their religion. Employers must "reasonably accommodate" the religious practices of their employees.

VI. DUE PROCESS AND EQUAL PROTECTION

A. **DUE PROCESS**
Both the Fifth and the Fourteenth Amendments provide that no person shall be deprived "of life, liberty, or property, without due process of law."

   1. **Procedural Due Process**
      Procedural due process requires that any government decision to take away the life, liberty, or property of an individual be accompanied by procedural safeguards to ensure fairness.

   2. **Substantive Due Process**
      Substantive due process focuses on the content (substance) of legislation.

      a. **Compelling Interest Test**
         A statute can restrict an individual's fundamental right (such as all First Amendment rights) only if the statute promotes a compelling or overriding governmental interest (speed limits, for example, protect public safety).

      b. **Rational Basis Test**
         Restrictions on business activities must relate rationally to a legitimate government purpose. Most business regulations qualify.

B. **EQUAL PROTECTION**
The Fourteenth Amendment prohibits a state from denying any person "the equal protection of the laws." The due process clause of the Fifth Amendment applies the equal protection clause to the federal government.

   1. **What Equal Protection Means**
      Equal protection means that the government must treat similarly situated individuals in a similar manner. If a law distinguishes among individuals, the basis for the distinction (classification) is examined.

      a. **Minimal Scrutiny**
         In matters of economic or social welfare, the classification will be considered valid if there is any conceivable *rational basis* on which it might relate to any legitimate government interest.

b. Intermediate Scrutiny

Laws using classifications based on gender or legitimacy must be substantially related to important government objectives.

c. Strict Scrutiny

A law that inhibits some persons' exercise of a fundamental right or a classification based on a suspect trait must be necessary to promote a compelling government interest.

2. The Difference between Substantive Due Process and Equal Protection

A law that limits the liberty of *all* persons to do something may violate substantive due process. A law that limits the liberty of only *some* persons may violate equal protection.

VII. PRIVACY RIGHTS

There is no specific guarantee of this right, but it is derived from guarantees in the First, Third, Fourth, Fifth, and Ninth Amendments. There are a number of federal statutes that protect privacy in certain areas.

VIII. FINDING AND ANALYZING THE LAW

A. FINDING STATUTORY AND ADMINISTRATIVE LAW

1. Publication of Statutes

Federal statutes are arranged by date of enactment in *United States Statutes at Large*. State statutes are collected in similar state publications. Statutes are also published in codified form (the form in which they appear in the federal and state codes) in other publications.

2. Finding a Statute in a Publication

Statutes are usually referred to in their codified form. In the codes, laws are compiled by subject. For example, the *United States Code* (U.S.C.) arranges by subject most federal laws. Each subject is assigned a title number and each statute a section number within a title.

3. Publication of Administrative Rules

Rules and regulations adopted by federal administrative agencies are published initially in the *Federal Register*. They are also compiled by subject in the *Code of Federal Regulations* (C.F.R.).

4. Finding an Administrative Rule in a Publication

In the C.F.R., administrative rules are arranged by subject. Each subject is assigned a title number and each rule a section number within a title.

B. FINDING CASE LAW

1. Publication of Court Opinions

State appellate court opinions are often published by the state in consecutively numbered volumes. They may also be published in units of the *National Reporter System*, by West Publishing Company. Federal court opinions appear in other West publications.

2. Finding a Court Opinion in a Publication

After a decision is published, it can be referred to by the name of the case and the volume, name, and page number of one or more reporters. This information is called the **citation**.

C. READING AND UNDERSTANDING CASE LAW

1. Plaintiffs and Defendants

In the title of a case (*Adams v. Jones*), the *v.* means **versus** (against). Adams is the **plaintiff** (the person who filed the suit) and Jones the **defendant** (the person against whom the suit was brought). An appellate court may place the name of the appellant first (*Jones v. Adams.*).

2. **Appellants and Appellees**
    An **appellant** (or **petitioner**) is the party who appeals a case to another court or jurisdiction from the one in which the case was brought. An **appellee** (or **respondent**) is the party against whom an appeal is taken.

3. **Judges and Justices**
    These terms are designations given to judges in different courts.

4. **Decisions and Opinions**
    An opinion contains a court's reasons for its decision, the rules of law that apply, and the judgment.

TRUE-FALSE QUESTIONS

(Answers at the Back of the Book)

____ 1. Law is a body of enforceable rules governing relationships among individuals and between individuals and their society.

____ 2. The doctrine of *stare decisis* obligates judges to follow precedents established within their jurisdictions.

____ 3. Common law develops from rules of law announced in court decisions.

____ 4. A federal statute takes precedence over the U.S. Constitution.

____ 5. In most states, the same courts can grant legal or equitable remedies.

____ 6. Congress can regulate any activity that substantially affects commerce.

____ 7. A state law that substantially impinges on interstate commerce is unconstitutional.

____ 8. The Bill of Rights protects individuals against various types of interference by the federal government only.

____ 9. Any restriction on commercial speech is unconstitutional.

____ 10. A right to privacy is not specifically guaranteed in the U.S. Constitution.

FILL-IN QUESTIONS

(Answers at the Back of the Book)

The common law system, on which the American legal system is based, involves the application of principles applied in earlier cases _____(with similar facts/whether or not the facts are similar). This use of previous case law, or _____ (precedent/preeminent), is known as the doctrine of *stare decisis*, and _____
_____ (emphasizes a flexible/permits a predictable) resolution of cases.

MULTIPLE-CHOICE QUESTIONS

(Answers at the Back of the Book)

____ 1. In a suit between Best Products, Inc., and Central Sales Corporation, the court applies the doctrine of *stare decisis*. This means that the court follows rules of law established by

a. all courts.
b. courts of higher rank only.
c. courts of lower rank only.
d. no courts.

_____ **2.** In a suit between Delta Data Company and Eagle Information, Inc., the court applies the doctrine of *stare decisis*. This requires the court to find cases that, compared to the case before it, has

a. entirely different facts.
b. no facts, only conclusions of law.
c. precisely identical facts.
d. similar facts.

_____ **3.** In a suit between Fine Manufacturing Company and Great Goods, Inc., the court orders a rescission. This is

a. an action to cancel a contract and return the parties to the positions they held before the contract's formation.
b. an award of damages.
c. an order to do or refrain from doing a particular act.
d. an order to perform what was promised.

_____ **4.** In a given case, most courts may grant

a. equitable remedies, legal remedies, or both.
b. equitable remedies only.
c. equitable or legal remedies, but not both.
d. legal remedies only.

_____ **5.** Eagle Shipping Company challenges a Georgia state statute, claiming that it unlawfully interferes with interstate commerce. A court will likely

a. balance Georgia's interest in regulating the matter against the burden on interstate commerce.
b. balance the burden on Georgia against the merit and purpose of interstate commerce.
c. strike the statute.
d. uphold the statute.

_____ **6.** An Illinois state statute bans certain advertising to prevent consumers from being misled. A court would likely hold this statute to be

a. an unconstitutional restriction of speech.
b. constitutional under the First Amendment.
c. justified by the need to protect individuals' rights.
d. necessary to protect state interests.

_____ **7.** Procedures used in South Dakota and other states in making decisions to take life, liberty, or property are the focus of constitutional provisions covering

a. equal protection.
b. procedural due process.
c. substantive due process.
d. the right to privacy.

_____ **8.** A Connecticut statute that limits the liberty of *all* persons to engage in a certain activity may violate constitutional provisions covering

a. equal protection.
b. procedural due process.
c. substantive due process.
d. the right to privacy.

____ 9. Metro City enacts an ordinance that restricts most vendors from doing business in a heavily trafficked area. This ordinance might be upheld under constitutional provisions covering

   a. equal protection.
   b. procedural due process.
   c. substantive due process.
   d. the right to privacy.

____ 10. If Montana enacts a statute that directly conflicts with a federal law

   a. both laws are invalid.
   b. both laws govern concurrently.
   c. Montana's statute takes precedence.
   d. the federal law takes precedence.

SHORT ESSAY QUESTIONS

1. What is *stare decisis*? Why is it important?

2. What is the significance of the commerce clause?

ISSUE SPOTTERS

(Answers at the Back of the Book)

1. The First Amendment provides protection for the free exercise of religion. A state legislature enacts a law that outlaws all religions that do not derive from the Judeo-Christian tradition. Is this law valid within that state? Why or why not?

2. Alpha Corporation learns that a federal administrative agency is considering a rule that will have a negative impact on the firm's ability to do business. Does the firm have any opportunity to express its opinion about the pending rule?

3. Can a state, in the interest of energy conservation, ban all advertising by power utilities if conservation could be accomplished by less restrictive means? Why or why not?

Chapter 2:
Ethics and Professional Responsibility

WHAT THIS CHAPTER IS ABOUT

The concepts set out in this chapter include the nature of business ethics and the relationship between ethics and business. Ultimately, the goal of this chapter is to provide you with basic tools for analyzing ethical issues in a business context.

CHAPTER OUTLINE

I. BUSINESS ETHICS
Ethics is the study of what constitutes right and wrong behavior. Ethics focuses on morality and the application of moral principles in everyday life.

A. WHAT IS BUSINESS ETHICS?
Business ethics focuses on what constitutes ethical behavior in the world of business. Business ethics is *not* a separate kind of ethics.

B. WHY IS BUSINESS ETHICS IMPORTANT?
An understanding of business ethics is important to the long-run viability of a business, the well being of its officers and directors, and the welfare of its employees.

II. SETTING THE RIGHT ETHICAL TONE
Some unethical conduct is founded on the lack of sanctions.

A. THE IMPORTANCE OF ETHICAL LEADERSHIP
Management must set and apply ethical standards to which they are committed. Employees will likely follow their example. Ethical conduct can be furthered by not tolerating unethical behavior, setting realistic employee goals, and periodic employee review.

B. CREATING ETHICAL CODES OF CONDUCT
Most large corporations have codes of conduct that indicate the firm's commitment to legal compliance and to the welfare of those who are affected by corporate decisions and practices. Large firms may also emphasize ethics in other ways (for example, with training programs).

C. CORPORATE COMPLIANCE PROGRAMS
Components of a comprehensive corporate ethical-compliance program include an ethical code of conduct, an ethics committee, training programs, and internal audits to monitor compliance. These components should be integrated. The Sarbanes-Oxley Act of 2002 requires firms to set up confidential systems for employees to report suspected illegal or unethical financial practices.

D. CONFLICTS AND TRADE-OFFS
A firm's duty to its shareholders should be weighed against duties to others who may have a greater stake in a particular decision. For example, an employer should consider whether it has an ethical duty to loyal, long-term employees not to replace them with workers who will accept lower pay and whether this duty prevails over a duty to improve profitability by restructuring.

III. BUSINESS ETHICS AND THE LAW
The minimal acceptable standard for ethical business behavior is compliance with the law. Ethical standards, such as those in a company's policies or codes of ethics, must also guide decisions.

A. LAWS REGULATING BUSINESS
Because there are many laws regulating business, it is possible to violate one without realizing it. Ignorance of the law is no excuse.

B. "GRAY AREAS" IN THE LAW
There are many "gray areas" in which it is difficult to predict how a court will rule. The best course is to act responsibly and in good faith.

C. TECHNOLOGICAL DEVELOPMENTS AND LEGAL UNCERTAINTIES
How laws apply in the context of cyberspace is not certain.

IV.   APPROACHES TO ETHICAL REASONING
Ethical reasoning is the process by which an individual examines a situation according to his or her moral convictions or ethical standards. Fundamental ethical reasoning approaches include the following.

A. DUTY-BASED ETHICS

1. Religious Ethical Standards
Religious standards provide that when an act is prohibited by religious teachings, it is unethical and should not be undertaken, regardless of the consequences. Religious standards also involve compassion.

2. Kantian Ethics
Immanual Kant believed that people should be respected because they are qualitatively different from other physical objects. Kant's *categorical imperative* is that individuals should evaluate their actions in light of what would happen if everyone acted the same way.

3. The Principle of Rights
According to the principle that persons have rights (to life and liberty, for example), a key factor in determining whether a business decision is ethical is how that decision affects the rights of others, including employees, customers and society.

B. OUTCOME-BASED ETHICS: UTILITARIANISM
Utilitarianism is a belief that an action is ethical if it produces the greatest good for the greatest number. This approach is often criticized, because it tends to reduce the welfare of people to plus and minus signs on a cost-benefit worksheet.

V.   PROFESSIONAL RESPONSIBILITY
Professionals must exercise the standard of care, knowledge, and judgment generally accepted by members of their professional group.

A. ACCOUNTANT'S DUTY OF CARE

1. Standard of Care
Accountants must comply with generally accepted accounting principles (GAAP) and generally accepted auditing standards (GAAS) (though compliance does not guarantee relief from liability). If an accountant conforms to GAAP and acts in good faith, he or she will not be liable to a client for incorrect judgment.

2. Violations of GAAP and GAAS
A violation of GAAP and GAAS is considered *prima facie* evidence of negligence. Compliance, however, does not necessarily relieve an accountant of liability: an accountant may be held to a higher standard established by state statute and by judicial decisions.

B. ATTORNEY'S DUTY OF CARE

1. Standard of Care
All attorneys owe a duty to provide competent and diligent representation. The standard is that of a reasonably competent general practitioner of ordinary skill, experience, and capacity.

2. Liability for Malpractice

An attorney who fails to exercise reasonable care and professional judgment breaches the duty of care.

C. STATUTORY DUTIES OF ACCOUNTANTS

1. The Duty of Accountants under Securities Laws

An accountant may be liable to anyone who buys a security for misstatements and omissions of material facts in its registration statement (which they often prepare for filing with the Securities and Exchange Commission (SEC) before an offering of securities—see Chapter 21). An accountant must exercise due diligence. Failure to follow GAAP and GAAS is proof of a lack of due diligence. There may also be liability for false statements under the Securities Exchange Act of 1934.

2. Potential Criminal Liability of Accountants

An accountant may be found criminally liable for violations of the Securities Act of 1933, the Securities Exchange Act of 1934, the Internal Revenue Code, and the Sarbanes-Oxley Act of 2002. Under the Sarbanes-Oxley Act, for example, an accountant's false or misleading certified audit statement may result in a fine of up to $5 million and imprisonment of up to twenty years.

VI.   DEFYING THE RULES: THE ENRON CASE

Unethical conduct resulted in the single largest bankruptcy of a U.S. business firm.

A. THE UNETHICAL CONDUCT

Managers took advantage of accounting standards to overestimate future earnings, which resulted in inflated reports of current earnings. To maintain these exaggerations, the company created subsidiaries to which it could shift unreported losses and assets with inflated values. Many of these shifts occurred outside the U.S. to avoid federal income taxes. When questioned, management refused to investigate and reveal financial improprieties.

B. WHO WAS AFFECTED?

This misconduct affected the firm's managers, employees, suppliers, and shareholders, and the community and society in general.

VII.   THE SARBANES-OXLEY ACT OF 2002

This act imposes requirements on a public accounting firm that provides auditing services to an *issuer* (a certain company that sells securities to investors).

A. THE PUBLIC COMPANY ACCOUNTING OVERSIGHT BOARD

This board, which reports to the Securities and Exchange Commission, oversees the audit of public companies subject to securities laws to protect public investors and ensure that public accounting firms comply with the provisions of the act.

B. APPLICABILITY TO PUBLIC ACCOUNTING FIRMS

Public accounting firms are firms and associated persons that are "engaged in the practice of public accounting or preparing or issuing audit reports."

1. Auditor Independence

- It is unlawful to perform for an issuer both audit and non-audit services.
- The issuer's audit committee must preapprove most auditing services.
- A public accounting firm cannot provide audit services to an issuer if the lead audit partner or the reviewing partner provided those services to the issuer in each of the prior five years.
- Reports to an issuer's audit committee must be timely and indicate critical accounting policies and practices, alternatives discussed, and other communications with the issuer's management.
- A public accounting firm cannot provide audit services to an issuer if the issuer's chief executive officer, chief financial officer, chief accounting officer, or controller worked for the auditor and participated in an audit of the issuer within the preceding year.

2. Document Destruction
The act prohibits destroying or falsifying records to obstruct or influence a federal investigation or in relation to a bankruptcy. Penalties include fines and imprisonment up to twenty years.

VIII. BUSINESS ETHICS ON A GLOBAL LEVEL

A. MONITORING THE EMPLOYMENT PRACTICES OF FOREIGN SUPPLIERS
Concerns include the treatment of foreign workers who make goods imported and sold in the United States by U.S. firms. Should a U.S firm refuse to deal with certain suppliers or monitor their workplaces to make sure that the workers are not being mistreated?

B. THE FOREIGN CORRUPT PRACTICES ACT
The Foreign Corrupt Practices Act (FCPA) of 1977 applies to U.S. companies and accountants.

1. U.S. Companies
The FCPA also covers business firms' directors, officers, shareholders, employees, and agents.

a. What Is Prohibited?
The FCPA prohibits the bribery of most foreign government officials to get them to act in their official capacities to provide business opportunities.

b. What Is Permitted?
The FCPA permits payments to (1) minor officials whose duties are ministerial, (2) foreign officials if the payments are lawful in the foreign country, or (3) private foreign companies or other third parties unless the U.S. firm knows payments will be made to a foreign government.

2. Accountants

a. What Is Required?
All companies must (1) keep detailed records that "accurately and fairly" reflect the company's financial activities and (2) have an accounting system that provides "reasonable assurance" that all transactions are accounted for and legal.

b. What Is Prohibited?
The FCPA prohibits false statements to accountants and false entries in accounts.

3. Penalties
Firms: fines up to $2 million. Officers or directors: fines up to $100,000 (cannot be paid by the company); imprisonment up to five years.

4. Other Nations
A treaty signed by members of the Organization for Economic Cooperation and Development makes the bribery of foreign officials a crime.

TRUE-FALSE QUESTIONS

(Answers at the Back of the Book)

____ 1. Ethics is the study of what constitutes right and wrong behavior.

____ 2. The *minimal* acceptable standard for ethical behavior is compliance with the law.

____ 3. According to utilitarianism, it does not matter how many people benefit from an act.

____ 4. The best course towards accomplishing legal and ethical behavior is to act responsibly and in good faith.

____ 5. The legality of an action is always clear.

____ 6. To foster ethical behavior among employees, managers should apply ethical standards to which they are committed.

____ 7. If an act is legal, it is ethical.

____ 8. Professionals must exercise the standard of care, knowledge, and judgment set by codes of ethics, court decisions, and state statutes.

____ 9. Compliance with GAAP and GAAS will relieve an accountant of liability.

____ 10. Bribery of public officials is only an ethical issue.

FILL-IN QUESTIONS
(Answers at the Back of the Book)

_____ (Religious standards/ Kantian ethics/ The principle of rights) provide(s) that when an act is prohibited by religious teachings, it is unethical and should not be undertaken, regardless of the consequences. According to _____ (religious standards/ Kantian ethics/ the principle of rights), individuals should evaluate their actions in light of what would happen if everyone acted the same way. According to _____ (religious standards/ Kantian ethics/ the principle of rights), a key factor in determining whether a business decision is ethical is how that decision affects the rights of others.

MULTIPLE-CHOICE QUESTIONS
(Answers at the Back of the Book)

____ 1. Beth is a marketing executive for Consumer Products Company. Compared to Beth's personal actions, her business actions require the application of

a. more complex ethical standards.
b. simpler ethical standards.
c. the same ethical standards.
d. no ethical standards.

____ 2. Pete, an employee of Quality Sales, Inc., takes a duty-based approach to ethics. Pete believes that he must

a. achieve the greatest good for the most people.
b. avoid unethical behavior regardless of the consequences.
c. conform to society's standards.
d. place his employer's interest first.

____ 3. Jill, chief financial officer of Kwik Delivery Company, adopts religious ethical standards. These involve an element of

a. compassion.
b. cost-benefit analysis.
c. discretion.
d. utilitarianism.

____   4. Eve, an employee of First Federal Bank, takes an outcome-based approach to ethics. Eve believes that she must

a. achieve the greatest good for the most people.
b. avoid unethical behavior regardless of the consequences.
c. conform to society's standards.
d. place his employer's interest first.

____   5. Don is a manager with Engineering Aviation Systems. At a company ethics meeting, Don's most effective argument against utilitarianism is that it

a. gives profits priority over costs.
b. ignores the practical costs of a given set of circumstances.
c. justifies human costs that many persons find unacceptable.
d. requires complex cost-benefit analyses of simple situations.

____   6. Tina, the president of United Sales, Inc., tries to ensure that United's actions are legal and ethical. To ensure this result, the best course of Tina and United is to act in

a. good faith.
b. ignorance of the law.
c. regard for the firm's shareholders only.
d. their own self interest.

____   7. Greg, an accountant, prepares for Fine Distribution, Inc. (FDI), a financial statement that omits a material fact. The statement is included in FDI's registration statement, which Holly reads before buying FDI stock on which she later suffers a loss. Greg may avoid liability to Holly if he

a. did not have a contract with Holly
b. did not prepare the registration statement
c. exercised due diligence in preparing the financial statement.
d. lacked criminal intent.

____   8. Lily is injured in an auto accident, but Mega Insurance Company refuses to pay her claim. She hires Nick, an attorney, who fails to file a suit against Mega before the time for filing runs out. Lily sues Nick. She will

a. lose, because clients are responsible for their own losses.
b. lose, because Nick could not reasonably have been expected to file on time.
c. win, because Mega refused to pay her claim.
d. win, because Nick committed malpractice.

____   9. Alan, an executive with Beta Corporation, follows the "principle of rights" theory, under which an action may be ethical depending on how it affects

a. the right determination under a cost-benefit analysis.
b. the right of Alan to maintain his dignity.
c. the right of Beta to make a profit.
d. the rights of others.

____   10. Gamma, Inc., a U.S. corporation, makes a side payment to the minister of commerce of another country for a favorable business contract. In the United States, this payment would be considered

a. illegal only.
b. unethical only.
c. illegal and unethical.
d. none of the above.

SHORT ESSAY QUESTIONS

1.   What is the difference between legal and ethical standards? How are legal standards affected by ethical standards?

2.   What is the accountants' duty of care in the context of their role in business financial systems?

ISSUE SPOTTERS

(Answers at the Back of the Book)

1.   If, like Robin Hood, a person robs the rich to pay the poor, does his or her benevolent intent make his or her actions ethical?

2.   Delta Tools, Inc., markets a product that under some circumstances is capable of seriously injuring consumers. Does Delta owe an ethical duty to remove this product from the market, even if the injuries result only from misuse?

3.   Acme Corporation decides to respond to what it sees as a moral obligation to correct for past discrimination by adjusting pay differences among its employees. Does this raise an ethical conflict between Acme's employees? Between Acme and its employees? Between Acme and its shareholders?

Chapter 3:
Traditional and Online Dispute Resolution

WHAT THIS CHAPTER IS ABOUT

This chapter explains which courts have power to hear what disputes and when and outlines what happens before, during, and after a civil trial. The chapter also covers alternative dispute resolution and online dispute resolution.

CHAPTER OUTLINE

I. **THE JUDICIARY'S ROLE IN AMERICAN GOVERNMENT**
The power of **judicial review**: the courts can decide whether the laws or actions of the executive branch and the legislative branch are constitutional.

II. **BASIC JUDICIAL REQUIREMENTS**

A. **JURISDICTION**
To hear a case, a court must have jurisdiction over (1) the defendant or the property involved and (2) the subject matter.

1. **Jurisdiction over Persons or Property**
A court has *in personam* (personal) jurisdiction over state residents. Long arm statutes permit courts to exercise jurisdiction over nonresidents who have *minimum contacts* with the state (for example, do business there). A court has *in rem* jurisdiction over property within its borders.

2. **Jurisdiction over Subject Matter**
A court of **general jurisdiction** can decide virtually any type of case. A court's jurisdiction may be **limited** by the subject of a suit, the amount of money in controversy, or whether a proceeding is a trial or appeal.

3. **Jurisdiction of the Federal Courts**

a. **Federal Questions**
Any suit based on the Constitution, a treaty, or a federal law can originate in a federal court.

b. **Diversity of Citizenship**
Federal jurisdiction covers cases involving (1) citizens of different states, (2) a foreign government and citizens of a state or of different states, or (3) citizens of a state and citizens or subjects of a foreign government. The amount in controversy must be more than $75,000.

4. **Exclusive v. Concurrent Jurisdiction**
Exclusive: when cases can be tried only in federal courts or only in state courts. Concurrent: When both federal and state courts can hear a case.

B. **JURISDICTION IN CYBERSPACE**
Whether a court can compel the appearance of a party *outside* the physical limits of the court's jurisdiction depends on the amount of business the party transacts over the Internet with parties *within* the court's jurisdiction.

C. INTERNATIONAL JURISDICTIONAL ISSUES

The minimum-contact standard can apply in an international context. As in cyberspace, a business should attempt to comply with the laws of any jurisdiction in which it targets customers.

D. VENUE

Venue is concerned with the most appropriate location for a trial.

E. STANDING TO SUE

Standing is the interest (injury or threat) that a plaintiff has in a case. A plaintiff must have standing to bring a suit, and the controversy must be justiciable (real, as opposed to hypothetical or purely academic).

III. THE STATE AND FEDERAL COURT SYSTEMS

A. STATE COURT SYSTEMS

1. Trial Courts

Trial courts are courts in which trials are held and testimony is taken.

2. Appellate, or Reviewing, Courts

Courts that hear appeals from trial courts look at *questions of law* (what law governs a dispute) but not *questions of fact* (what occurred in the dispute), unless a trial court's finding of fact is clearly contrary to the evidence. Decision of a state's highest court on state law is final.

B. THE FEDERAL COURT SYSTEM

1. U.S. District Courts

The federal equivalent of a state trial court of general jurisdiction. There is at least one federal district court in every state. Other federal trial courts include the U.S. Tax Court and the U.S. Bankruptcy Court.

2. U.S. Courts of Appeals

The U.S. (circuit) courts of appeals for twelve of the circuits hear appeals from the federal district courts located within their respective circuits. The court of appeals for the thirteenth circuit (the federal circuit) has national jurisdiction over certain cases.

3. The United States Supreme Court

The Supreme Court, the highest level of the federal court system, can review any case decided by any of the federal courts of appeals, and it has authority over some cases decided in state courts. To appeal a case to the Supreme Court, a party asks for a writ of *certiorari*. Whether the Court issues the writ is within its discretion.

IV. FOLLOWING A STATE COURT CASE

A. THE PLEADINGS

1. The Plaintiff's Complaint

Filed by the plaintiff with the clerk of the trial court. Contains (1) a statement alleging the facts for the court to take jurisdiction, (2) a short statement of the facts necessary to show that the plaintiff is entitled to a remedy, and (3) a statement of the remedy the plaintiff is seeking.

2. The Summons

Served on the defendant, with the complaint. Notifies the defendant to answer the complaint (usually within twenty to thirty days).

3. The Defendant's Response

No response results in a default judgment for the plaintiff.

a. Answer
Admits the allegations in the complaint or denies them and sets out any defenses. May include a counterclaim against the plaintiff.

b. Motion to Dismiss
The defendant may file a motion to dismiss. If the court denies the motion, the defendant must file an answer. If the court grants the motion, the plaintiff must file an amended complaint.

B. PRETRIAL MOTIONS

1. Motion to Dismiss
(See above.) Either party may file a motion to dismiss if they have agreed to settle the case. A court may file such a motion itself.

2. Motion for Judgment on the Pleadings
Any party can file this motion (after the pleadings have been filed), when no facts are disputed and only questions of law are at issue. A court may consider only those facts stated in the pleadings.

3. Motion for Summary Judgment
Any party can file this motion, if there is no disagreement about the facts and the only question is which laws apply. A court can consider evidence outside the pleadings.

C. DISCOVERY
The process of obtaining information from the opposing party or from witnesses may include depositions; interrogatories; and requests for admissions, documents, objects, entry on land, and physical or mental examinations. Information stored electronically, such as computer data, can be the object of a request. This may include data that was not intentionally saved, such as concealed notes.

D. PRETRIAL CONFERENCE
This is an informal discussion between the judge and the attorneys, after discovery, to identify the issues, consider a settlement, and plan the trial.

E. JURY SELECTION
The process by which a jury is chosen is *voir dire*—the jurors are questioned, and a party may ask that some not be sworn.

F. AT THE TRIAL
First, each side presents opening statements. Second, the plaintiff presents his or her case, offering evidence, including the testimony of witnesses. The defendant can challenge the evidence and cross-examine the witnesses.

1. Motion for a Directed Verdict
After the plaintiff's case, the defendant can ask the judge to direct a verdict on the ground the plaintiff presented no evidence to justify relief. If the motion is not granted, the defendant presents his or her case, after which this motion can be filed again.

2. Jury Verdict
In a jury trial, the jury decides the facts and the amount of the award, if any, to be paid by the losing party. This is the verdict.

G. POSTTRIAL MOTIONS

1. Motion for Judgment *N.O.V.*
The defendant can file this motion, if he or she previously moved for a directed verdict. The standards for granting this motion are the same as those for granting a motion to dismiss or for a directed verdict.

2. Motion for a New Trial

This motion is granted if the judge believes that the jury erred but that it is not appropriate to grant a judgment for the other side.

H. THE APPEAL

1. Filing the Appeal

Appellant files a notice of appeal with the clerk of the trial court, and the record on appeal, an abstract, and a brief with the reviewing court. Appellee files an answering brief. The parties can give oral arguments.

2. Appellate Review

Appellate courts do not usually reverse findings of fact unless they are contradicted by the evidence presented at the trial in the lower court.

a. Options of an Appellate Court

(1) Affirm: enforce the lower court's order; (2) reverse (if an error was committed during the trial); or (3) remand: send back to the court that originally heard the case for a new trial.

b. Appeal to a Higher Appellate Court

If the reviewing court is an intermediate appellate court, the case may be appealed to the state's highest court. If a federal question is involved, the case may go to the United States Supreme Court.

I. ENFORCING THE JUDGMENT

A judgment may not be enforceable, particularly if a losing party does not have sufficient assets or insurance to cover it.

V. THE COURTS ADAPT TO THE ONLINE WORLD

A. Electronic Filing

To save time, storage space, etc., courts are switching from paper to electronic document filing, using the Internet, e-mail, and CD-ROMs.

B. Courts Online

Most courts have Web sites. What is available on the sites varies.

C. Cyber Courts and Proceedings

The future may see the use of virtual courtrooms, in which proceedings take place only on the Internet.

VI. ALTERNATIVE DISPUTE RESOLUTION (ADR)

A. NEGOTIATION

Parties come together informally, with or without attorneys, to try to settle or resolve their differences without involving independent third parties.

B. MEDIATION

Parties come together informally with a mediator, who may propose solutions for the parties. A mediator is often an expert in a particular field.

C. ARBITRATION

An arbitrator—the third party hearing the dispute—decides the dispute. The decision may be legally binding.

1. Arbitration Clauses

Disputes are often arbitrated because of an arbitration clause in a contract entered into before the dispute. Courts enforce such clauses.

    2. Arbitration Statutes
Most states have statutes under which arbitration clauses are enforced. The Federal Arbitration Act (FAA) enforces arbitration clauses in contracts involving interstate commerce.

    3. The Arbitration Process
At an arbitration hearing, the parties make their arguments, present evidence, and call and examine witnesses, and the arbitrator makes a decision. The decision is called an award, even if no money is involved.

D. OTHER TYPES OF ADR

    1. Early Neutral Case Evaluation
Parties select a neutral third party (generally an expert) to evaluate their positions, with no hearing and no discovery. The evaluation is a basis for negotiating a settlement.

    2. Mini-trial
A private proceeding in which attorneys briefly argue each party's case. A third party indicates how a court would likely decide the issue.

    3. Summary Jury Trial
Like a mini-trial, but a jury renders a nonbinding verdict. Negotiations follow. If no settlement is reached, either side can seek a full trial.

VII. ONLINE DISPUTE RESOLUTION
Many Web sites offer online dispute resolution (ODR) services to help resolve small- to medium-sized business liability claims.

A. WHAT LAW APPLIES IN AN ODR PROCEEDING?
Most ODR services do not apply the law of a specific jurisdiction. Results are based on general, common legal principles.

B. NEGOTIATION AND MEDIATION SERVICES

    1. Online Negotiation
A settlement may be negotiated through blind bidding: one party submits an offer to be shown to the other party if it falls within a previously agreed range. There is a limited time to respond.

    2. Mediation Providers—SquareTrade
SquareTrade resolves disputes involving $100 or more between eBay customers. SquareTrade also resolves other disputes related to online transactions, using software to walk participants through a step-by-step resolution process.

C. ARBITRATION PROGRAMS

    1. Internet Corporation for Assigned Names and Numbers (ICANN)
The federal government set up ICANN as a nonprofit corporation to oversee the distribution of domain names. ICANN has issued rules and authorized organizations to resolve related disputes.

    2. Resolution Forum, Inc. (RFI)
RFI, a nonprofit entity associated with the Center for Legal Responsibility at South Texas College of Law, offers arbitration in an online conference room via a standard browser, using a password.

    3. Virtual Magistrate Project (VMAG)
VMAG resolves disputes involving users of online systems; victims of wrongful messages, postings and files; and system operators subject to complaints or similar demands. Online-related contract, intellectual property, property, and tort disputes. The goal is resolution within seventy-two hours. Appeal of a result may be made to a court.

TRUE-FALSE QUESTIONS

(Answers at the Back of the Book)

_____ 1. Under a long arm statute, a state court can obtain jurisdiction over an out-of-state defendant.

_____ 2. Doing substantial business in a jurisdiction over the Internet can be enough to support a court's jurisdiction over an out-of-state defendant.

_____ 3. The United States Supreme Court is the final authority for any case decided by a state court.

_____ 4. Suits involving federal questions originate in federal district courts.

_____ 5. An answer may admit or deny the allegations in a complaint.

_____ 6. A motion for summary judgment may be supported by sworn statements and other materials.

_____ 7. Only a losing party may appeal to a higher court.

_____ 8. Most lawsuits go to trial.

_____ 9. In mediation, a mediator makes a decision on the matter in dispute.

_____ 10. Most states do not enforce arbitration clauses.

FILL-IN QUESTIONS

(Answers at the Back of the Book)

A motion _____ (to dismiss/for summary judgment) alleges that even if the facts in a complaint are true, their legal consequences are such that there is no reason to go on with the suit and no need for the defendant to file an answer. A motion _____ (to dismiss/for judgment on the pleadings) is filed after the complaint, answer, and any counterclaim and reply have been filed, when no facts are disputed and only questions of law are at issue. A motion for _____ (summary judgment/a new trial) is proper if there is no disagreement on the facts and the only question is which laws apply to the facts.

MULTIPLE-CHOICE QUESTIONS

(Answers at the Back of the Book)

_____ 1. Ace Corporation, which is based in Texas, advertises on the Web. A court in Illinois would be most likely to exercise jurisdiction over Ace if Ace

a. conducted substantial business with Illinois residents at its site.
b. interacted with any Illinois resident through its Web site.
c. only advertised passively at its Web site.
d. all of the above.

_____ 2. Alpha Company files a suit against Beta Corporation. Before the trial, Alpha can obtain from Beta

a. access to related documents in Beta's possession.
b. accurate information about Beta's trade secrets.
c. an admission of the truth of matters not related to the trial.
d. all of the above.

_____ 3. Eagle Company, which is based in Florida, owns commercial property in Georgia. A dispute arises over the ownership of the property with Holly, a resident of Alabama. Holly files a suit against Eagle in Georgia. In this suit, Georgia has

a. diversity jurisdiction.
b. *in personam* jurisdiction.
c. *in rem* jurisdiction.
d. no jurisdiction.

_____ 4. Central Business Corporation was incorporated in Delaware, has its main office in New Jersey, and does business in New York. Central is subject to the jurisdiction of

a. Delaware, New Jersey, or New York.
b. Delaware or New Jersey only.
c. Delaware or New York only.
d. New Jersey or New York only.

_____ 5. Standard Marketing, Inc., loses its suit against Top Sales Corporation. Standard's best ground for an appeal is the trial court's interpretation of

a. the conduct of the witnesses during the trial.
b. the credibility of the evidence that Top presented.
c. the dealings between the parties before the suit.
d. the law that applied to the issues in the case.

_____ 6. John files a suit against Kay, and loses. John appeals, and loses again. The United States Supreme Court is

a. required to hear the case if John appeals again.
b. required to hear the case if John lost in a federal court.
c. required to hear the case if John lost in a state court.
d. not required to hear the case.

_____ 7. Ann serves a complaint on Bob, who files a motion to dismiss. If the motion is denied

a. Ann will be given time to file an amended complaint.
b. Ann will have a judgment entered in her favor.
c. Bob will be given time to file another response.
d. Bob will have a judgment entered in his favor.

_____ 8. Carol files a suit against Don. Before going to trial, the parties meet with their attorneys to represent them, to try to resolve the dispute without involving a third party. This is

a. arbitration.
b. litigation.
c. mediation.
d. negotiation.

_____ 9. Sam files a suit against Tina. They meet, and their attorneys present the case to a jury. The jury renders a non-binding verdict, after which the parties try to reach an agreement. This is

a. a mini-trial.
b. arbitration.
c. a summary jury trial.
d. early neutral case evaluation.

———   10. Jill submits a claim against Ken to LetsSettle.com, an online dispute resolution forum. An appeal of this dispute may be made to a court by

    a. Jill only.
    b. Ken only.
    c. Jill or Ken.
    d. none of the above.

SHORT ESSAY QUESTIONS

1. What is jurisdiction? How does jurisdiction over a person or property differ from subject matter jurisdiction? What does a long arm statute do?

2. What are the advantages and disadvantages of alternative dispute resolution?

ISSUE SPOTTERS

(Answers at the Back of the Book)

Sue contracts with Tom to deliver a quantity of computers to Sue's Computer Store. They disagree over the amount, the delivery date, the price, and the quality. Sue files a suit against Tom in a state court.

1. Their state requires that their dispute be submitted to mediation or nonbinding arbitration. If the dispute is not resolved, or if either party disagrees with the decision of the mediator or arbitrator, will a court hear the case?

2. At the trial, after Sue calls her witnesses, offers her evidence, and otherwise presents her side of the case, Tom has at least two choices between courses of actions. Tom can call his first witness. What else might he do?

3. After the trial, the judge issues a judgment that includes a grant of relief for Sue, but the relief is not as much as Sue wanted. Neither Sue nor Tom is satisfied with this result. Who can appeal to a higher court?

Chapter 4:
Torts and Cyber Torts

WHAT THIS CHAPTER IS ABOUT

Torts consist of wrongful conduct by one person that causes injury to another. *Tort* is French for "wrong." For acts that cause physical injury or that interfere with physical security and freedom of movement, tort law provides remedies, typically damages.

This chapter outlines intentional torts, negligence, and strict liability. These categories include torts that are specifically related to business and cyber torts.

CHAPTER OUTLINE

I. THE BASIS OF TORT LAW

Two notions serve as the basis of all torts: wrongs and compensation. Tort law recognizes that some acts are wrong because they cause injuries to others. Most crimes involve torts, but not all torts are crimes. A tort action is a *civil* action in which one person brings a personal suit against another, usually for damages.

II. INTENTIONAL TORTS AGAINST PERSONS

Intentional torts involve acts that were intended or could be expected to bring about consequences that are the basis of the tort. A **tortfeasor** (one committing a tort) must intend to commit an act, the consequences of which interfere with the personal or business interests of another in a way not permitted by law.

A. ASSAULT AND BATTERY

1. Assault
An intentional act that creates in another person a reasonable apprehension or fear of immediate harmful or offensive contact.

2. Battery
An intentional and harmful or offensive physical contact. Physical injury need not occur. Whether the contact is offensive is determined by the reasonable person standard.

3. Compensation
A plaintiff may be compensated for emotional harm or loss of reputation resulting from a battery, as well as for physical harm.

4. Defenses to Assault and Battery

a. Consent
When a person consents to an act that damages him or her, there is generally no liability for the damage.

b. Self-Defense
An individual who is defending his or her life or physical well-being can claim self-defense.

c. Defense of Others
An individual can act in a reasonable manner to protect others who are in real or apparent danger.

    d. Defense of Property
    Reasonable force may be used in attempting to remove intruders from one's home, although force that is likely to cause death or great bodily injury can never be used just to protect property.

B. FALSE IMPRISONMENT

1. What False Imprisonment Is
The intentional confinement or restraint of another person without justification. The confinement can be accomplished through the use of physical barriers, physical restraint, or threats of physical force.

2. The Defense of Probable Cause
In some states, a merchant is justified in delaying a suspected shoplifter if the merchant has probable cause. The detention must be conducted in a reasonable manner and for only a reasonable length of time.

C. INTENTIONAL INFLICTION OF EMOTIONAL DISTRESS
Intentional infliction of emotional distress is an act that amounts to extreme and outrageous conduct resulting in severe emotional distress to another (a few states require physical symptoms). Stalking is one way to commit it. Repeated annoyance, with threats, is another.

D. DEFAMATION
Defamation is wrongfully hurting another's good reputation through false statements. Doing it orally is **slander**; doing it in writing is **libel**.

1. Types of False Utterances That Are Torts *Per Se*
Proof of injury is not required when one falsely states that another has a loathsome communicable disease, has committed improprieties while engaging in a profession or trade, or has committed or been imprisoned for a serious crime, or that an unmarried woman is unchaste.

2. The Publication Requirement
The statement must be published (communicated to a third party). Anyone who republishes or repeats a defamatory statement is liable.

3. Defenses against Defamation

    a. Truth
    The statement is true. It must be true in whole, not in part.

    b. Privilege
    The statement is privileged: absolute (made in a judicial or legislative proceeding) or qualified (for example, made by one corporate director to another and was about corporate business).

    c. Public Figure
    The statement is about a public figure, made in a public medium, and related to a matter of general public interest. To recover damages, a public figure must prove a statement was made with **actual malice** (knowledge of its falsity or reckless disregard for the truth).

E. INVASION OF THE RIGHT TO PRIVACY
Four acts qualify as invasions of privacy:

1. The use of a person's name, picture, or other likeness for commercial purposes without permission. (This is **appropriation**—see below.)

2. Intrusion on an individual's affairs or seclusion.

3. Publication of information that places a person in a false light.

4. Public disclosure of private facts about an individual that an ordinary person would find objectionable.

F. APPROPRIATION
The use of one person's name or likeness by another, without permission and for the benefit of the user. An individual's right to privacy includes the right to the exclusive use of his or her identity.

G. MISREPRESENTATION (FRAUD)
Fraud is the use of misrepresentation and deceit for personal gain. Puffery (seller's talk) is not fraud. The elements of fraudulent misrepresentation—

1. **Misrepresentation** of material facts or conditions with knowledge that they are false or with reckless disregard for the truth.

2. **Intent** to induce another to rely on the misrepresentation.

3. **Justifiable reliance** by the deceived party.

4. **Damages** suffered as a result of reliance.

5. **Causal connection** between the misrepresentation and the injury.

H. WRONGFUL INTERFERENCE

1. **Wrongful Interference with a Contractual Relationship**
   Occurs when there is a contract between two parties and a third party who knows of the contract intentionally causes either of the two parties to break it.

2. **Wrongful Interference with a Business Relationship**
   If there are two yogurt stores in a mall, placing an employee of Store A in front of Store B to divert customers to Store A constitutes the tort of wrongful interference with a business relationship.

3. **Defenses to Wrongful Interference**
   A person is not liable if the interference is justified or permissible (such as bona fide competitive behavior).

III. INTENTIONAL TORTS AGAINST PROPERTY

A. TRESPASS TO LAND
Trespass to land occurs if a person, without permission, enters onto, above, or below the surface of land owned by another; causes anything to enter onto the land; or remains on the land or permits anything to remain on it.

1. **Trespass Criteria, Rights, and Duties**
   Posted signs *expressly* establish trespass. Entering onto property to commit an illegal act *impliedly* does so. Trespassers are liable for any property damage. Owners may have a duty to post notice of any danger.

2. **Defenses against Trespass to Land**
   Defenses against trespass include that the trespass was warranted or that the purported owner had no right to possess the land in question.

B. TRESPASS TO PERSONAL PROPERTY
Occurs when an individual unlawfully harms the personal property of another or interferes with an owner's right to exclusive possession and enjoyment. Defenses include that the interference was warranted.

C. CONVERSION

1. **What Conversion Is**
   An act depriving an owner of personal property without the owner's permission and without just cause. Conversion is the civil side of crimes related to theft. Buying stolen goods is conversion.

2. Defenses

Defenses to conversion include that the purported owner does not own the property or does not have a right to possess it that is superior to the right of the holder. Necessity is also a defense.

D. DISPARAGEMENT OF PROPERTY

Occurs when economically injurious falsehoods are made about another's product or ownership of property. Torts can be specifically referred to as **slander of quality** (product) or **slander of title** (ownership of property).

IV. UNINTENTIONAL TORTS (NEGLIGENCE)

A. THE ELEMENTS OF NEGLIGENCE

1. What Negligence Is

Someone's failure to live up to a required duty of care, causing another to suffer injury. The breach of the duty must create a risk of certain harmful consequences, whether or not that was the intent.

2. The Elements of Negligence

(1) A duty of care, (2) breach of the duty of care, (3) damage or injury as a result of the breach, and (4) the breach causes the damage or injury.

B. THE DUTY OF CARE AND ITS BREACH

1. The Reasonable Person Standard

The duty of care is measured according to the **reasonable person standard** (how a reasonable person would have acted in the same circumstances).

2. Duty of Landowners

Owners are expected to use reasonable care (guard against some risks and warn of others) to protect persons coming onto their property.

3. Duty of Professionals

A professional's duty is consistent with his or her knowledge, skill, and intelligence, including what is reasonable for that professional.

4. Factors for Determining a Breach of the Duty of Care

The nature of the act (whether it is outrageous or commonplace), the manner in which the act is performed (cautiously versus heedlessly), and the nature of the injury (whether it is serious or slight). Note: Failing to rescue a stranger in peril is not a breach of a duty of care.

C. THE INJURY REQUIREMENT AND DAMAGES

To recover damages (receive compensation), the plaintiff must have suffered some loss, harm, wrong, or invasion of a protected interest. Punitive damages (to punish the wrongdoer and deter others) may also be awarded.

D. CAUSATION

1. Causation in Fact

The breach of the duty of care must cause the injury—that is, "but for" the wrongful act, the injury would not have occurred.

2. Proximate Cause

There must be a connection between the act and the injury strong enough to justify imposing liability. Generally, the harm or the victim of the harm must have been foreseeable in light of all of the circumstances.

E. DEFENSES TO NEGLIGENCE

1. Assumption of Risk

One who voluntarily enters a risky situation, knowing the risk, cannot recover. This does not include a risk different from or greater than the risk normally involved in the situation.

2. **Superseding Cause**
    An unforeseeable intervening force breaks the connection between the breach of the duty of care and the injury or damage. Taking a defensive action (such as swerving to avoid an oncoming car) does not break the connection. Nor does someone else's attempt to rescue the injured party.

3. **Contributory Negligence**
    In some states, a plaintiff cannot recover for an injury if he or she was negligent. The last-clear-chance rule allows a negligent plaintiff to recover if the defendant had the last chance to avoid the damage.

4. **Comparative Negligence**
    In most states, the plaintiff's and the defendant's negligence is compared and liability prorated. Some states allow a plaintiff to recover even if his or her fault is greater than the defendant's. In many states, the plaintiff gets nothing if he or she is more than 50 percent at fault.

F. **SPECIAL NEGLIGENCE DOCTRINES AND STATUTES**

1. *Res Ipsa Loquitur*
    If negligence is very difficult to prove, a court may infer it, and the defendant must prove he or she was *not* negligent. This is only if the event causing the harm is one that normally does not occur in the absence of negligence and is caused by something within the defendant's control.

2. **Negligence *Per Se***
    A person who violates a statute providing for a criminal penalty is liable when the violation causes another to be injured, if (1) the statute sets out a standard of conduct, and when, where, and of whom it is expected; (2) the injured person is in the class protected by the statute; and (3) the statute was designed to prevent the type of injury suffered.

3. **"Danger Invites Rescue" Doctrine**
    A person can be liable to a party who is injured trying to protect another from the consequences of the first person's act.

4. **Special Negligence Statutes**
    Good Samaritan statutes protect those who aid others from being sued for negligence. Dram shop acts impose liability on bar owners for injuries caused by intoxicated persons who are served by those owners. A statute may impose liability on social hosts for acts of their guests.

V.   STRICT LIABILITY
Under this doctrine, liability for injury is imposed for reasons other than fault.

A. **ABNORMALLY DANGEROUS OR EXCEPTIONAL ACTIVITIES**
    The basis for imposing strict liability on an abnormally dangerous activity is that the activity creates an extreme risk. Balancing the risk against the potential for harm, it is fair to ask the person engaged in the activity to pay for injury caused by that activity.

B. **DANGEROUS ANIMALS**
    A person who keeps a dangerous animal is strictly liable for any harm inflicted by the animal.

C. **PRODUCT LIABILITY**
    A significant application of strict liability is in the area of product liability—liability of manufacturers, sellers, and others for harmful or defective products. See Chapter 13.

VI.   CYBER TORTS

A. **DEFAMATION ONLINE**
    Under the Communications Decency Act of 1996, Internet service providers (ISPs) are not liable for the defamatory remarks of those who use their services.

B. SPAM

Spam is junk e-mail. The federal government and some states regulate its use, which may constitute trespass to personal property. The First Amendment limits what the government can do to restrict it.

TRUE-FALSE QUESTIONS

(Answers at the Back of the Book)

——— **1.** To commit an intentional tort, a person must intend the consequences of his or her act or know with substantial certainty that certain consequences will result.

——— **2.** A reasonable apprehension or fear of harmful or offensive contact in the distant future is an assault.

——— **3.** A defamatory statement must be communicated to a third party to be actionable.

——— **4.** Puffery is fraud.

——— **5.** Conversion is wrongfully taking or retaining an individual's personal property and placing it in the service of another.

——— **6.** An *ordinary* person standard determines whether allegedly negligent conduct resulted in a breach of a duty of care.

——— **7.** Strict liability is liability without fault.

——— **8.** Bona fide competitive behavior can constitute wrongful interference with a contractual relationship.

——— **9.** An Internet service provider is not normally liable for its users' defamatory remarks.

——— **10.** The government does not regulate spam.

FILL-IN QUESTIONS

(Answers at the Back of the Book)

1. Basic defenses to _____ (negligence/intentional torts) include comparative negligence, contributory negligence, and assumption of risk.

2. One who voluntarily and knowingly enters into a risky situation normally cannot recover damages. This is the defense of _____ (contributory negligence/ assumption of risk).

3. When both parties' failure to use reasonable care combines to cause injury, in some states the injured party's recovery is prorated according to his or her own negligence. This is _____ (comparative/ contributory) negligence.

MULTIPLE-CHOICE QUESTIONS

(Answers at the Back of the Book)

——— **1.** Joe shoves Kay, who falls and suffers a concussion. This is an intentional tort

a. if Joe had a bad motive for shoving Kay.
b. if Joe intended to shove Kay.
c. if Kay was afraid of Joe.
d. only if Joe intended that Kay suffer a concussion.

____ 2. Alan, the owner of Beta Computer Store, detains Cathy, a customer, whom Alan suspects of shoplifting. This is false imprisonment if

    a. Alan detains Cathy for an unreasonably long time.
    b. Cathy did not shoplift.
    c. Cathy has probable cause to suspect Alan of deceit.
    d. Cathy protests her innocence.

____ 3. Fred drives across Gail's land. This is a trespass to land only if

    a. Fred damages the land.
    b. Fred does not have Gail's permission to drive on her land.
    c. Fred makes disparaging remarks about Gail's land.
    d. Gail is aware of Fred's driving on her land.

____ 4. Gil sends a letter to Holly in which he falsely accuses her of embezzling. This is defamation only if the letter is read by

    a. any third person.
    b. a public figure.
    c. Holly.
    d. Holly's employer.

____ 5. To protect its customers and other business invitees, Grocers Market must warn them of

    a. hidden and obvious dangers.
    b. hidden dangers.
    c. neither hidden nor obvious dangers.
    d. obvious dangers.

____ 6. Lee, a salesperson for Midsize Corporation, causes a car accident while on business. Lee and Midsize are liable to

    a. all those who were injured.
    b. only those who were uninsured.
    c. only those whose injuries could have been reasonably foreseen.
    d. only those with whom Lee was doing business.

____ 7. Ace Mining Company engages in blasting in its operations. This is subject to strict liability because

    a. Ace is a mining company.
    b. blasting is a dangerous activity.
    c. blasting is a negligent activity.
    d. mining can be done without blasting.

____ 8. Best Box Company advertises so effectively that Cardboard Products, Inc., stops doing business with Delta Packaging Corporation. Best is liable for

    a. appropriation.
    b. conversion.
    c. wrongful interference with a business relationship.
    d. none of the above.

_____ 9. Internet Services, Inc. (ISI), is an Internet service provider. ISI does not create, but disseminates, a defamatory statement by Jill, its customer, about Ron. Liability for the remark may be imposed on

    a. ISI and Jill.
    b. ISI or Jill, but not both.
    c. ISI only.
    d. Jill only.

_____ 10. Online Services Company (OSC) is an Internet service provider. Ads Unlimited, Inc., sends spam to OSC's customers, some of which then cancel OSC's services. Ads Unlimited is most likely liable for

    a. appropriation.
    b. disparagement of property.
    c. trespass to personal property.
    d. wrongful interference with a business relationship.

SHORT ESSAY QUESTIONS

1. What is a _tort_?

2. What are the elements of a cause of action based on negligence?

ISSUE SPOTTERS

(Answers at the Back of the Book)

1. Adam kisses the sleeve of Eve's blouse, to which she did not consent and which she finds offensive. Is Adam guilty of a tort?

2. If a student takes another student's business law textbook as a practical joke and hides it for several days before the final examination, has a tort been committed?

3. After less than a year in business, Superior Club surpasses Ordinary Club in number of members. Superior's marketing strategies attract many Ordinary members, who then change clubs. Does Ordinary have any recourse against Superior?

Chapter 5
Intellectual Property

WHAT THIS CHAPTER IS ABOUT

Intellectual property consists of the products of intellectual, creative processes. The law of trademarks, patents, copyrights, and related concepts protect many of these products (such as inventions, books, software, movies, and songs). This chapter outlines these laws, including their application in cyberspace.

CHAPTER OUTLINE

I. TRADEMARKS AND RELATED PROPERTY

A. TRADEMARKS
The Lanham Act protects trademarks at the federal level. Many states also have statutes that protect trademarks.

1. What Is a Trademark?
A distinctive mark, motto, device, or emblem that a manufacturer stamps, prints, or otherwise affixes to the goods it produces to distinguish them from the goods of other manufacturers.

2. The Federal Trademark Dilution Act of 1995
Prohibits dilution (unauthorized use of marks on goods or services, even if they do not compete directly with products whose marks are copied).

3. Trademark Registration
A trademark may be registered with a state or the federal government. Trademarks need not be registered to be protected.

a. Requirements for Federal Registration
A trademark may be filed with the U.S. Patent and Trademark Office on the basis of (1) use or (2) the intent to use the mark within six months (which may be extended to thirty months).

b. Renewal of Federal Registration
Between the fifth and sixth years and then every ten years (twenty years for marks registered before 1990).

4. Requirements for Trademark Protection
The extent to which the law protects a trademark is normally determined by how distinctive it is.

a. Strong Marks
Fanciful, arbitrary, or suggestive marks are considered most distinctive.

b. Descriptive Terms, Geographic Terms, and Personal Names
Descriptive terms, geographic terms, and personal names are not inherently distinctive and are not protected until they acquire a secondary meaning (which means that customers associate the mark with the source of a product)

c. Generic Terms
Terms such as *bicycle* or *computer* receive no protection, even if they acquire secondary meaning.

5. Trademark Infringement

This occurs when a trademark is copied to a substantial degree or used in its entirety by another.

B. SERVICE, CERTIFICATION, AND COLLECTIVE MARKS

Laws that apply to trademarks normally also apply to—

1. Service Marks

Used to distinguish the services of one person or company from those of another. Registered in the same manner as trademarks.

2. Certification Marks

Used by one or more persons, other than the owner, to certify the region, materials, mode of manufacture, quality, or accuracy of the owner's goods or services.

3. Collective Marks

Certification marks used by members of a cooperative, association, or other organization.

C. TRADE NAMES

Used to indicate part or all of a business's name. Trade names cannot be registered with the federal government but may be protected under the common law if they are used as trademarks or service marks.

D. TRADE DRESS

Trade dress is the image and appearance of a product, and is subject to the same protection as trademarks.

II. CYBER MARKS

A. ANTICYBERSQUATTING LEGISLATION

The Anticybersquatting Consumer Reform Act (ACRA) of 1999 amended the Lanham Act to make cybersquatting clearly illegal. Bad faith intent is an element (the ACRA lists "bad faith" factors). Damages may be awarded.

B. META TAGS

Words in a Web site's key-word field that determine the site's appearance in search engine results. Using others' marks as tags without permission constitutes trademark infringement.

C. DILUTION IN THE ONLINE WORLD

Using a mark, without permission, in a way that diminishes its distinctive quality. Tech-related cases have concerned the use of marks as domain names and spamming under another's logo.

D. LICENSING

Licensing is permitting a party to use a mark, copyright, patent, or trade secret for certain purposes. Use for other purposes is a breach of the license agreement.

III. PATENTS

A. WHAT IS A PATENT?

A grant from the federal government that conveys and secures to an inventor the exclusive right to make, use, and sell an invention for a period of 20 years (14 years for a design).

B. REQUIREMENTS FOR A PATENT

An invention, discovery, or design must be genuine, novel, useful, and not obvious in light of the technology of the time. A patent is given to the first person to invent a product, not to the first person to file for a patent.

C. PATENTS FOR SOFTWARE

The basis for software is often a mathematical equation or formula, which is not patentable, but a patent can be obtained for a process that incorporates a computer program.

D. PATENT INFRINGEMENT
Making, using, or selling another's patented design, product, or process without the patent owner's permission. The owner may obtain an injunction, damages, destruction of all infringing copies, attorneys' fees, and court costs.

E. BUSINESS PROCESS PATENTS
Business processes are patentable (but laws of nature, natural phenomena, and abstract ideas are not).

IV. COPYRIGHTS

A. WHAT IS A COPYRIGHT?
An intangible right granted by statute to the author or originator of certain literary or artistic productions. Protection is automatic; registration is not required.

B. COPYRIGHT PROTECTION
Protection lasts for the life of the author plus 70 years. Copyrights owned by publishing houses expire 95 years from the date of publication or 120 years from the date of creation, whichever is first. For works by more than one author, copyright expires 70 years after the death of the last surviving author.

C. WHAT IS PROTECTED EXPRESSION?
To be protected, a work must meet these requirements—

1. Fit a Certain Category
It must be a (1) literary work; (2) musical work; (3) dramatic work; (4) pantomime or choreographic work; (5) pictorial, graphic, or sculptural work; (6) film or other audiovisual work; or (7) a sound recording. The Copyright Act also protects computer software and architectural plans.

2. Be Fixed in a Durable Medium
From which it can be perceived, reproduced, or communicated.

3. Be Original
A compilation of facts (formed by the collection and assembling of preexisting materials of data) is copyrightable if it is original.

D. WHAT IS NOT PROTECTED?
Ideas, facts, and related concepts are not protected. If an idea and an expression cannot be separated, the expression cannot be copyrighted.

E. COPYRIGHT INFRINGEMENT
A copyright is infringed if a work is copied without the copyright holder's permission. A copy does not have to be exactly the same as the original—copying a substantial part of the original is enough.

1. Damages and Penalties
Actual damages (based on the harm to the copyright holder); damages under the Copyright Act, not to exceed $150,000; and criminal proceedings (which may result in fines or imprisonment).

2. Exception—The "Fair Use" Doctrine
The Copyright Act permits the fair use of a work for purposes such as criticism, news reporting, teaching (including multiple copies for classroom use), scholarship, or research. Factors in determining whether a use is infringement include the effect of the use on the market for the work.

F. COPYRIGHT PROTECTION FOR SOFTWARE
The Computer Software Copyright Act of 1980 provides protection.

1. What Is Protected?
The binary object code (the part of a software program readable only by computer); the source code (the part of a program readable by people); and the program structure, sequence, and organization.

2. What May or May Not Be Protected
The "look and feel"—the general appearance, command structure, video images, menus, windows, and other displays—of a program.

G. COPYRIGHTS IN DIGITAL INFORMATION
Copyright law is important in cyberspace in part because the nature of the Internet means that data is "copied" before being transferred online.

1. The Copyright Act of 1976
Copyright law requires the copyright holder's permission to sell a "copy" of a work. For these purposes, loading a file or program into a computer's random access memory (RAM) is the making of a "copy."

2. Further Developments in Copyright Law

a. No Electronic Theft Act of 1997
Extends criminal liability to the exchange of pirated, copyrighted materials, even if no profit is realized from the exchange, and to the unauthorized copying of works for personal use.

b. Digital Millennium Copyright Act of 1998
Imposes penalties on anyone who circumvents encryption software or other technological anti-piracy protection. Also prohibits the manufacture, import, sale, or distribution of devices or services for circumvention. ISP s are not liable for their customers' violations.

c. MP3 and File-Sharing Technology
MP3 file compression and music file sharing occur over the Internet through peer-to-peer (P2P) networking. Doing this without the permission of the owner of the music's copyright is infringement.

V. TRADE SECRETS

A. WHAT IS A TRADE SECRET?
Customer lists, formulas, plans, research and development, pricing information, marketing techniques, production techniques, and generally anything that provides an opportunity to obtain an advantage over competitors who do not know or use it.

B. TRADE SECRET PROTECTION
Protection of trade secrets extends both to ideas and their expression. Liability extends to those who misappropriate trade secrets by any means. Trade secret theft is also a federal crime.

C. TRADE SECRETS IN CYBERSPACE
The nature of technology (especially e-mail) undercuts a firm's ability to protect its confidential information, including trade secrets.

VI. INTERNATIONAL PROTECTION

A. THE BERNE CONVENTION
The Berne Convention is an international copyright treaty.

1. For Citizens of Countries That Have Signed the Berne Convention
If, for example, an American writes a book, the copyright in the book is recognized by every country that has signed the convention.

2. For Citizens of Other Countries
If a citizen of a country that has not signed the convention publishes a book first in a country that has signed, all other countries that have signed the convention recognize that author's copyright.

B. **THE TRIPS AGREEMENT**
Trade-Related Aspects of Intellectual Property Rights (TRIPS) Agreement is part of the agreement creating the World Trade Organization (WTO). Each member nation must not discriminate (in administration, regulation, or adjudication of intellectual property rights) against the rights' owners.

C. **WORLD INTELLECTUAL PROPERTY ORGANIZATION (WIPO) COPYRIGHT TREATY**
Current international law includes the WIPO Copyright Treaty of 1996, which the United States implemented in the Digital Millennium Copyright Act of 1998.

TRUE-FALSE QUESTIONS

(Answers at the Back of the Book)

1. To obtain a patent, an applicant must show that an invention is genuine, novel, useful, and not obvious in light of current technology.

2. To obtain a copyright, an author must show that a work is genuine, novel, useful, and not a copy of a current copyrighted work.

3. In determining whether the use of a copyrighted work is infringement under the fair use doctrine, one factor is the effect of that use on the market for the work.

4. A personal name is protected under trademark law if it acquires a secondary meaning.

5. A formula for a chemical compound is not a trade secret.

6. A trade name, like a trademark, can be registered with the federal government.

7. A copy must be exactly the same as an original work to infringe on its copyright.

8. Only the *intentional* use of another's trademark can be trademark infringement.

9. Using another's trademark in a domain name without permission violates federal law.

10. Trademark dilution requires proof that consumers are likely to be confused by the unauthorized use of the mark.

FILL-IN QUESTIONS

(Answers at the Back of the Book)

Copyright protection is automatic for the life of the author of a work plus _____ (70/95/120) years. Copyrights owned by publishing houses expire _____ (70/95/120) years from the date of the publication of a work or _____ (70/95/120) years from the date of its creation, whichever is first. For works by more than one author, a copyright expires _____ (70/95/120) years after the death of the last surviving author.

MULTIPLE-CHOICE QUESTIONS

(Answers at the Back of the Book)

1. Alpha, Inc., uses Beta Corporation's patented design in Alpha's plan for a similar product, without Beta's permission. This is
a. copyright infringement.
b. patent infringement.
c. trademark infringement.
d. none of the above.

____ **2.** Omega, Inc., uses a trademark on its products that no one, including Omega, has registered with the government. Under federal trademark law, Omega

a. can register the mark for protection.
b. cannot register a mark that has been used in commerce.
c. has committed trademark infringement.
d. must postpone registration until the mark has been out of use for three years.

____ **3.** Ann invents a new type of light bulb and applies for a patent. If Ann is granted a patent, the invention will be protected

a. for 10 years.
b. for 20 years.
c. for the life of the inventor plus 70 years.
d. forever.

____ **4.** The graphics used in "Grave Robbers," a computer game, are protected by

a. copyright law.
b. patent law.
c. trademark law.
d. trade secrets law.

____ **5.** Production techniques used to make "Grave Robbers," a computer game, are protected by

a. copyright law.
b. patent law.
c. trademark law.
d. trade secrets law.

____ **6.** Tech Corporation uses USA, Inc.'s trademark in Tech's ads without USA's permission. This is

a. copyright infringement.
b. patent infringement.
c. trademark infringement.
d. none of the above.

____ **7.** Clothes made by workers who are members of the Clothes Makers Union are sold with tags that identify this fact. This is

a. a certification mark.
b. a collective mark.
c. a service mark.
d. trade dress.

____ **8.** Tony owns Antonio's, a pub in a small town in Iowa. Universal Dining, Inc., opens a chain of pizza places in California called "Antonio's" and, without Tony's consent, uses "antoniosincalifornia" as part of the URL for the chain's Web site. This is

a. copyright infringement.
b. patent infringement.
c. trademark dilution.
d. none of the above.

____   9.   Data Corporation created and sells "Economix," financial computer software. Data's copyright in Economix is best protected under

   a.   the Berne Convention.
   b.   the Paris Convention.
   c.   the TRIPS Agreement.
   d.   none of the above.

____   10.   National Media, Inc. (NMI), publishes *Opinion* magazine, which contains an article by Paula. Without her permission, NMI puts the article into an online database. This is

   a.   copyright infringement.
   b.   patent infringement.
   c.   trademark infringement.
   d.   none of the above.

SHORT ESSAY QUESTIONS

1.   What does a copyright protect?

2.   What is a trade secret and how is it protected?

ISSUE SPOTTERS

(Answers at the Back of the Book)

1.   Delta Company discovers that it can extract data from the computer of Gamma, Inc., its major competitor, by making a series of phone calls over a high-speed modem. When Delta uses its discovery to extract Gamma's customer list, without permission, what recourse does Gamma have?

2.   Global Products develops, patents, and markets software. World Copies, Inc., sells Global's software without the maker's permission. Is this patent infringement? If so, how might Global save the cost of suing World for infringement and at the same time profit from World's sales?

3.   Eagle Corporation began marketing software in 1995 under the mark "Eagle." In 2005, Eagle.com, Inc., a different company selling different products, begins to use "eagle" as part of its URL and registers it as a domain name. Can Eagle Corporation stop this use of "eagle"? If so, what must the company show?

Chapter 6:
Criminal Law and Cyber Crimes

WHAT THIS CHAPTER IS ABOUT

This chapter defines what makes an act a crime, describes crimes that affect business (including cyber crimes), lists defenses to crimes, and outlines criminal procedure. Sanctions for crimes are different from those for torts or breaches of contract. Another difference between civil and criminal law is that an individual can bring a civil suit, but only the government can prosecute a criminal.

CHAPTER OUTLINE

I. CIVIL LAW AND CRIMINAL LAW

A. CIVIL LAW
Civil law consists of the duties that exist between persons or between citizens and their governments, excluding the duty not to commit crimes.

B. CRIMINAL LAW
A **crime** is a wrong against society proclaimed in a statute and, if committed, punishable by society through fines, imprisonment, or death. Crimes are offenses against society as a whole and are prosecuted by public officials, not victims.

II. CLASSIFICATION OF CRIMES
Felonies are serious crimes punishable by death or by imprisonment in a federal or state penitentiary for more than a year. A crime that is not a felony is a **misdemeanor**—punishable by a fine or by confinement (in a local jail) for up to a year. Petty offenses are minor misdemeanors.

III. CRIMINAL LIABILITY
Two elements must exist for a person to be convicted of a crime—

A. CRIMINAL ACT
A criminal statute prohibits certain behavior—an act of commission (doing something) or an act of omission (not doing something that is a legal duty).

B. INTENT TO COMMIT A CRIME
The wrongful mental state required to establish guilt depends on the crime.

IV. CORPORATE CRIMINAL LIABILITY
Corporations are liable for crimes committed by their agents and employees within the course and scope of employment. Directors and officers are personally liable for crimes they commit and may be liable for the actions of employees under their supervision.

V.   TYPES OF CRIMES

A. VIOLENT CRIME
These include murder, rape, assault and battery (see Chapter 4), and robbery (forcefully and unlawfully taking personal property from another). They are classified by degree, depending on intent, weapon, and victim's suffering.

B. PROPERTY CRIME
Robbery could also be in this category.

1. Burglary
Burglary is the unlawful entry into a building with the intent to commit a felony.

2. Larceny
Larceny is wrongfully taking and carrying away another's personal property with the intent of depriving the owner permanently of the property (without force or intimidation, which are elements of robbery).

a. Property
The definition of property includes computer programs, computer time, trade secrets, cellular phone numbers, long-distance phone time, and natural gas.

b. Grand Larceny and Petit Larceny
In some states, grand larceny is a felony and petit larceny a misdemeanor. The difference depends on the value of the property taken.

3. Obtaining Goods by False Pretenses
This includes, for example, buying goods with a check written on an account with insufficient funds.

4. Receiving Stolen Goods
The recipient need not know the identity of the true owner of the goods.

5. Arson
Arson is the willful and malicious burning of a building (and in some states, personal property) owned by another. Every state has a statute that covers burning a building to collect insurance.

6. Forgery
Fraudulently making or altering any writing in a way that changes the legal rights and liabilities of another is forgery.

C. PUBLIC ORDER CRIME
Examples: public drunkenness, prostitution, gambling, and illegal drug use.

D. WHITE-COLLAR CRIME

1. Embezzlement
Fraudulently appropriating another's property or money by one who has been entrusted with it (without force or intimidation).

2. Mail and Wire Fraud

a. The Crime
It is a federal crime to (1) mail or cause someone else to mail something written, printed, or photocopied for the purpose of executing (2) a scheme to defraud (even if no one is defrauded). Also a crime to use wire, radio, or television transmissions to defraud.

b. The Punishment
Fine of up to $1,000, imprisonment for up to five years, or both. If a violation affects a financial institution, the fine may be up to $1 million, the imprisonment up to thirty years, or both.

3. **Bribery**

   a. **Bribery of Public Officials**

   This is attempting to influence a public official to act in a way that serves a private interest by offering the official a bribe. The crime is committed when the bribe (anything the recipient considers valuable) is offered.

   b. **Commercial Bribery**

   Attempting, by a bribe, to obtain proprietary information, cover up an inferior product, or secure new business is commercial bribery.

   c. **Bribery of Foreign Officials**

   A crime occurs when attempting to bribe foreign officials to obtain business contracts. The Foreign Corrupt Practices Act of 1977 (see Chapter 2) makes this a crime.

4. **Bankruptcy Fraud**

   Filing a false claim against a debtor; fraudulently transferring assets to favored parties; or fraudulently concealing property before or after a petition for bankruptcy is filed.

5. **The Theft of Trade Secrets**

   Under the Economic Espionage Act of 1996, it is a federal crime to steal trade secrets, or to knowingly buy or possess another's stolen secrets. Penalties include up to ten years' imprisonment, fines up to $500,000 (individual) or $5 million (corporation), and forfeiture of property.

6. **Insider Trading**

   Using inside information (information not available to the general public) about a publicly traded corporation to profit from the purchase or sale of the corporation's securities (see Chapter 21).

E. **ORGANIZED CRIME**

1. **Money Laundering**

   Transferring the proceeds of crime through legitimate businesses is money laundering. Financial institutions must report transactions of more than $10,000.

2. **The Racketeer Influenced and Corrupt Organizations Act**

   Two offenses under the Racketeer Influenced and Corrupt Organizations Act (RICO) of 1970 constitute "racketeering activity."

   a. **Activities Prohibited by RICO**

   (1) Use income from racketeering to buy an interest in an enterprise, (2) acquire or maintain such an interest through racketeering activity' (3) conduct or participate in an enterprise through racketeering activity, or 4) conspire to do any of the above.

   b. **Civil Liability**

   Civil penalties include divestiture of a defendant's interest in a business or dissolution of the business. Private individuals can recover treble damages, plus attorneys' fees.

   c. **Criminal Liability**

   RICO is often used to prosecute white-collar crimes. Penalties include fines of up to $25,000 per violation, imprisonment for up to 20 years, or both.

VI. DEFENSES TO CRIMINAL LIABILITY

A. **INFANCY**

Cases involving persons who have not reached the age of majority are handled in juvenile courts. In some states, a child over a certain age (usually fourteen) charged with a felony may be tried in an adult court.

B. INTOXICATION

Involuntary intoxication is a defense to a crime if it makes a person incapable of understanding that the act committed was wrong or incapable of obeying the law. *Voluntary* intoxication may be a defense if the person was so intoxicated as to lack the required state of mind.

C. INSANITY

1. The Model Penal Code Test

Most federal courts and some states use this test: a person is not responsible for criminal conduct if at the time, as a result of mental disease or defect, the person lacks substantial capacity either to appreciate the wrongfulness of the conduct or to conform his or her conduct to the law.

2. The *M'Naghten* Test

Some states use this test: a person is not responsible if at the time of the offense, he or she did not know the nature and quality of the act or did not know that the act was wrong.

3. The Irresistible Impulse Test

Some states use this test: a person operating under an irresistible impulse may know an act is wrong but cannot refrain from doing it.

D. MISTAKE

1. Mistake of Fact

Defense if it negates the mental state necessary to commit a crime.

2. Mistake of Law

A person not knowing a law was broken may have a defense if (1) the law was not published or reasonably made known to the public or (2) the person relied on an official statement of the law that was wrong.

E. CONSENT

Consent is a defense if it cancels the harm that the law is designed to prevent, unless the law forbids an act without regard to the victim's consent.

F. DURESS

1. What Duress Is

Duress occurs when a person's threat induces another person to do something that he or she would not otherwise do.

2. When Duress Is a Defense

(1) The threat is one of serious bodily harm, (2) the threat is immediate and inescapable, (3) the threatened harm is greater than the harm caused by the crime, and (4) the defendant is involved through no fault of his or her own.

G. JUSTIFIABLE USE OF FORCE

1. Nondeadly Force

People can use as much nondeadly force as seems necessary to protect themselves, their dwellings, or other property or to prevent a crime.

2. Deadly Force

Deadly force can be used in self-defense if there is a reasonable belief that imminent death or serious bodily harm will otherwise result, if the attacker is using unlawful force, and if the defender did not provoke the attack.

H. ENTRAPMENT

This occurs when a law enforcement agent suggests that a crime be committed, pressures or induces an individual to commit it, and arrests the individual for it.

I. **STATUTE OF LIMITATIONS**
A statute of limitation provides that the state has only a certain amount of time to prosecute a crime.

J. **IMMUNITY**
A state can grant immunity from prosecution or agree to prosecute for a less serious offense in exchange for information. This is often part of a plea bargain between the defendant and the prosecutor.

VII. CONSTITUTIONAL SAFEGUARDS AND CRIMINAL PROCEDURES
Most of these safeguards apply not only in federal courts but also in state courts by virtue of the due process clause of the Fourteenth Amendment.

A. **FOURTH AMENDMENT**
Protection from unreasonable searches and seizures. No warrants for a search or an arrest can be issued without probable cause.

B. **FIFTH AMENDMENT**
No one can be deprived of "life, liberty, or property without due process of law." No one can be tried twice (double jeopardy) for the same offense. No one can be required to incriminate himself or herself.

C. **SIXTH AMENDMENT**
Guarantees a speedy trial, trial by jury, a public trial, the right to confront witnesses, and the right to a lawyer in some proceedings.

D. **EIGHTH AMENDMENT**
Prohibits excessive bail and fines, and cruel and unusual punishment.

E. **EXCLUSIONARY RULE**
Evidence obtained in violation of the Fourth, Fifth, and Sixth Amendments, as well as all "fruit of the poisonous tree" (evidence derived from illegally obtained evidence), must be excluded.

F. *MIRANDA* **RULE**
A person in police custody who is to be interrogated must be informed that he or she has the right to remain silent; anything said can and will be used against him or her in court; he or she has the right to consult with an attorney; and if he or she is indigent, a lawyer will be appointed. Exceptions to this rule include "public safety."

G. **CRIMINAL PROCEDURES AND SENTENCING**

1. **Arrest**
Requires a warrant based on probable cause (a substantial likelihood that the person has committed or is about to commit a crime). To make an arrest without a warrant, an officer must also have probable cause.

2. **Indictment or Information**
A formal charge is called an **indictment** if issued by a grand jury and an **information** if issued by a government prosecutor.

3. **Trial**
Criminal trial procedures are similar to those of a civil trial, but the standard of proof is higher: the prosecutor must establish guilt beyond a reasonable doubt.

4. **Sentencing Guidelines**
    These guidelines cover possible penalties for federal crimes. A sentence is based on a defendant's criminal record, seriousness of the offense, and other factors.

VIII. CYBER CRIME

A. CYBER THEFT
Computers make it possible for employees and others to commit crimes (such as fraud) involving serious financial losses. The Internet has made identity theft and consequent crimes easier.

B. CYBER STALKING
Harassing a person in cyberspace (such as via e-mail). Prohibited by federal law and most states. Some states require a "credible threat" that puts the person in reasonable fear for his or her safety or the safety of the person's family.

C. HACKING AND CYBER TERRORISM
Using one computer to break into another is hacking. This is often part of cyber theft. Cyber terrorism is exploiting computers for such serious impacts as spreading a virus through a computer network.

D. PROSECUTING CYBER CRIMES
Jurisdictional issues and the anonymous nature of technology can hinder the investigation and prosecution of crimes committed in cyberspace.

1. **The Computer Fraud and Abuse Act**
    The Computer Access Device and Computer Fraud and Abuse Act of 1984 provides for criminal prosecution of a person who accesses a computer online, without authority, to obtain classified, restricted, or protected data (restricted government info, financial records, etc.), or attempts to do. Penalties include fines and up to five years' imprisonment.

2. **Other Federal Statutes**
    Electronic Fund Transfer Act of 1978, Anticounterfeiting Consumer Protection Act of 1996, National Stolen Property Act of 1988, and more.

TRUE-FALSE QUESTIONS

(Answers at the Back of the Book)

____ 1. Only the government prosecutes criminal defendants.

____ 2. A crime punishable by imprisonment is a felony.

____ 3. Burglary involves taking another's personal property from his or her person or immediate presence.

____ 4. Embezzlement requires physically taking property for another's possession.

____ 5. Stealing a computer program is larceny.

____ 6. Offering a bribe is only one element of the crime of bribery.

____ 7. Receiving stolen goods is a crime only if the recipient knows the true owner.

____ 8. Generally, a person is not responsible for a criminal act if, as a result of a mental defect, he or she lacked substantial capacity to appreciate the wrongfulness of the act.

____   9.   A person who accesses a computer online, without authorization, to obtain protected data commits a federal crime.

____   10.   RICO is often used to prosecute acts classified as white-collar crimes.

FILL-IN QUESTIONS

(Answers at the Back of the Book)

Specific constitutional safeguards for those accused of crimes apply in all federal courts, and most of them also apply in state courts under the due process clause of the Fourteenth Amendment. The safeguards include (1) the Fourth Amendment protection from _____ (unexpected/unreasonable) searches and seizures, (2) the Fourth Amendment requirement that no warrants for a search or an arrest can be issued without _____ (probable/possible) cause, (3) the Fifth Amendment requirement that no one can be deprived of "life, liberty, or property without _____ (consent/due process of law)," (4) the Fifth Amendment prohibition against double _____ (immunity/jeopardy), (5) the Sixth Amendment guaranties of a speedy _____ (appeal/trial), _____ (appeal to/trial by) a jury, a public trial, the right to confront _____ (counsel/witnesses), and the right to legal counsel, and (6) the Eighth Amendment prohibitions against excessive _____(bail/bail and fines) and cruel and unusual punishment.

MULTIPLE-CHOICE QUESTIONS

(Answers at the Back of the Book)

____   1.   Carl wrongfully takes a box from a Delta, Inc., shipping container, puts it in his truck, and drives away. This is

a. burglary.
b. embezzlement.
c. forgery.
d. larceny.

____   2.   Nora is charged with the commission of a crime. For a conviction, most crimes require

a. a specified state of mind and performance of a prohibited act.
b. neither a specified state of mind nor performance of a prohibited act.
c. only a specified state of mind or intent.
d. only the performance of a prohibited act.

____   3.   Adam signs Beth's name, without her consent, to the back of a check payable to Beth. This is

a. burglary.
b. embezzlement.
c. forgery.
d. larceny.

____   4.   Owen, a bank teller, deposits into his account checks that bank customers give to him to deposit into their accounts. This is

a. burglary.
b. embezzlement.
c. forgery.
d. larceny.

___ 5. Jay is charged with the commission of a crime. For a conviction, the standard to find Jay guilty is

a. a preponderance of the evidence.
b. beyond all doubt.
c. beyond a reasonable doubt.
d. clear and convincing evidence.

___ 6. Nick is charged with the crime of mail fraud. For a conviction, Nick must be found to have

a. had a scheme to defraud and used the mails.
b. had a scheme to defraud only.
c. neither schemed to defraud nor used the mails.
d. used the mails only.

___ 7. Sue, a government agent, arrests Tim for the commission of a crime. Tim claims that Sue entrapped him. This is a valid defense if Sue

a. did not tell Tim that she was a government agent.
b. pressured Tim into committing the crime.
c. set a trap for Tim, who was looking to commit the crime.
d. was predisposed to commit the crime.

___ 8. John is arrested on suspicion of the commission of a crime. Individuals who are arrested must be told of their right to

a. confront witnesses.
b. protection against unreasonable searches.
c. remain silent.
d. trial by jury.

___ 9. While away from her business, Kate is arrested on the suspicion of the commission of a crime. At Kate's trial, under the exclusionary rule

a. biased individuals must be excluded from the jury.
b. business records must be excluded from admission as evidence.
c. illegally obtained evidence must be excluded from admission as evidence.
d. the arresting officer must be excluded from testifying.

___ 10. Eve is arrested on suspicion of the commission of a crime. A grand jury issues a formal charge against Eve. This is

a. an arraignment.
b. an indictment.
c. an information.
d. an inquisition.

SHORT ESSAY QUESTIONS

1. What are some of the significant differences between criminal law and civil law?

2. What constitutes civil liability under the Racketeer Influenced and Corrupt Organizations Act (RICO) of 1968 and what are the penalties?

ISSUE SPOTTERS

(Answers at the Back of the Book)

1. Bob drives off in Fred's car mistakenly believing that it is his. Is this theft?

2. Ellen takes her roommate's credit card, intending to charge expenses that she incurs on a vacation. Her first stop is a gas station, where she uses the card to pay for gas. With respect to the gas station, has she committed a crime? If so, what is it?

3. Ben downloads consumer credit files from a computer of Consumer Credit Agency, without permission, over the Internet. Ben sells the data to Donna. Has Ben committed a crime? If so, what is it?

Chapter 7:
Contracts: Nature, Classification, Agreement, and Consideration

WHAT THIS CHAPTER IS ABOUT

Contract law concerns the formation and keeping of promises, the excuses our society accepts for breaking such promises, and what promises are considered contrary to public policy and therefore legally void. This chapter introduces the basic terms and concepts of contract law, and covers agreement and consideration—two of the elements for a valid contract—in more detail.

CHAPTER OUTLINE

I. THE NATURE AND FUNCTION OF CONTRACTS

Contract law assures the parties to private agreements that the promises they make will be enforceable. The law of contracts is followed in business agreements to avoid problems—for example, when price changes or adverse economic factors make it costly to comply with a promise.

A. DEFINITION OF A CONTRACT

A **contract** is an agreement that can be enforced in court. It is formed by two or more parties who promise to perform or refrain from performing some act now or in the future.

B. REQUIREMENTS OF A CONTRACT

1. **Agreement**
   Includes an offer and an acceptance. One party must offer to enter into a legal agreement, and another party must accept the offer.

2. **Consideration**
   Promises must be supported by legally sufficient and bargained-for consideration.

3. **Contractual Capacity**
   This concerns characteristics that qualify the parties to a contract as competent.

4. **Legality**
   A contract's purpose must be to accomplish a goal that is not against public policy.

5. **Defenses to the Enforcement of a Contract**

   a. **Genuineness of Assent**
      The apparent consent of both parties must be genuine.

   b. **Form**
      A contract must be in whatever form the law requires (some contracts must be in writing).

C. FREEDOM OF CONTRACT AND FREEDOM FROM CONTRACT

1. **Freedom of Contract**
   Generally, everyone may enter freely into contracts. This freedom is a strongly held public policy, and courts rarely interfere with contracts that have been voluntarily made.

2. Freedom from Contract

Illegal bargains, agreements unreasonably in restraint of trade, and unfair contracts between one party with a great amount of bargaining power and another with little power are generally not enforced. Contracts are not enforceable if they are contrary to public policy, fairness, and justice.

II.   TYPES OF CONTRACTS

Each category signifies a legal distinction regarding a contract's formation, performance, or enforceability.

A.   CONTRACT FORMATION

1. Bilateral versus Unilateral Contracts

a. Bilateral Contract

This is a promise for a promise—to accept the offer, the offeree need only promise to perform.

b. Unilateral Contract

This is a promise for an act—the offeree can accept only by performance. A problem arises when the promisor attempts to revoke the offer after the promisee has begun performance but before the act has been completed.

1) Revocation—Traditional View

The promisee can accept only by performing fully. Offers are revocable until accepted.

2) Revocation—Modern-Day View

The offer cannot be revoked once performance begins.

2. Formal versus Informal Contracts

A formal contract requires a special form or method of creation to be enforceable (such as a contract under seal, a formal writing with a special seal attached). All contracts that are not formal are informal, and except for certain contracts that must be in writing, no special form is required.

3. Express versus Implied Contracts

An express contract fully and explicitly states the terms of the agreement in words (oral or written). An implied-in-fact contract is implied from the conduct of the parties.

B.   CONTRACT PERFORMANCE

1. Executed Contract

This is a contract that has been fully performed on both sides.

2. Executory Contract

This is a contract that has not been fully performed by one or more parties.

C.   CONTRACT ENFORCEABILITY

1. Valid Contract

A valid contract has all the elements necessary for contract formation.

2. Voidable Contract

This is a valid contract that can be avoided by one or more parties (for example, contracts by minors are voidable at the minor's option).

3. Void Contract

This has no legal force or binding effect (for example, a contract is void if its purpose was illegal).

4. Unenforceable Contract

An unenforceable contract cannot be enforced because of certain legal defenses (for example, if a contract that must be in writing is not in writing).

D. QUASI CONTRACTS
In the absence of an actual contract, a court may impose a quasi contract to avoid the unjust enrichment of one party at the expense of another. Cannot be invoked if there is an actual contract that covers the area in controversy.

III. AGREEMENT
The elements of an agreement are an offer and an acceptance—one party offers a bargain to another, who accepts.

A. REQUIREMENTS OF THE OFFER
An **offer** is a promise or commitment to do or refrain from doing some specified thing in the future. An offer has three elements—

1. Intention
The offeror must intend to be bound by the offer.

a. How to Determine the Offeror's Intent
The offeror's intent is what a reasonable person in the offeree's position would conclude the offeror's words and actions meant. Offers in obvious anger, jest, or undue excitement do not qualify.

b. What Does Not Constitute an Offer?
Nonoffers include: (1) expressions of opinion, (2) statements of intention, (3) preliminary negotiations, and (4) advertisements, catalogues, price lists, and circulars. Auctions are a special situation—the bidder is the offeror; the seller is the offeree.

c. Agreements to Agree
Agreements to agree to a material term of a contract at some future date may be enforced if the parties clearly intended to be bound.

2. Definiteness
All of the major terms must be stated with reasonable definiteness in the offer (or, if the offeror directs, in the offeree's acceptance).

3. Communication
The offeree must know of the offer.

B. TERMINATION OF THE OFFER

1. Termination by Action of the Parties

a. Revocation of the Offer
The offeror usually can revoke the offer (even if he or she promised to keep it open), by express repudiation or by acts that are inconsistent with the offer and are made known to the offeree.

1) Communicated to the Offeree
A revocation becomes effective when the offeree or offeree's agent receives it.

2) Offers to the General Public
An offer made to the general public can be revoked in the same manner the offer was originally communicated.

b. Irrevocable Offers

1) When an Offeree Changes Position in Justifiable Reliance
The offer may not be revoked, under the doctrine of promissory estoppel (see below).

2) A Merchant's Firm Offer
The offer may be irrevocable (see Chapter 11).

3) Option Contract

An option contract is a promise to hold an offer open for a period of time. If no time is specified, a reasonable time is implied.

c. Rejection of the Offer by the Offeree

The offeree may reject an offer by words or conduct evidencing intent not to accept. A rejection is effective on receipt. Asking about an offer is not a rejection.

d. Counteroffer by the Offeree

The offeree's attempt to include different terms is a rejection of the original offer and a simultaneous making of a new offer. The **mirror image rule** requires the acceptance to match the offer exactly.

2. Termination by Operation of Law

a. Lapse of Time

An offer terminates automatically when the period of time specified in the offer has passed.

1) When the Time Begins to Run

Time begins to run when the offeree receives an offer. If there is a delay, time runs from the date the offeree would have received it (if the offeree knows or should know of the delay).

2) If No Time Is Specified

If no time is specified, a reasonable time is implied.

b. Destruction of the Subject Matter

An offer is automatically terminated.

c. Death or Incompetence of the Offeror or Offeree

An offeree's power of acceptance is terminated. Exceptions include irrevocable offers (see above).

d. Supervening Illegality of the Proposed Contract

When a statute or court decision makes an offer illegal, the offer is automatically terminated.

C. ACCEPTANCE

1. Who Can Accept?

Usually, only the offeree (or the offeree's agent) can accept.

2. Unequivocal Acceptance

The offeree must accept the offer unequivocally. This is the mirror image rule (see above).

3. Silence as Acceptance

Ordinarily, silence cannot operate as an acceptance. Silence or inaction can constitute acceptance in the following circumstances—

a. Receipt of Offered Services

If an offeree receives the benefit of offered services even though he or she had an opportunity to reject them and knew that they were offered with the expectation of compensation.

b. Prior Dealings

The offeree had prior dealings with the offeror that lead the offeror to understand silence will constitute acceptance.

4. Communication of Acceptance

    a. Bilateral Contract
    A bilateral contract is formed when acceptance is communicated. The offeree must use reasonable efforts to communicate acceptance.

    b. Unilateral Contract
    Communication is normally unnecessary, unless the offeror requests it or has no way of knowing the act has been performed.

  5. Mode and Timeliness of Acceptance (in Bilateral Contracts)
  Acceptance is timely if it is made before the offer is terminated.

    a. Authorized Means of Communication
    If an offeree uses a mode of communication expressly or impliedly authorized by the offeror, acceptance is effective on dispatch. This is the **mailbox rule** (deposited acceptance rule).

      1) Express
      When an offeror specifies how acceptance should be made and the offeree uses that mode, the acceptance is effective even if the offeror never receives it.

      2) Implied
      When an offeror does not specify how acceptance should be made, the offeree may use the same means the offeror used to make the offer or a faster means.

      3) Exceptions

        a) If an acceptance is not properly dispatched, in most states it will not be effective until it is received.

        b) If an offeror conditions an offer on receipt of acceptance by a certain time, acceptance is effective only on timely receipt.

        c) If both a rejection and an acceptance are sent, whichever is received first is effective.

    b. Unauthorized Means of Communication
    If an offeree uses a mode of communication that was not authorized by the offeror, acceptance is effective when received.

IV. CONSIDERATION
Consideration is the value given in return for a promise.

A. ELEMENTS OF CONSIDERATION
There are two elements to consideration: something of legal value and a bargained-for exchange.

  1. Something of Legal Value
  Something of legal value must be given in exchange for a promise. The "something" may be (1) a promise to do something that one had no legal duty to do, (2) performing an act that one had no legal duty to perform, or (3) refraining from doing something that one could otherwise do.

  2. Bargained-for Exchange
  The consideration given by the promisor must induce the promisee to incur legal detriment, and the detriment incurred must induce the promisor to make the promise. A gift does not have this.

B. ADEQUACY OF CONSIDERATION
Adequacy of consideration refers to the fairness of a bargain. Normally, a court will not question the adequacy of consideration.

1. **Extreme Cases**
    Extremely inadequate consideration may indicate fraud, duress, incapacity, undue influence, or a lack of bargained-for exchange.

2. **Unconscionability**
    A contract may be unconscionable (and unenforceable) if consideration is so one-sided under the circumstances as to be unfair. (See Chapter 8.)

C. CONTRACTS THAT LACK CONSIDERATION

1. **Preexisting Duty**
    A promise to do what one already has a legal duty to do does not constitute consideration (no legal detriment is incurred). Exceptions include—

    a. **Unforeseen Difficulties**
        If a party runs into extraordinary difficulties that were unforeseen when a contract was formed, some courts will enforce an agreement to pay more. Ordinary business risks are not included.

    b. **Rescission and New Contract**
        The parties can rescind a contract to the extent that it is executory.

2. **Past Consideration**
    An act already done cannot be consideration for a later promise.

3. **Illusory Promises**
    If a contract expresses such uncertainty of performance that the promisor has not definitely promised anything, it is unenforceable.

D. SETTLEMENT OF CLAIMS

1. **Accord and Satisfaction**
    Concerns a debtor's offer of payment and a creditor's acceptance of a lesser amount than the creditor originally purported to be owed.

    a. **Accord**
        The agreement under which one of the parties undertakes to give or perform, and the other to accept, in satisfaction of a claim, something other than that which was originally agreed on.

    b. **Satisfaction**
        Takes place when the accord is executed.

    c. **The Amount of the Debt Must Be Unliquidated (in Dispute)**

        1) **Unliquidated Debt—Consideration**
           When the amount of a debt is in dispute, acceptance of a lesser sum discharges the debt. Consideration is given by the parties' giving up a legal right to contest the amount of debt.

        2) **Liquidated Debt—No Consideration**
           Acceptance of less than the entire amount of a liquidated debt is not satisfaction, and the balance of the debt is still owed. The debtor gives no consideration, because he or she has a preexisting obligation to pay the entire debt.

2. **Release**
    A **release** (a promise to refrain from pursuing a valid claim) bars any further recovery beyond the terms stated in the release. Releases are generally binding if they are (1) given in good faith, (2) stated in a signed writing, and (3) accompanied by consideration.

3. **Covenant Not to Sue**

The parties substitute a contractual obligation for some other type of legal action based on a valid claim. If the obligation is not met, an action can be brought for breach of contract.

E. **PROMISSORY ESTOPPEL**

Under the doctrine of **promissory estoppel** (detrimental reliance), a person who relies on the promise of another may be able to recover if—

1. The promise was clear and definite.
2. The reliance is justifiable.
3. The reliance is of a substantial and definite character.
4. Justice will be better served by enforcement of the promise.

TRUE-FALSE QUESTIONS

(Answers at the Back of the Book)

____ 1. A unilateral contract is accepted by a promise to perform.

____ 2. An oral contract is an implied contract.

____ 3. An unenforceable contract is a valid contract that can be avoided by at least one of the parties to it.

____ 4. An executed contract is one that has been fully performed.

____ 5. A quasi contract arises from a mutual agreement between two parties.

____ 6. A contract does not need to contain reasonably definite terms to be enforced.

____ 7. A counteroffer terminates an offer.

____ 8. There are no irrevocable offers.

____ 9. The mirror image rule does not require an acceptance to match exactly an offer to create a contract.

____ 10. Inadequate consideration may indicate fraud, duress, or undue influence.

FILL-IN QUESTIONS

(Answers at the Back of the Book)

The elements necessary for an effective offer are (1) a _____ (serious/subjective) intent by the _____ (offeror/offeree) to be bound by the offer; (2) _____ (detailed/reasonably definite) contractual terms; and (3) communication of the offer to the _____ (offeror/offeree).

MULTIPLE-CHOICE QUESTIONS

(Answers at the Back of the Book)

____ 1. National Transport, Inc., agrees to deliver paper to Office Company, which promises to pay for the service. National delivers the paper. This contract is

a. executory on National's part.
b. executory on Office's part.
c. fully executed.
d. fully non-executed.

——   **2.**   Mary enters into an implied-in-fact contract with Nick. The parties' conduct

a.   defines the contract's terms.
b.   determines the facts.
c.   factors in the implications of the contract.
d.   is irrelevant in terms of the facts.

——   **3.**   Dan, a doctor, renders aid to Eve, who is injured. Dan can recover the cost of from Eve

a.   even if Eve was not aware of Dan's help.
b.   only if Eve was aware of Dan's help.
c.   only if Eve was *not* aware of Dan's help.
d.   under no circumstances.

——   **4.**   Rita calls Sam on the phone and agrees to buy his laptop computer for $500. This is

a.   an express contract.
b.   an implied-in-fact contract.
c.   an implied-in-law contract.
d.   a quasi contract.

——   **5.**   Ann's contract with Bob is voidable. If the contract is avoided

a.   both parties are released from it.
b.   neither party is released from it.
c.   only Ann is released from it.
d.   only Bob is released from it.

——   **6.**   Ann offers to buy from Bill a used computer, with a monitor and printer, for $400. Bill says, "OK, but $200 more for the monitor and printer." Bill has

a.   accepted the offer.
b.   made a counteroffer without rejecting the offer.
c.   rejected the offer and made a counteroffer.
d.   rejected the offer without making a counteroffer.

——   **7.**   Jill offers to sell her car to Kelly, stating that the offer will stay open for thirty days. Jill may revoke the offer

a.   before Kelly accepts the offer.
b.   before thirty days have expired, whether or not Kelly has accepted the offer.
c.   only after Kelly accepts the offer.
d.   only after thirty days.

——   **8.**   Leo offers to sell Mona a computer. Mona sends an acceptance via the mail. This acceptance is effective when it is

a.   in transit.
b.   received.
c.   sent.
d.   written.

____ 9. Best Office Company promises to pay Carl $1,000 to repair the roof on Best's building. Carl fixes the roof. The act of fixing the roof

   a. imposes a moral obligation on Best to pay Carl.
   b. imposes no obligation on Best unless it is satisfied with the job.
   c. is not sufficient consideration because it is not goods or money.
   d. is the consideration that creates Best's obligation to pay Carl.

____ 10. General Contractor Corporation (GCC) begins constructing a building for High-rise Apartments, Inc. In mid-project, GCC asks for $150,000 more, claiming an increase in ordinary business expenses. High-rise agrees. This agreement is

   a. enforceable as an accord and satisfaction.
   b. enforceable because of unforeseen difficulties.
   c. unenforceable as an illusory promise.
   d. unenforceable due to the preexisting duty rule.

SHORT ESSAY QUESTIONS

1. What are the basic elements of a contract?

2. What is the function of contract law?

ISSUE SPOTTERS

(Answers at the Back of the Book)

1. Ira receives from the local tax collector a notice of property taxes due. The notice is for tax on Jan's property, but Ira believes that the tax is his and pays it. Can Ira recover from Jan the amount paid?

2. One morning, when Ben's new car—with an $18,000 market value—doesn't start, he yells in anger, "I'd sell this car to anyone for $500." Carl drops $500 in Ben's lap. Is the car Ben's?

3. Before Paula starts her first year of college, Ross promises to pay her $5,000 if she graduates. She goes to college, borrowing and spending more than $5,000. At the start of he last semester, she reminds Ross of the promise. Ross sends her a note that says, "I revoke the promise." Is Ross's promise binding?

Chapter 8:
Contracts: Capacity, Legality, Assent, and Form

WHAT THIS CHAPTER IS ABOUT

If a party to a contract lacks capacity, an essential element for a valid contract is missing, and the contract is void. Also, to be enforceable, a contract must not violate any statutes or public policy. If the parties have not genuinely assented to the terms of the contract, or it is not in the proper form, it may be unenforceable.

CHAPTER OUTLINE

I. CONTRACTUAL CAPACITY

A. MINORS
A minor can enter into any contract that an adult can enter into, as long as it is not prohibited by law (for example, the sale of alcoholic beverages).

1. Disaffirmance
A minor can disaffirm a contract by manifesting an intent not to be bound. A contract can ordinarily be disaffirmed at any time during minority or for a reasonable time after a minor comes of age.

2. Obligations on Disaffirmance
A minor cannot disaffirm a fully executed contract without returning whatever goods have been received or paying their reasonable value.

a. What the Adult Recovers

1) **In Most States**
   If the goods (or other consideration) are in the minor's control, the minor must return them (without added compensation).

2) **In a Growing Number of States**
   If the goods have been used, damaged, or ruined, the adult must be restored to the position he or she held before the contract.

b. What the Minor Recovers
A minor can recover all property that he or she transferred to an adult as consideration, even if it is in a third party's hands. If it cannot be returned, the adult must pay the minor its value.

3. Misrepresentation of Age

a. In Most States
A minor who misrepresents his or her age can still disaffirm a contract. In some states, he or she is not liable for fraud, because indirectly that might force the minor to perform the contract.

b. In Some States
Some states prohibit disaffirmance; some courts refuse to allow minors to disaffirm executed contracts unless they can return the consideration; some courts allow a minor to disaffirm but hold the minor liable for damages for fraud.

4. **Contracts for Necessaries**
   Necessaries are food, clothing, shelter, medicine, and hospital care—whatever a court believes is necessary to maintain a person's status. A minor may disaffirm a contract for necessaries but will be liable for the reasonable value.

5. **Contracts for Insurance and Loans**
   In most states, minors can disaffirm insurance contracts and recover all premiums paid. A minor must repay a loan made to buy necessaries if the lender personally verified the money was so spent.

6. **Ratification**
   Ratification is the act of accepting and thereby giving legal force to an obligation that was previously unenforceable.

   a. **Express Ratification**
      When a minor states orally or in writing that he or she intends to be bound by a contract.

   b. **Implied Ratification**
      When a minor performs acts inconsistent with disaffirmance or fails to disaffirm an executed contract within a reasonable time after reaching the age of majority.

B. **INTOXICATED PERSONS**

1. **If a Person Is Sufficiently Intoxicated to Lack Mental Capacity**
   Any contract he or she enters into is voidable at the option of the intoxicated person, even if the intoxication was voluntary.

2. **If a Person Understands the Legal Consequences of a Contract**
   Despite intoxication, the contract is usually enforceable.

C. **MENTALLY INCOMPETENT PERSONS**

1. **Persons Adjudged Mentally Incompetent by a Court**
   If a person has been adjudged mentally incompetent by a court of law and a guardian has been appointed, a contract by the person is void.

2. **Incompetent Persons Not So Adjudged by a Court**

   a. **Voidable Contracts**
      A contract is voidable (at the option of the person) if a person does not know he or she is entering into the contract or lacks the capacity to comprehend its nature, purpose, and consequences.

   b. **Valid Contracts**
      If a mentally incompetent person understands the nature and effect of entering into a certain contract, the contract will be valid.

II.   LEGALITY

A. **CONTRACTS CONTRARY TO STATUTE**

1. **Usury**
   All states limit the rate of interest that may be charged for a loan.

2. **Gambling**
   All states regulate gambling.

3. **Sabbath (Sunday) Laws**

a. Prohibited Contracts
In some states, all contracts entered into on a Sunday are illegal. Other states prohibit only the sale of certain merchandise (such as alcoholic beverages) on a Sunday.

b. Exceptions
Contracts for necessities and works of charity; executed contracts.

4. Licensing Statutes
In some states, the lack of a required business license bars the enforcement of work-related contracts.

a. Illegal Contracts
If the statute's purpose is to protect the public from unauthorized practitioners, a contract with an unlicensed individual is illegal.

b. Enforceable Contracts
If the purpose of the statute is to raise revenue, a contract entered into with an unlicensed practitioner is enforceable.

B. CONTRACTS CONTRARY TO PUBLIC POLICY

1. Contracts in Restraint of Trade
Competition in the economy is favored so contracts that restrain trade or violate an antitrust statute (see Chapter 22) are prohibited.

a. Covenant Not to Compete
This is enforceable if it is reasonable, determined by the length of time and the size of the area in which the party agrees not to compete.

b. Reformation of an Illegal Covenant Not to Compete
A court may reform an unreasonable covenant not to compete by changing it to reflect the true intentions of the parties.

2. Unconscionable Contracts or Clauses
A bargain that is unfairly one-sided is **unconscionable**.

a. Procedural Unconscionability
This relates to a party's lack of knowledge or understanding of contract terms because of small print, "legalese," etc. An **adhesion contract** (drafted by one party for his benefit) may be held unconscionable.

b. Substantive Unconscionability
This relates to the parts of a contract that are so unfairly one-sided they "shock the conscience" of the court.

3. Exculpatory Clauses
Contract clauses attempting to release parties of negligence or other wrongs. Usually held to be contrary to public policy.

C. THE EFFECT OF ILLEGALITY
Generally, an illegal contract is void. No party can sue to enforce it and no party can recover for its breach. Exceptions include—

1. Justifiable Ignorance of the Facts
A party who is innocent may recover benefits conferred in a partially executed contract or enforce a fully performed contract.

2. Members of Protected Classes
When a statute is designed to protect a certain class of people, a member of that class can enforce a contract in violation of the statute (the other party to the contract cannot enforce it).

3. **Withdrawal from an Illegal Agreement**
   If the illegal part of an agreement has not been performed, the party rendering performance can withdraw and recover the performance or its value.

4. **Fraud, Duress, or Undue Influence**
   A party induced to enter into an illegal bargain by fraud, duress, or undue influence can enforce the contract or recover for its value.

5. **Severable, or Divisible Contracts**
   If a contract can be divided into parts, a court may enforce a legal portion but not an illegal part.

III.   GENUINENESS OF ASSENT

In most cases in which assent is not genuine, the innocent party can choose to rescind the contract, or enforce it and seek damages.

A. MISTAKES

1. **Unilateral Mistakes**
   When one contracting party makes a mistake as to some material fact, he or she is not entitled to relief from the contract. Exceptions are—

   a. **Other Party's Knowledge**
      A contract may not be enforceable if the other party to the contract knows or should have known that a mistake was made.

   b. **Mathematical Mistakes**
      A contract may not be enforceable if a mistake in addition, subtraction, division, or multiplication was inadvertent.

2. **Bilateral (Mutual) Mistakes**
   When both parties make a mistake as to some material fact, either party can rescind the contract. (If the mistake concerns the later value or quality of the object of the contract, however, either party can enforce the contract.)

B. FRAUDULENT MISREPRESENTATION

1. **The Elements of Fraud**
   These are (1) misrepresentation of a material fact, (2) an intent to deceive, and (3) an innocent party's justifiable reliance on the misrepresentation.

2. **Misrepresentation Must Occur**

   a. **Statements of Opinion**
      Statements of opinion are generally not subject to claims of fraud. But when a naïve purchaser relies on an expert's opinion, the innocent party may be entitled to rescission or reformation.

   b. **Misrepresentation by Conduct**
      Misrepresentation can occur by, for example, concealment, which prevents the other party from learning of a material fact.

3. **Intent to Deceive (*Scienter*)**
   The misrepresenting party must know that facts have been falsely represented. This occurs when a party (1) knows a fact is not as stated; (2) makes a statement that he or she believes not to be true or makes it recklessly, without regard to the truth; or (3) says or implies that a statement is made on a basis such as personal knowledge when it is not.

4. **Reliance on the Misrepresentation**
   The misrepresentation must be an important factor in inducing the party to contract. Reliance is not justified if the party knows the true facts or relies on obviously extravagant statements, or the defect is obvious.

5. **Injury to the Innocent Party**
   To rescind a contract, most courts do not require proof of injury. To recover damages, proof of injury is required.

C. UNDUE INFLUENCE

If a contract enriches a party at the expense of another who is dominated by the enriched party, the contract is voidable. The essential feature is that the party taken advantage of does not exercise free will.

D. DURESS

Duress involves coercive conduct—forcing a party to enter into a contract by threatening the party with a wrongful act. Economic need is not enough.

IV. THE STATUTE OF FRAUDS—REQUIREMENT OF A WRITING

The Statute of Frauds stipulates what types of contracts must be in writing to be enforceable. If one of these contracts is not in writing, it is not void but the Statute of Frauds is a defense to its enforcement.

A. CONTRACTS INVOLVING INTERESTS IN LAND

Land includes all objects permanently attached, such as trees. Contracts for transfer of interests in land, such as leases, must be in writing.

B. THE ONE-YEAR RULE

1. **When a Contract Must Be in Writing to Be Enforceable**
   A contract must be in writing if performance is objectively impossible within a year of the date of the contract's formation.

2. **When a Contract Need Not Be in Writing to Be Enforceable**
   A contract need not be in writing if performance within one year is possible—even if it is improbable, unlikely, or takes longer.

C. COLLATERAL PROMISES

1. **What Collateral Promises Must Be in Writing to Be Enforceable**
   A promise ancillary to a principal transaction and made by a third party to assume the debts or obligations of the primary party (only if the primary party does not perform).

2. **Exception—"Main Purpose" Rule**
   An oral promise to answer for the debt of another is enforceable if the guarantor's main purpose is to secure a personal benefit.

D. PROMISES MADE IN CONSIDERATION OF MARRIAGE

Prenuptial agreements must be in writing to be enforceable.

E. CONTRACTS FOR SALES OF GOODS

The Uniform Commercial Code (UCC) requires a writing for a sale of goods priced at $500 or more ($5,000 or more under the 2003 amendments to the UCC) [UCC 2–201].

F. EXCEPTIONS TO THE STATUTE OF FRAUDS

1. **Partial Performance**

   a. **Contracts for the Transfer of Interests in Land**
      If a buyer pays part of the price, takes possession, and makes permanent improvements and the parties cannot be returned to their pre-contract status quo, a court may grant specific performance.

    b. Contracts Covered by the UCC
    Under the UCC, an oral contract is enforceable to the extent that a seller accepts payment or a buyer accepts delivery of the goods.

  2. Admissions
  In some states, if a party admits in pleadings, testimony, or in court that a contract was made, the contract will be enforceable.

  3. Promissory Estoppel
  An oral contract may be enforced if (1) a promisor makes a promise on which the promisee justifiably relies to his or her detriment, (2) the reliance was foreseeable to the promisor, and (3) injustice can be avoided only by enforcing the promise.

  4. Special Exceptions under the UCC
  Oral contracts that may be enforceable under the UCC include those for customized goods and those between merchants that have been confirmed in writing (see Chapter 11).

V.   THE STATUTE OF FRAUDS—SUFFICIENCY OF THE WRITING

There must be at least a memo, confirmation, invoice, sales slip, check, fax, or several documents stapled together or in the same envelope that include—

A. THE SIGNATURE OF THE PARTY TO BE CHARGED

The writing must be signed (initialed) by the party who refuses to perform. The signature can be anywhere in the writing.

B. ESSENTIAL TERMS

  1. Contracts Covered by the UCC
  The writing must include a quantity term. Other terms need not be stated exactly, if they adequately reflect the parties' intentions.

  2. Other Contracts
  The writing must name the parties, subject matter, consideration, and quantity. In some states, a sale of land must include the price and a description of the property.

TRUE-FALSE QUESTIONS

(Answers at the Back of the Book)

____ 1. Some states impose a duty of restitution on minors who disaffirm contracts.

____ 2. A contract that exculpates one party for negligence or other wrongdoing will usually be viewed as unconscionable.

____ 3. A contract that calls for the performance of an illegal act may be enforceable.

____ 4. A contract with an unlicensed practitioner is always enforceable.

____ 5. A covenant not to compete is never enforceable.

____ 6. A unilateral mistake does not generally afford the mistaken party a right to relief from the contract.

____ 7. When both parties are mistaken as to the same material fact, neither party can rescind the contract.

____ 8. To constitute fraud, misleading statements must be consciously false and have been made with an intent to mislead another.

____   **9.**   To rescind a contract for fraud, a plaintiff must prove that he or she suffered an injury.

____   **10.**   To be enforceable, a contract for a sale of goods priced at $300 or more must be in writing.

FILL-IN QUESTIONS

(Answers at the Back of the Book)

The act of accepting and giving legal force to an obligation that previously was not enforceable is _____ (disaffirmance/ratification). In relation to contracts entered into by minors or persons who are intoxicated or mentally incompetent, this is an act or an expression in words by which the person, on or after reaching majority or regaining sobriety or mental competence, indicates intent to be bound by a contract.

Disaffirmance or ratification may be express or implied. For example, a person's continued use and payments on something bought when he or she was incompetent is inconsistent with a desire to _____ (disaffirm/ratify) and _____ (indicates/does not indicate) an intent to be bound by the contract. In general, any act or conduct showing an intent to affirm the contract will be deemed _____ (disaffirmance/ratification).

MULTIPLE-CHOICE QUESTIONS

(Answers at the Back of the Book)

____   **1.**   While a minor, Kay buys a car. After reaching the age of majority, Kay still maintains and operates the car. With regard to Kay's contract to buy the car, a court would likely hold that Kay

   a. disaffirmed it.
   b. emancipated it.
   c. ratified it.
   d. rescinded it.

____   **2.**   Eve, a sixteen-year-old minor, buys a car from Fine Autos and wrecks it. To disaffirm the contract and satisfy a duty of restitution, Eve must

   a. only return the car.
   b. only pay for the damage.
   c. return the car and pay for the damage.
   d. none of the above.

____   **3.**   Jill sells her business to Kyle and, as part of the agreement, promises not to engage in a business of the same kind within thirty miles for three years. This promise is most likely

   a. an unreasonable restraint of trade.
   b. unreasonable in terms of geographic area and time.
   c. unreasonable in terms of Kyle's "goodwill" and "reputation."
   d. valid and enforceable.

____   **4.**   Luke is an unlicensed contractor in a state that requires a license to protect the public from unauthorized contractors. Mary hires Luke to build an office building. This contract is

   a. enforceable only after Mary learns of Luke's status.
   b. enforceable only before Mary learns of Luke's status.
   c. enforceable only if no problems arise.
   d. unenforceable.

____ 5. Fred signs a covenant not to compete with his employer, General Sales Corporation. This covenant is enforceable if it

   a. is not ancillary to the sale of a business.
   b. is reasonable in terms of geographic area and time.
   c. is supported by consideration.
   d. requires both parties to obtain business licenses.

____ 6. Adam persuades Beth to contract for his company's services by telling her that his employees are the "best and the brightest." Adam's statement is

   a. duress.
   b. fraud.
   c. puffery.
   d. undue influence.

____ 7. Carol sells to Dan ten shares of Eagle Corporation stock. Dan believes that it will increase in value, but it later drops in price. From Carol, Dan can most likely recover

   a. the difference between the stock's purchase price and its later value.
   b. the stock's later value only.
   c. the stock's purchase price only.
   d. none of the above.

____ 8. Standard Business Company agrees to hire Tim as a sales representative for six months. Their contract is oral. This contract is enforceable by

   a. neither Standard nor Tim.
   b. Standard only.
   c. Standard or Tim.
   d. Tim only.

____ 9. Ed borrows $1,000 from First State Bank. Fran orally promises the bank that she will repay the debt if Ed does not. This promise is enforceable by

   a. Ed only.
   b. Ed or First State Bank.
   c. First State Bank only.
   d. neither Ed nor First Bank.

____ 10. Jay and Kim enter into a contract for Jay's sale to Kim of eleven computers for $500 each. After Kim takes possession, but before she makes payment, this contract is enforceable

   a. enforceable only if it is in writing.
   b. enforceable only if it is oral.
   c. enforceable whether it is oral or in writing.
   d. not enforceable.

SHORT ESSAY QUESTIONS

1. Who has protection under the law relating to contractual capacity and what protection do they have?

2. What is required to satisfy the writing requirement of the Statute of Frauds?

ISSUE SPOTTERS

(Answers at the Back of the Book)

1. International Airlines, Inc., prints on its tickets that it is not liable for any injury to a passenger caused by the airline's negligence. If the cause of an accident is found to be the airline's negligence, can it use the clause as a defense to liability?

2. In selling a house, Matt tells Nora that the wiring is of a certain quality. Matt knows nothing about the quality, until he later learns that it is not as he represented. He says nothing to Nora, who buys the house. When she discovers the truth, can she rescind the deal?

3. Paula orally agrees with Quality Corporation to work in New York for two years. She moves her family to New York and begins work. Three months later, she is fired for no stated cause. Could she successfully sue for reinstatement or pay?

Chapter 9:
Contracts: Third Party Rights, Discharge, Breach, and Remedies

WHAT THIS CHAPTER IS ABOUT

A party to a contract can assign the rights arising from it to another party or delegate the duties of the contract by having another person perform them. A third party also acquires rights to enforce a contract when the contracting parties intend that the contract benefit the third party (who is known as an *intended* beneficiary). This chapter also discusses performance and, as the title states, discharge and breach of contract, as well as contractual remedies.

CHAPTER OUTLINE

I.   ASSIGNMENTS AND DELEGATIONS
Assignment and delegation occur after the original contract is made, when one of the parties transfers to another party an interest or duty in the contract.

A. ASSIGNMENTS

1.   **What an Assignment Is**
Parties to a contract have rights and duties. One party has a *right* to require the other to perform, and the other has a *duty* to perform. The transfer of the *right* to a third person is an assignment.

2.   **Rights That Cannot Be Assigned**

a.   **Statute Prohibits Assignment**
(Such as assignment of future workers' compensation benefits.)

b.   **Contract Is Personal**
The rights under the contract cannot be assigned unless all that remains is a money payment.

c.   **Assignment Materially Increases or Alters Risk or Duties of Obligor**

d.   **Contract Stipulates That It Cannot Be Assigned**
Exceptions: a contract cannot prevent an assignment of (1) a right to receive money, (2) rights in real property (known as restraints against alienation), (3) rights in negotiable instruments (see Chapter 14), or (4) a right to receive damages for breach of a sales contract or for payment of an amount owed under the contract.

B. DELEGATIONS
Duties are delegated. The party making the delegation is the delegator; the party to whom the duty is delegated is the delegatee.

1.   **Duties That Cannot Be Delegated**
Any duty can be delegated, unless (1) performance depends on the personal skill or talents of the obligor, (2) special trust has been placed in the obligor, (3) performance by a third party will vary materially from that expected by the obligee (the one to whom performance is owed) under the contract, or (4) the contract expressly prohibits it.

2. **Effect of a Delegation**
    The obligee (the one to whom performance is owed) must accept performance from the delegatee, unless the duty is one that cannot be delegated. If the delegatee fails to perform, the delegator is still liable.

3. **Liability of the Delegatee**
    If the delegatee makes a promise of performance that will directly benefit the obligee, there is an "assumption of duty." Breach of this duty makes the delegatee liable to the obligee, and the obligee can sue both the delegatee and the delegator.

4. **"Assignment of All Rights"**
    A contract that provides in general words for an assignment of all rights (for example, "I assign the contract" or "I assign all my rights under the contract") is both an assignment of rights and a delegation of duties.

II. THIRD PARTY BENEFICIARIES
Only intended beneficiaries acquire legal rights in a contract.

A. INTENDED BENEFICIARIES
An intended beneficiary is one for whose benefit a contract is made. If the contract is breached, he or she can sue the promisor.

1. **Types of Intended Beneficiaries**

    a. **Creditor Beneficiaries**
        A creditor beneficiary benefits from a contract in which a promisor promises to pay a debt that the promisee owes to him or her.

    b. **Donee Beneficiaries**
        A donee beneficiary benefits from a contract made for the express purpose of giving a gift to him or her.

2. **When the Rights of an Intended Beneficiary Vest**
    To enforce a contract against the original parties, the rights of the third party must first vest (take effect). The rights vest when (1) the third party manifests assent to the contract or (2) the third party materially alters his or her position in detrimental reliance

3. **Modification or Rescission of the Contract**
    Until the third party's rights vest, the others can modify or rescind the contract without the third party's consent. If the contract reserves the power to rescind or modify, vesting does not terminate the power.

B. INCIDENTAL BENEFICIARIES
The benefit that an incidental beneficiary receives from a contract between other parties is unintentional. An incidental beneficiary cannot enforce a contract to which he or she is not a party.

C. INTENDED OR INCIDENTAL BENEFICIARY?

1. **Reasonable Person Test**
    A beneficiary is intended if a reasonable person in his or her position would believe that the promisee intended to confer on the beneficiary the right to sue to enforce the contract.

2. **Other Factors Indicating an Intended Beneficiary**
    (1) Performance is rendered directly to the third party, (2) the third party has the right to control the performance, or (3) the third party is expressly designated as beneficiary in the contract.

III.   CONTRACT DISCHARGE

A. CONDITIONS OF PERFORMANCE
If performance is contingent on a condition and it is not satisfied, a party does not have to perform.

B. DISCHARGE BY PERFORMANCE
Most contracts are discharged by the parties' doing what they promised to do. Discharge can be accomplished by tender. If performance has been tendered and the other party refuses to perform, the party making the tender can sue for breach.

1.   Complete versus Substantial Performance

a. Complete Performance
Express conditions fully occur in all aspects. Any deviation is a breach of contract and discharges the other party.

b. Substantial Performance
Performance that does not vary greatly from the performance promised in the contract. If one party fulfills the terms of the contract with substantial performance, the other party is obligated to perform (but may obtain damages for the minor deviations).

2.   Performance to the Satisfaction of Another

a. Personal Satisfaction of One of the Parties
When the subject matter of the contract is personal, performance must actually satisfy the party (a condition precedent).

b. Satisfaction of a Reasonable Person
Contracts involving mechanical fitness, utility, or marketability need only be performed to the satisfaction of a reasonable person.

c. Satisfaction of a Third Party
When the satisfaction of a third party is required, most courts require the work to be satisfactory to a reasonable person.

3.   Material Breach of Contract
A **breach of contract** is the nonperformance of a contractual duty. A breach is material when performance is not at least substantial. The nonbreaching party is excused from performing.

4.   Anticipatory Repudiation
This occurs when, before either party has a duty to perform, one party refuses to perform. It can discharge the nonbreaching party, who can sue to recover damages and also seek a similar contract elsewhere.

C. DISCHARGE BY AGREEMENT
Any contract can be discharged by an agreement of the parties.

1.   Discharge by Rescission
Rescission is the process by which a contract is canceled and the parties are returned to the positions they occupied prior to forming it.

a. Executory Contracts
Can be rescinded. The parties must make another agreement, which must satisfy the legal requirements for a contract. Their promises not to perform are consideration for the second contract.

    b. Enforceable Even if Made Orally

       Unless the new agreement falls within the Statute of Frauds, or the original contract was subject to the UCC and required a writing.

    c. Executed Contracts

       Can be rescinded only if the party who has performed receives consideration to call off the deal.

2. Discharge by Novation

  Occurs when the parties to a contract and a new party get together and agree to substitute the new party for one of the original parties. Requirements are (1) a previous valid obligation, (2) an agreement of all the parties to a new contract, (3) the extinguishment of the old obligation (discharge of the prior party), and (4) a new, valid contract .

3. Discharge by Accord and Satisfaction

  The parties agree to accept performance that is different from the performance originally promised.

    a. Accord

       An accord is an executory contract to perform an act that will satisfy an existing duty. An accord suspends, but does not discharge, the duty.

    b. Satisfaction

       The performance of the accord discharges the original contract.

    c. If the Obligor Refuses to Perform

       The obligee can sue on the original obligation or seek a decree for specific performance on the accord.

D. DISCHARGE BY OPERATION OF LAW

1. Contract Alteration

  An innocent party can treat a contract as discharged if the other party materially alters a term (such as quantity or price) without consent.

2. Statutes of Limitations

  Statutes of limitations limit the period during which a party can sue based on a breach of contract.

3. Bankruptcy

  A discharge in bankruptcy (Chapter 16) normally bars enforcement of most of a debtor's contracts.

4. When Performance Is Impossible

    a. Objective Impossibility

       Performance is objectively impossible in the event of (1) a party's death or incapacity, (2) destruction of the specific subject matter of a contract, or (3) change in law that makes performance illegal.

    b. Commercial Impracticability

       Performance may be excused if it becomes much more difficult or expensive than contemplated when the contract was formed.

    c. Temporary Impossibility

       An event that makes it temporarily impossible to perform will suspend performance until the impossibility ceases.

IV. DAMAGES

Damages compensate a nonbreaching party for the loss of a bargain and, under special circumstances, for additional losses. Generally, the party is placed in the position he or she would have occupied if the contract been performed.

A. TYPES OF DAMAGES

1. Compensatory Damages

Compensatory damages compensate a party for the *loss* of a bargain—the difference between the promised performance and the actual performance.

a. Incidental Damages

These are added expenses that are caused directly by a breach of contract (such as those incurred to obtain performance from another source).

b. Measurement of Compensatory Damages

1) Sale of Goods

Usual measure is the difference between the contract price and the market price. If a buyer breaches and the seller has not yet made the goods, the measure is lost profit on the sale.

2) Sale of Land

If specific performance (see below) is unavailable, or if the buyer breaches, the measure of damages is the difference between the land's contract price and its market price.

3) Construction Contracts

a) **Owner's Breach Before, During, or After Construction**

Contractor can recover (1) before construction: only profits (contract price, less cost of materials and labor); (2) during construction: profits, plus cost of partial construction; (3) after construction: the contract price, plus interest.

b) **Contractor's Breach**

Owner can recover, before construction is complete, the cost of completion.

2. Consequential Damages

These damages give an injured party the entire *benefit* of the bargain—foreseeable losses caused by special circumstances beyond the contract. The breaching party must know (or have reason to know) that special circumstances will cause the additional loss.

3. Punitive Damages

Punitive damages punish a guilty party and make an example to deter similar, future conduct. Awarded for a tort, but not for a contract breach.

4. Nominal Damages

These damages (such as $1) establish that even if no loss resulted, a defendant acted wrongfully.

B. MITIGATION OF DAMAGES

An injured party has a duty to mitigate damages. For example, persons whose jobs have been wrongfully terminated have a duty to seek other jobs. The damages they receive are their salaries, less the income they received (or would have received) in similar jobs.

C. LIQUIDATED DAMAGES VERSUS PENALTIES

1. Liquidated Damages Provision—Enforceable

Specifies a certain amount to be paid in the event of a breach to the nonbreaching party for the loss.

2. Penalty Provision—Unenforceable

Specifies a certain amount to be paid in the event of a breach *to penalize the breaching party.*

3. **How to Determine If a Provision Will Be Enforced**
Ask (1) When the contract was made, was it clear that damages would be difficult to estimate in the event of a breach? (2) Was the amount set as damages a reasonable estimate? If either answer is "no," the provision will not be enforced.

V.   EQUITABLE REMEDIES

A. RESCISSION AND RESCISSION
Rescission is an action to undo, or cancel, a contract—to return nonbreaching parties to the positions they occupied prior to the transaction. Rescission is available if fraud, mistake, duress, or failure of consideration is present. The rescinding party must give prompt notice to the breaching party, and the parties must make **restitution** by returning to each other goods, property, or money previously conveyed.

B. SPECIFIC PERFORMANCE
This remedy calls for the performance of the act promised in the contract.

1. **When Specific Performance Is Available**
Damages must be an inadequate remedy. If goods are unique, a court will grant specific performance. Specific performance is usually granted to a buyer on the breach of a contract for the sale of land (every parcel of land is unique).

2. **When Specific Performance Is Not Available**
Contracts for sales of goods (other than unique goods) rarely qualify, because substantially identical goods can be bought or sold elsewhere. Courts normally refuse to grant specific performance of personal service contracts.

C. REFORMATION
This remedy is used when the parties have imperfectly expressed their agreement in writing. Reformation allows the contract to be rewritten to reflect the parties' true intentions.

1. **When Reformation Is Available**
(1) In cases of fraud or mutual mistake; (2) to prove the correct terms of an oral contract; (3) if a covenant not to compete is for a valid purpose (such as the sale of a business), but the area or time constraints are unreasonable, some courts will reform the restraints to make them reasonable.

2. **When Reformation Is Not Available**
If the area or time constraints in a covenant not to compete are unreasonable, some courts will throw out the entire covenant.

VI.   RECOVERY BASED ON QUASI CONTRACT
When there is no enforceable contract, quasi contract prevents unjust enrichment. The law implies a promise to pay the reasonable value for benefits received.

A. WHEN QUASI-CONTRACTUAL RECOVERY IS USEFUL
This remedy is useful when a party has partially performed under a contract that is unenforceable. The party may recover the reasonable value (fair market value).

B. REQUIREMENTS
The party seeking recovery must show (1) he or she conferred a benefit on the other party, (2) he or she had the reasonable expectation of being paid, (3) he or she did not act as a volunteer in conferring the benefit, and (4) the other party would be unjustly enriched by retaining it without paying.

VII.   ELECTION OF REMEDIES
To prevent double recovery, a nonbreaching party must choose which remedy to pursue. This doctrine has been eliminated in contracts for sales of goods—UCC remedies are cumulative (see Chapter 12).

TRUE-FALSE QUESTIONS

(Answers at the Back of the Book)

_____ 1. Third parties do not have rights under contracts to which they are not parties.

_____ 2. If a delegatee fails to perform, the delegator must do so.

_____ 3. Complete performance occurs when a contract's conditions fully occur.

_____ 4. A material breach of contract does not excuse the nonbreaching party from further performance.

_____ 5. Objective impossibility discharges a contract.

_____ 6. Liquidated damages are uncertain in amount.

_____ 7. On rescission, the parties essentially return to the positions they were in before the contract.

_____ 8. On a breach of contract, a nonbreaching party has a duty to mitigate damages that he or she suffers.

_____ 9. Quasi-contractual recovery is possible only when there is an enforceable contract.

_____ 10. Consequential damages are foreseeable damages that arise from a party's breach of a contract.

FILL-IN QUESTIONS

(Answers at the Back of the Book)

The usual measure of compensatory damages under a contract for a sale of goods is the difference between _____ (the contract price and the market price/the market price and lost profits on the sale). The usual remedy for a seller's breach of a contract for a sale of land is _____ (specific performance/rescission and restitution). If this remedy is unavailable or if the buyer breaches, in most states the measure of damages is the difference between _____ (the contract price and the market price/the market price and lost profits on the sale).

MULTIPLE-CHOICE QUESTIONS

(Answers at the Back of the Book)

_____ 1. Jim and Kay enter into a contract that intentionally benefits Lora. Lora's rights under this contract will vest

   a. if she manifest assent to it or if she materially alters her position in detrimental reliance on it.
   b. only if she manifests assent to it.
   c. only if she materially alters her position in detrimental reliance on it.
   d. under no circumstances.

_____ 2. Sam and Tony want to discharge their obligations under a prior contract by executing and performing a new agreement. They must execute and perform

   a. an accord and satisfaction.
   b. an assignment.
   c. a novation.
   d. a nullification.

_____ **3.** Lee and Mary want Nick to replace Lee as a party to their contract. They can best accomplish this by agreeing to

a. an accord and satisfaction.
b. an assignment.
c. a novation.
d. a nullification.

_____ **4.** Adam contracts with Beth to deliver Beth's goods to her customers. This contract, like most contracts, will be discharged by

a. accord and satisfaction.
b. agreement.
c. operation of law.
d. performance.

_____ **5.** Carl contracts with Diane to build a store on her property. If, before construction begins, the county enacts a law that prohibits building a store on that property, then

a. Carl is in breach of contract.
b. Diane is in breach of contract.
c. the contract is discharged.
d. the contract is suspended until the parties choose a new location.

_____ **6.** Ann pays Bob $1,000 to design a computer network for her business. The next day, Bob tells Ann that he has accepted a job with CompuWeb and cannot design her network, but he does not return her payment. Ann can recover

a. $1,000.
b. Bob's pay from CompuWeb.
c. $1,000 plus Bob's pay from CompuWeb.
d. nothing.

_____ **7.** Sue contracts to sell a quantity of CD players to Tom for $1,000, payable in advance. Tom pays the money, but Sue fails to perform. Tom can

a. neither rescind the contract nor obtain restitution of the $1,000.
b. obtain restitution of the $1,000 but not rescind the contract.
c. rescind the contract and obtain restitution of the $1,000.
d. rescind the contract but not obtain restitution of the $1,000.

_____ **8.** Eagle Corporation contracts to sell to Frosty Malts, Inc., six steel mixers for $5,000. When Eagle fails to deliver, Frosty buys mixers from Great Company, for $6,500. Frosty's measure of damages is

a. $6,500.
b. $5,000.
c. $1,500 plus incidental damages.
d. nothing.

____   9.   General Construction (GC) contracts to build a store for Home Stores, Inc. (HIS), for $1 million. In mid-project, HSI repudiates the contract, and GC stops working. GC incurred costs of $600,000 and would have made a profit of $100,000. GC's measure of damages is

    a. $1 million.
    b. $700,000.
    c. $100,000.
    d.   nothing.

____   10.   Owen contracts with Paul to buy a computer for $1,500. Owen tells Paul that if the goods are not delivered on Monday, he will lose $2,000 in business. Paul ships the computer late. Owen can recover

    a. $3,500.
    b. $2,000.
    c. $1,500.
    d.   nothing.

SHORT ESSAY QUESTIONS

1.   What effect does a material breach have on the nonbreaching party? What is the effect of a nonmaterial breach?

2.   What are damages designed to do in a breach of contract situation?

ISSUE SPOTTERS

(Answers at the Back of the Book)

1.   Eagle Construction contracts with Fred to build a store. The work is to begin on May 1 and be done by November 1, so that Fred can open for the holiday buying season. Eagle does not finish until November 15. Fred opens but, due to the delay, loses some sales. Is Fred's duty to pay for the construction of the store discharged?

2.   Greg contracts to build a storage shed for Holly, who pays Greg in advance, but Greg completes only half the work. Holly pays Ira $500 to finish the shed. If Holly sues Greg, what would be the measure of recovery?

3.   Excel Engineering, Inc., signs a contract to design a jet for Flight, Inc. The contract excludes liability for design and construction errors. An error in design causes the jet to crash. Is the clause that excluded liability enforceable?

Chapter 10:
E-Contracts

WHAT THIS CHAPTER IS ABOUT

E-contracts include any contract entered into in e-commerce, whether business to business (B2B) or business to consumer (B2C), and any contract involving the computer industry. This chapter reviews some of the problems of e-contracts.

CHAPTER OUTLINE

I. FORMING CONTRACTS ONLINE

Disputes arising from contracts entered into online concern the terms and the parties' assent to those terms.

A. ONLNE OFFERS

Terms should be conspicuous and clearly spelled out. On a Web site, this can be done with a link to a separate page that contains the details. Subjects include remedies, forum selection, payment, taxes, refund and return policies, disclaimers, and privacy policies. A click-on acceptance box should also be included.

B. ONLNE ACCEPTANCES

A *shrink-wrap agreement* is an agreement whose terms are expressed inside a box in which a product is packaged. Usually, the agreement is not between a seller and a buyer, but a manufacturer and the product's user. Terms generally concern warranties, remedies, and other issues.

1. Shrink-Wrap Agreements—Enforceable Contract Terms

Courts often enforce shrink-wrap agreements, reasoning that the seller proposed an offer that the buyer accepted after an opportunity to read the terms. Also, it is more practical to enclose the full terms of sale in a box.

2. Shrink-Wrap Agreements—Terms that May Not Be Enforced

If a court finds that the buyer learned of the shrink-wrap terms *after* the parties entered into a contract, the court might conclude that those terms were proposals for additional terms, which were not part of the contract unless the buyer expressly agreed to them.

3. Click-On Agreements

A *click-on agreement* is when a buyer, completing a transaction on a computer, indicates his or her assent to be bound by the terms of the offer by clicking on a button that says, for example, "I agree." The terms may appear on a Web site through which a buyer obtains goods or services, or on a computer screen when software is loaded.

4. Browse-Wrap Terms

Browse-wrap terms do not require a user to assent to the terms before going ahead with an online transaction. Offerors of these terms generally assert that they are binding without the user's active consent. Critics argue that a user should at least be required to navigate past the terms before they should be considered binding.

II. E-SIGNATURES

How are e-signatures created and verified, and what is their legal effect?

A. E-SIGNATURE TECHNOLOGIES

Methods for creating and verifying e-signatures include—

1. **Digital Signatures**
   Asymmetric (different) cryptographic keys provide private code for one party and public software for another party, who reads the code to verify the first party's identity. A cybernotary issues the keys.

2. **Signature Dynamics**
   One party signs a digital pad with a stylus. A measurement of the signature, with time and date, is encrypted in a biometric token and attached to a document. Another party can use the token to verify the signature.

3. **Other Forms**
   A smart card is a credit-card size device embedded with code that can be read by a computer to establish a person's identity or signature. Other possibilities include retina- and face-scanning.

B. **STATE LAWS GOVERNING E-SIGNATURES**
   Most states have laws governing e-signatures, although the laws are not uniform. The Uniform Electronic Transactions Act (UETA), issued in 1999, was an attempt by the National Conference of Commissioners on Uniform State Laws (NCCUSL) to create more uniformity.

C. **FEDERAL LAW ON E-SIGNATURES AND E-DOCUMENTS**
   In 2000, Congress enacted the Electronic Signatures in Global and National Commerce (E-SIGN) Act to provide that no contract, record, or signature may be denied legal effect solely because it is in an electronic form. Some documents are excluded (such as those governed by UCC Articles 3, 4, and 9.)

III. PARTNERING AGREEMENTS

Through a partnering agreement, a seller and a buyer agree in advance on the terms to apply in all transactions subsequently conducted electronically. These terms may include access and identification codes. A partnering agreement, like any contract, can prevent later disputes.

IV. THE UNIFORM ELECTRONIC TRANSACTIONS ACT

The UETA removes barriers to e-commerce by giving the same legal effect to e-records and e-signatures as to paper documents and signatures.

A. **THE SCOPE AND APPLICABILITY OF THE UETA**
   The UETA applies only to e-records and e-signatures in a transaction (an interaction between two or more people relating to business, commercial, or government activities). The UETA does not apply to laws governing wills or testamentary trusts, the UCC (except Articles 2 and 2A), the UCITA, and other laws excluded by the states that adopt the UETA.

B. **THE FEDERAL E-SIGN ACT AND THE UETA**

   1. **Does the E-SIGN Act Preempt the UETA?**
      If a state enacts the UETA without modifying it, the E-SIGN Act does not preempt it. The E-SIGN Act preempts modified versions of the UETA to the extent that they are inconsistent with the E-SIGN Act.

   2. **Can the States Enact Alternative Procedures or Requirements?**
      Under the E-SIGN Act, states may enact alternative procedures or requirements for the use or acceptance of e-records or e-signatures if—

      a. The procedures or requirements are consistent with the E-SIGN Act.
      b. The procedures do not give greater legal effect to any specific type of technology.
      c. The state law refers to the E-SIGN Act if the state adopts the alternative after the enactment of the E-SIGN Act.

C. **HIGHLIGHTS OF THE UETA**
   Individual state versions of the UETA as enacted may vary.

   1. **The Parties Must Agree to Conduct Their Transaction Electronically**
      This agreement may be implied by the circumstances and the parties' conduct (for example, giving out a business card with an e-mail address on it). Consent may also be withdrawn.

2. **Parties Can "Opt Out"**
    Parties can waive or vary any or all of the UETA, but the UETA applies in the absence of an agreement to the contrary.

3. **Attribution**
    The effect of an e-record in a transaction is determined from its context and circumstances. Attribution refers to the identification of a party.

    a. **Names and "Signatures"**
        A person's name is not necessary to give effect to an e-record, but if, for example, a person types his or her name at the bottom of an e-mail purchase order, that typing qualifies as a "signature" and is attributed to the person.

    b. **Relevant Evidence**
        Any relevant evidence can prove that an e-record or e-signature is, or is not, attributable to a certain person.

    c. **Issues Arising outside the UETA**
        State laws other than the UETA apply to issues that relate to agency, authority, forgery, or contract formation.

4. **Notarization**
    A document can be notarized by a notary's e-signature.

5. **The Effect of Errors**
    If the parties agree to a security procedure and one party does not detect an error because it did not follow the procedure, the conforming party can avoid the effect of the error [UETA 10].

    a. **When Other State Laws Determine the Effect of an Error**
        Other state laws determine the effect if the parties do not agree on a security procedure.

    b. **To Avoid the Effect of an Error**
        A party must (1) promptly notify the other party of the error and of his or her intent not to be bound by it and (2) take reasonable steps to return any benefit or consideration received. If restitution cannot be made, the transaction may be unavoidable.

6. **Timing**

    a. **When Is an E-Record "Sent"?**
        When it is directed from the sender's place of business to the intended recipient in a form readable by the recipient's computer at the recipient's place of business with the closest relation to the deal (or either party's residence, if there is no place of business). Once an e-record leaves the sender's control or comes under the recipient's control, it is sent.

    b. **When Is an E-Record "Received"?**
        When it enters the recipient's processing system in a readable form—even if no person is aware of its receipt [UETA 15].

V. THE UNIFORM COMPUTER INFORMATION TRANSACTIONS ACT
The Uniform Computer Information Transactions Act (UCITA) is also a draft of legislation suggested to the states by the NCCUSL to validate e-contracts to license or buy software, or contracts that give access to, or allow the distribution of, computer information. Only two states adopted it, and the NCCUSL has withdrawn its support of UCITA.

TRUE-FALSE QUESTIONS
(Answers at the Back of the Book)

____ 1. A shrink-wrap agreement is normally not enforced.

____ 2. A click-on agreement is normally enforced.

_____   3.   State e-signature laws are not uniform.

_____   4.   Under federal law, a signature may be denied legal effect simply because it is in electronic form.

_____   5.   The Uniform Electronic Transactions Act (UETA) is a federal law.

_____   6.   The UETA does not apply to a transaction unless the parties agree to apply it.

_____   7.   Under the UETA, a person's name is not necessary to give effect to an electronic record.

_____   8.   Under the UETA, a contract is enforceable even if it is in electronic form.

_____   9.   An e-record is considered received under the UETA only if a person is aware of its receipt.

_____   10.   Under the UETA, once an e-record leaves the sender's control or comes under the recipient's control, it is sent.

FILL-IN QUESTIONS

(Answers at the Back of the Book)

Parties _____ (must/need not) participate in e-commerce to make binding contracts, according to the UETA. E-records are valid under the _____ (E-SIGN Act only/UETA only/E-SIGN Act and the UETA). The UETA supports all e-transactions, _____ (and creates/ but does not create) rules for them. The UETA _____ (applies/ does not apply) unless contracting parties agree to use e-commerce in their transactions.

MULTIPLE-CHOICE QUESTIONS

(Answers at the Back of the Book)

_____   1.   Alpha Corporation attempts to enter into shrink-wrap agreements with buyers of its products. A shrink-wrap agreement is an agreement whose terms are expressed

    a.   in code at the end of a computer program.
    b.   inside a box in which a product is packaged.
    c.   in small print at the end of a paper contract signed by both parties.
    d.   on a computer screen.

_____   2.   Beta, Inc., includes a shrink-wrap agreement with its products. A court would likely enforce this agreement if a buyer used the product

    a.   after having had an opportunity to read the agreement.
    b.   before having had an opportunity to read the agreement.
    c.   only after actually reading the agreement.
    d.   none of the above.

_____   3.   Gamma Company agrees to sell software to Holly from Gamma's Web site. To complete the deal, Holly clicks on a button that, with reference to certain terms, states, "I agree." The parties have

    a.   a binding contract that does not include the terms.
    b.   a binding contract that includes only the terms to which Holly later agrees.
    c.   a binding contract that includes the terms.
    d.   no contract.

____ **4.** Local Delivery Company and Regional Trucking, Inc., attempt to enter into a contract in electronic form. Under the Electronic Signatures in Global and National Commerce Act (E-SIGN Act), because this contract is in electronic form, it

a. may be denied legal effect.
b. may not be denied legal effect.
c. will be limited to certain terms.
d. will not be enforced.

____ **5.** International Investments, Inc., enters into contracts in e-commerce and in traditional commerce. The UETA applies, if at all, only to those transactions in which the parties agree to use

a. e-commerce.
b. traditional commerce.
c. e-commerce or traditional commerce.
d. none of the above.

____ **6.** American Sales Company and B2C Corporation enter into a contract over the Internet. The contract says nothing about the UETA. The UETA applies to

a. none of the contract.
b. only the part of the contract that does not involve computer information.
c. only the part of the contract that involves computer information.
d. the entire contract.

____ **7.** Digital Tech, Inc., e-mails an e-record, as part of a business deal, to E-Engineering Corporation. Under the UETA, an e-record is considered sent

a. only when it leaves the sender's control.
b. only when it comes under the recipient's control.
c. when it leaves the sender's control or comes under the recipient's control.
d. when it is midway between the sender and recipient.

____ **8.** New Software, Inc. (NSI), and Open Source Company (OSC) agree to follow a certain security procedure in transacting business. NSI fails to follow the procedure and, for this reason, does not detect an error in its deal with OSC. OSC can avoid the effect of the error

a. only if NSI's name is affixed to the e-record evidencing the error.
b. only if OSC takes reasonable steps to return any benefit or consideration received.
c. under any circumstances.
d. under no circumstances.

____ **9.** First Financial Corporation and Great Applications, Inc., enter into a contract that falls under the UETA. The UETA covers contracts that are also covered by

a. laws governing wills and trusts only.
b. the Uniform Commercial Code only.
c. the Uniform Commercial Information Transactions Act only.
d. none of the above.

____ **10.** Delta Company and Epsilon, Inc., engage in e-commerce without expressly opting in or out of the UETA. The UETA covers

a. none of the contract.
b. only the part of the contract that does not involve e-commerce.
c. only the part of the contract that involves e-signatures.
d. the entire contract.

SHORT ESSAY QUESTIONS

1.   Are shrink-wrap and click-on agreements enforceable?

2.   What are some of the provisions of the UETA?

ISSUE SPOTTERS

(Answers at the Back of the Book)

1.   Applied Products, Inc., does business with Best Suppliers, Inc., online. Under the UETA, what determines the effect of the electronic documents evidencing the parties' deal? Is a party's "signature" necessary?

2.   Technical Support, Inc., and United Services Corporation enter into a contract that may be subject to the E-SIGN Act and the UETA. Does one of these statutes take precedence over the other?

3.   Computer Applications Corporation and Digitized Data, Inc., agree to a contract in e-commerce. Assuming the deal falls under the UETA, what effect might the UETA have in this situation?

Chapter 11:
Sales and Leases: Formation, Title, and Risk

WHAT THIS CHAPTER IS ABOUT

This chapter introduces two parts of the Uniform Commercial Code: Article 2, which covers sales of goods, and Article 2A, which covers leases. The chapter also discusses three important concepts: identification, risk of loss, and insurable interest.

CHAPTER OUTLINE

I. THE SCOPE OF THE UCC

The UCC provides rules to deal with all phases of a commercial sale: Articles 2 and 2A cover contracts for sales or leases of goods; Articles 3, 4, and 4A cover payments by checks, notes, and other means; Article 7 covers warehouse documents; and Article 9 covers transactions that involve collateral.

II. THE SCOPE OF ARTICLE 2—SALES

Article 2 governs contracts for sales of goods.

A. WHAT IS A SALE?

A **sale** is "the passing of title from the seller to the buyer for a price" [UCC 2–106(1)]. The price may be payable in money, goods, or services.

B. WHAT ARE GOODS?

Goods are tangible and movable. Goods may include minerals, crops, etc. If a transaction involves both goods and services, a court determines which aspect is dominant. Serving food or drink is a sale of goods [UCC 2–314(1)].

C. WHO IS A MERCHANT?

UCC 2–104: Special rules apply to those who (1) deal in goods of the kind involved; (2) by occupation, hold themselves out as having knowledge and skill peculiar to the practices or goods involved in the transaction; (3) employ a merchant as a broker, agent, or other intermediary.

III. THE SCOPE OF ARTICLE 2A—LEASES

Article 2A governs contracts for leases of goods. A **lease agreement** is the lessor and lessee's bargain, in their words and deeds, including course of dealing, usage of trade, and course of performance [UCC 2A–103(k)].

IV. THE FORMATION OF SALES AND LEASE CONTRACTS

The following summarizes how the UCC *changes* the common law of contracts.

A. OFFER

An agreement sufficient to constitute a contract can exist even if verbal exchanges, correspondence, and conduct do not reveal exactly when it became binding [UCC 2–204(2), 2A–204(2)].

1. Open Terms

A sales or lease contract will not fail for indefiniteness even if one or more terms are left open, as long as (1) the parties intended to make a contract and (2) there is a reasonably certain basis for the court to grant an appropriate remedy [UCC 2–204(3), 2A–204(3)].

a. **Open Price Term**

1) If the parties have not agreed on a price, a court will determine "a reasonable price at the time for delivery" [UCC 2–305(1)].

2) If either the buyer or the seller is to determine the price, the price is to be fixed in good faith [UCC 2–305(2)].

3) If a price is not fixed through the fault of one party, the other can cancel the contract or fix a reasonable price [UCC 2–305(3)].

b. **Open Payment Term**
When parties do not specify payment terms—

1) Payment is due at the time and place at which the buyer is to receive the goods [UCC 2–310(a)].

2) The buyer can tender payment in cash or a commercially acceptable substitute (a check or credit card) [UCC 2–511(2)].

c. **Open Delivery Term**
When no delivery terms are specified—

1) The buyer normally takes delivery at the seller's place of business [UCC 2–308(a)]. If the seller has no place of business, the seller's residence is used. When goods are located in some other place and both parties know it, delivery is made there.

2) If the time for shipment or delivery is not clearly specified, a court will infer a "reasonable" time [UCC 2–309(1)].

d. **Duration of an Ongoing Contract**
A party who wishes to terminate an indefinite but ongoing contract must give reasonable notice to the other party [UCC 2–309(2), (3)].

e. **Options and Cooperation Regarding Performance**

1) When no specific shipping arrangements have been made but the contract contemplates shipment of the goods, the seller has the right to make arrangements [UCC 2–311].

2) When terms relating to an assortment of goods are omitted, the buyer can specify the assortment [UCC 2–311].

f. **Open Quantity Term**
If parties do not specify a quantity, there is no basis for a remedy. Exceptions include [UCC 2–306]—

1) **Requirements Contract**
The buyer agrees to buy and the seller agrees to sell all or up to a stated amount of what the buyer needs or requires. There is consideration: the buyer gives up the right to buy from others.

2) **Output Contract**
The seller agrees to sell and the buyer agrees to buy all or up to a stated amount of what the seller produces. Because the seller forfeits the right to sell goods to others, there is consideration.

3) **The UCC Imposes a Good Faith Limitation**
The quantity under these contracts is the amount of requirements or output that occurs during a normal production year.

2. Merchant's Firm Offer

If a merchant gives assurances in a signed writing that an offer will remain open, the offer is irrevocable, without consideration, for the stated period, or if no definite period is specified, for a reasonable period (neither to exceed three months) [UCC 2–205, 2A–205].

a. The offer must be written and signed by the offeror. When a firm offer is contained in a form contract prepared by the offeree, a separate firm-offer assurance must be signed as well.

b. The other party need not be a merchant.

B. ACCEPTANCE

1. Any Reasonable Means

When an offeror does not specify a means of acceptance, acceptance can be by any reasonable means [UCC 2–206(1), 2A–206(1)].

2. Promise to Ship or Prompt Shipment

a. Promise or Shipment of Conforming Goods

An offer to buy goods for current or prompt shipment can be accepted by a promise to ship or by a prompt shipment [UCC 2–206(1)(b)].

b. Shipment of Nonconforming Goods

Prompt shipment of nonconforming goods is both an acceptance and a breach, unless the seller (1) seasonably notifies the buyer that it is offered only as an accommodation and (2) indicates clearly that it is not an acceptance.

3. Communication of Acceptance

To accept a unilateral offer, the offeree must notify the offeror of performance if the offeror would not otherwise know [UCC 2–206(2)].

4. Additional Terms

If the offeree's response indicates a definite acceptance of the offer, a contract is formed, even if the acceptance includes terms in addition to, or different from, the original offer [UCC 2–207(1)]. This is contrary to the common law mirror image rule.

a. Not Conditioned on the Offeror's Assent

Does the contract include the additional terms?

1) When the Seller or Buyer Is a Nonmerchant

Additional terms are considered proposals and not part of the contract. The contract is on the offeror's terms [UCC 2–207(2)].

2) When Both Parties Are Merchants

Additional terms are part of the contract unless (1) the offer expressly states no other terms; (2) they materially alter the original contract; or (3) the offeror objects to the modified terms in a timely fashion [UCC 2–207(2)].

b. Conditioned on the Offeror's Assent

If the additional terms are conditioned on the offeror's assent, the offeree's response is not an acceptance.

c. Additional Terms May Be Stricken

Regardless of what parties write down, they have a contract according to their conduct [UCC 2–207(3)]. If they do not act in accord with added terms, the terms are not part of a contract.

C. CONSIDERATION

An agreement modifying a sales or lease contract needs no consideration to be binding [UCC 2–209(1), 2A–208(1)].

1. **Modification Must Be Sought in Good Faith [UCC 1–203]**

2. **When a Modification Must Be in Writing to Be Enforceable**

   a. Contract prohibits changes except by a signed writing.

   b. If a consumer (nonmerchant) is dealing with a merchant, and the merchant's form prohibits oral modification, the consumer must sign a separate acknowledgment [UCC 2–209(2), 2A–208(2)].

   c. Any modification that brings a *sales* contract under the Statute of Frauds must be in writing to be enforceable [UCC 2–209(3)].

D. **STATUTE OF FRAUDS**
   To be enforceable, a sales contract must be in writing if the goods are $500 or more and a lease if the payments are $1,000 or more [UCC 2–201, 2A–201].

   1. **Sufficiency of the Writing**
      A writing is sufficient if it indicates the parties intended to form a contract and is signed by the party against whom enforcement is sought. A sales contract is not enforceable beyond the quantity stated. A lease must identify and describe the goods and the lease term.

   2. **Transactions between Merchants**
      The writing requirement is met if one merchant sends a signed written confirmation to the other.

      a. **Contents of the Confirmation**
         The confirmation must indicate the terms of the agreement, and the merchant receiving it must have reason to know of its contents.

      b. **Objection within Ten Days**
         Unless the merchant who receives the confirmation objects in writing within ten days, the confirmation is enforceable [UCC 2–201(2)].

   3. **Exceptions**
      An oral contract for a sale or lease that should otherwise be in writing will be enforceable in cases of [UCC 2–201(3), 2A–201(4)]—

      a. **Specially Manufactured Goods**
         The seller (or lessor) makes a substantial start on the manufacture of the goods, or makes commitments for it, and the goods are unsuitable for resale to others in the ordinary course of the business.

      b. **Admissions**
         The party against whom enforcement of a contract is sought admits in pleadings or court proceedings that a contract was made.

      c. **Partial Performance**
         Some payment has been made and accepted or some goods have been received and accepted (enforceable to that extent).

E. **UNCONSCIONABILITY**

   1. **What an Unconscionable Contract (or Clause) Is**
      An unconscionable contract or clause is a contract or clause so one-sided and unfair (at the time it was made) that enforcing it would be unreasonable.

   2. **What a Court Can Do**
      A court can (1) refuse to enforce the contract, (2) enforce the contract without the unconscionable clause, or (3) limit the clause to avoid an unconscionable result [UCC 2–302, 2A–108].

V.   TITLE, RISK, AND INSURABLE INTEREST

A. IDENTIFICATION

For an interest in goods to pass from seller to buyer or lessor to lessee, the goods must (1) exist and (2) be identified as subject to the contract. Identification gives the buyer (1) a right to obtain insurance and (2) a right to obtain the goods from the seller.

B. PASSAGE OF TITLE

Title passes—

1. **According to the Parties' Agreement**

    Parties can agree on when and under what conditions title will pass.

2. **At the Time and Place at Which the Seller Performs**

    If the parties do not specify a time, title passes on delivery [UCC 2–401(2)]. The delivery terms determine when this occurs.

    a. **Shipment Contracts**

        If the seller is required or authorized to ship goods by carrier, title passes at time and place of shipment [UCC 2–401(2)(a)]. All contracts are shipment contracts unless they say otherwise.

    b. **Destination Contracts**

        If the seller is required to deliver goods to a certain destination, title passes when the goods are tendered there [UCC 2–401(2)(b)].

    c. **Delivery without Movement of the Goods**

        If a buyer is to pick up goods, passing title turns on whether a seller must give a document of title (bill of lading, warehouse receipt).

        1) **When a Document of Title Is Required**

            Title passes when and where the document is delivered. The goods do not need to move (for example, they can stay in a warehouse).

        2) **When No Document of Title Is Required**

            If the goods have been identified, title passes when and where the contract was made. If the goods have not been identified, title does not pass until identification [UCC 2–401(3)].

C. RISK OF LOSS

The question of who suffers a financial loss if goods are damaged, destroyed, or lost (who bears the *risk of loss*) is determined by the parties' contract. If the contract does not state who bears the risk, the UCC has rules to determine it.

1. **Delivery with Movement of the Goods—Carrier Cases**

    When goods are to be delivered by truck or other paid transport—

    a. **Contract Terms**

        1) **F.O.B.** (Free on board)—delivery is at seller's expense to a specific location. Risk passes at the location [UCC 2–319(1)].

        2) **F.A.S.** (Free alongside)—seller delivers goods next to the ship that will carry them, and risk passes to buyer [UCC 2–319(2)].

        3) **C.I.F. or C.&F.** (Cost, insurance, and freight)—seller puts goods in possession of a carrier before risk passes [UCC 2–320(2)].

        4) **Delivery Ex-ship** (From the carrying vessel)—risk passes to buyer when goods leave the ship or are unloaded [UCC 2–322].

    b. **Shipment Contracts**
Risk passes to the buyer or lessee when the goods are delivered to a carrier [UCC 2–509(1)(a), 2A–219(2)(a)].

    c. **Destination Contracts**
Risk passes to the buyer or lessee when the goods are tendered to the buyer at the destination [UCC 2–509(1)(b), 2A–219(2)(b)].

2. **Delivery without Movement of the Goods**
When goods are to be picked up by the buyer or lessee—

    a. **If the Seller or Lessor Is a Merchant**
Risk passes only on buyer or lessee taking possession of the goods.

    b. **If the Seller or Lessor Is Not a Merchant**
Risk passes on tender of delivery [UCC 2–509(3), 2A–219(c)].

    c. **If a Bailee Holds the Goods**
Risk passes when (1) buyer receives a negotiable document of title for the goods, (2) bailee acknowledges buyer's (or in a lease, lessee's) right to the goods, or (3) buyer receives a nonnegotiable document of title, presents the document to the bailee, and demands the goods. If the bailee refuses to honor the document, the risk remains with the seller [UCC 2–503(4)(b), 2–509(2), 2A–219(2)(b)].

3. **Conditional Sales**

    a. **Sale or Return (or Sale and Return)**
A seller delivers goods to a buyer who may retain any part and pay accordingly. Balance is returned or held by the buyer as a bailee.

        1) **Title and Risk Pass to the Buyer with Possession**
Title and risk stay with the buyer until he or she returns the goods to the seller within the specified time. A sale is final if the buyer fails to return the goods in time. Goods in the buyer's possession are subject to the claims of the buyer's creditors.

        2) **Consignment**
A consignment is a sale or return. Goods in consignee's (buyer's) possession are subject to his or her creditors' claims.

    b. **Sale on Approval**
A seller offers to sell goods, and the buyer takes them on a trial basis. Title and risk remain with seller until buyer accepts goods.

        1) **What Constitutes Acceptance**
Any act inconsistent with trial purpose or the seller's ownership; or by the buyer's choice not to return the goods on time.

        2) **Return**
Return is at seller's expense and risk [UCC 2–327(1)]. Goods are not subject to claims of the buyer's creditors until acceptance.

4. **Risk of Loss When a Sales or Lease Contract Is Breached**
Generally, the party in breach bears the risk of loss.

    a. **When the Seller or Lessor Breaches**
Risk passes to buyer or lessee when defects are cured or buyer or lessee accepts the goods in spite of the defects. If, after acceptance, a buyer discovers a latent defect, acceptance can be revoked and the risk goes back to the seller [UCC 2–510(2), 2A–220(1)].

b. **When the Buyer or Lessee Breaches**
Risk shifts to buyer or lessee (if goods have been identified), where it stays for a commercially reasonable time after seller or lessor learns of the breach. Buyer or lessee is liable to the extent of any deficiency in seller or lessor's insurance [UCC 2–510(3), 2A–220(2)].

D. **INSURABLE INTEREST**
A party buying insurance must have a "sufficient interest" in the insured item. More than one party can have an interest at the same time.

1. **Insurable Interest of the Buyer or Lessee**
A buyer or lessee has an insurable interest in goods the moment they are identified, even before risk of loss passes [UCC 2–501(1), 2A–218(1)].

2. **Insurable Interest of the Seller or Lessor**
A seller or lessor has an insurable interest in goods as long as he or she holds title or a security interest in the goods [UCC 2–501(2), 2A–218(3)].

TRUE-FALSE QUESTIONS

(Answers at the Back of the Book)

____   1.   Article 2 of the UCC governs sales of goods.

____   2.   Under the UCC, a sale occurs when title passes from a seller to a buyer for a price.

____   3.   Under the UCC, an agreement modifying a contract needs new consideration to be binding.

____   4.   If a contract for a sale of goods is missing a term, it will not be enforceable.

____   5.   An unconscionable contract is a contract so one-sided and unfair, at the time it is made, that enforcing i t would be unreasonable.

____   6.   Before an interest in specific goods can pass from a seller to a buyer, the goods must exist and be identified to the contract.

____   7.   Under all circumstances, title passes at the time and place that the buyer accepts the goods.

____   8.   Unless a contract provides otherwise, it is normally assumed to be a shipment contract.

____   9.   Under a destination contract, the risk of loss passes at time and place of shipment.

____   10.   If a seller is a merchant, the risk of loss to goods held by the seller passes to a buyer on delivery.

FILL-IN QUESTIONS

(Answers at the Back of the Book)

_____ (F.A.S./F.O.B.) means that delivery is at a seller's expense to a specific location—the place of shipment or a place of destination. When the term is _____ (F.A.S./F.O.B.) place of *shipment*, risk passes when the seller puts the goods into a carrier's possession. When the term is _____ (F.A.S./F.O.B.) place of *destination*, risk passes when the seller tenders delivery. _____ (F.A.S./ F.O.B.) requires a seller at his or her own expense and risk to deliver goods alongside the ship that will transport them at which point risk passes.

MULTIPLE-CHOICE QUESTIONS

(Answers at the Back of the Book)

____   1.   Alpha Electronics, Inc., sells computers and computer accessories to persons who order them. Alpha is a merchant with respect to

   a.   computers only.
   b.   computer accessories only.
   c.   computers and computer accessories.
   d.   none of the above.

____   2.   A-One Products Corporation and Best Manufacturing, Inc., enter into a contract for a sale of goods that does not include a price term. In a suit between A-One and Best over the price, a court will

   a.   determine a reasonable price.
   b.   impose the lowest market price for the goods.
   c.   refuse to enforce the agreement.
   d.   return the parties to the positions they held before the contract.

____   3.   Coastal Sales Corporation sends its purchase order form to Delta Products, Inc., for sixty display stands. Delta responds with its own form. Additional terms in Delta's form automatically become part of the contract unless

   a.   Coastal objects to the new terms within a reasonable period of time.
   b.   Coastal's form expressly required acceptance of its terms.
   c.   the additional terms materially alter the original contract.
   d.   any of the above.

____   4.   Mountain Boots, Inc., and National Shoe Company orally agree to a sale of 100 pair of hiking boots for $5,000. National gives Mountain a check for $500 as a down payment. At this point, the contract is

   a.   enforceable to at least the extent of $500.
   b.   fully enforceable because it is for specially made goods.
   c.   fully enforceable because it is oral.
   d.   none of the above.

____   5.   Eve enters a contract with Fancy Furniture, Inc. In a later suit, Eve claims that a clause in the contract is unconscionable. If the court agrees, it may

   a.   enforce, limit, or refuse to enforce the contract or the disputed clause.
   b.   enforce the contract without the disputed clause only.
   c.   limit the application of the disputed clause only.
   d.   refuse to enforce the contract only.

____   6.   Alpha Products, Inc., sells ten computers to Beta Sales Corporation. They agree to ship the computers "F.O.B. Alpha" via Gamma Shipping Company. The computers are destroyed in transit. The loss is suffered by

   a.   Alpha.
   b.   Beta.
   c.   Gamma.
   d.   none of the above.

_____ 7. Stan buys a CD player from Tom, his neighbor, who agrees to keep the player until Stan picks it up. Before Stan can get it, the player is stolen. The loss is suffered by

a. Stan only.
b. Tom only.
c. Stan and Tom.
d. none of the above.

_____ 8. Retail Floor Stores buys tile from Superior Tile Corporation. Town Storage holds the tile in a warehouse. The tile is delivered to Retail by the transfer of a negotiable warehouse receipt. A fire later damages the tile. The loss is suffered by

a. Retail.
b. Superior.
c. Town.
d. none of the above.

_____ 9. Omega Engineering, Inc., buys ten drafting tables from Quality Supply Corporation. They agree to ship the tables "F.O.B. Omega" via State Trucking Company. The tables are destroyed in transit. The loss is suffered by

a. Omega.
b. Quality.
c. State.
d. none of the above.

_____ 10. Standard Goods, Inc., ships fifty defective hard drives to Top Business Corporation. Top rejects the drives and ships them back to Standard, via United Transport, Inc. The drives are lost in transit. The loss is suffered by

a. Standard.
b. Top.
c. United.
d. none of the above.

SHORT ESSAY QUESTIONS

1. For purposes of UCC Article 2, what is a sale? What are goods?

2. When does risk pass (a) under a shipment contract; (b) under a destination contract; (c) when the buyer is to pick up the goods and (1) the seller is a merchant and (2) the seller is not a merchant; (d) when a bailee holds the goods?

ISSUE SPOTTERS

(Answers at the Back of the Book)

1. E-Design, Inc., orders 150 computer desks. Fine Supplies, Inc., ships 150 printer stands. Is this an acceptance of the offer or a counteroffer? If it is an acceptance, is it a breach of the contract? What if Fine told E-Design it was sending printer stands as "an accommodation"?

2.   Fine Farms in Washington sells Green Produce in Alaska a certain size of apples to be shipped "F.O.B. Seattle." The apples that Fine delivers to the shipping company for transport are too small. The apples are lost in transit. Who suffers the loss?

3.   Chocolate, Inc., sells five hundred cases of cocoa mix to Dessert Company, which pays with a bad check. Chocolate does not discover that the check is bad until after Dessert sells the cocoa to Eden Food Stores, which suspects nothing. Can Chocolate recover the cocoa from Eden?

Chapter 12:
Sales and Leases: Performance and Breach

WHAT THIS CHAPTER IS ABOUT

This chapter examines the basic obligations of a seller and a buyer under a sales contract, and a lessor and a lessee under a lease contract, and the remedies each party has if the contract is breached. The general purpose of the remedies is to put a nonbreaching party "in as good a position as if the other party had fully performed."

CHAPTER OUTLINE

I. PERFORMANCE OBLIGATIONS

The obligations of good faith and commercial reasonableness underlie every contract within the UCC [UCC 1–203]. The obligation of the seller or lessor is to tender and deliver conforming goods. The obligation of the buyer or lessee is to accept and pay for the goods [UCC 2–301, 2A–516(1)].

II. OBLIGATIONS OF THE SELLER OR LESSOR

A seller or lessor must have and hold conforming goods at the disposal of the buyer or lessee and give whatever notice is reasonably necessary to enable the buyer or lessee to take delivery [UCC 2–503(1), 2A–508(1)].

A. TENDER OF DELIVERY

At a reasonable hour, in a reasonable manner, and the goods must be kept available for a reasonable time [UCC 2–503(1)(a)]. Goods must be tendered in a single delivery unless parties agree otherwise [UCC 2–612, 2A–510] or, under the circumstances, a party can request delivery in lots [UCC 2–307].

B. PLACE OF DELIVERY

Parties may agree on a particular destination, or the contract or the circumstances may indicate a place.

1. Noncarrier Cases

a. Seller's Place of Business
If the contract does not designate a place of delivery, and the buyer is to pick up the goods, the place is the seller's place of business or if none, the seller's residence [UCC 2–308].

b. Identified Goods That Are Not at the Seller's Place of Business
Wherever they are is the place of delivery [UCC 2–308].

2. Carrier Cases

a. Shipment Contract
The seller must [UCC 2–504]—

1) Put the goods into the hands of a carrier.

2) Make a contract for the transport of the goods that is reasonable according to their nature and value.

3) Tender to the buyer any documents necessary to obtain possession of the goods from the carrier.

4) Promptly notify the buyer that shipment has been made.

5) If a seller fails to meet these requirements, and this causes a material loss or a delay, the buyer can reject the shipment.

b. Destination Contract
The seller must give the buyer appropriate notice and any necessary documents of title [UCC 2–503].

C. THE PERFECT TENDER RULE
A seller or lessor must deliver goods in conformity with every detail of the contract. If goods or tender fail in any respect, the buyer or lessee can accept the goods, reject them, or accept part and reject part . [UCC 2–601, 2A–509].

D. EXCEPTIONS TO THE RULE

1. Agreement of the Parties
Parties can agree in their contract that, for example, the seller can repair or replace any defective goods within a reasonable time.

2. Cure

a. Within the Contract Time for Performance
If nonconforming goods are rejected, the seller or lessor can notify the buyer or lessee of an intention to repair, adjust, or replace the goods and can then do so within the contract time for performance [UCC 2–508, 2A–513].

b. After the Time for Performance Expires
The seller or lessor can cure if there were reasonable grounds to believe the nonconformance would be acceptable. ("Reasonable grounds" include nonconforming tender with a price allowance.)

c. Substantially Restricts the Buyer's Right to Reject
If the buyer or lessee refuses goods but does not notice of the nature of the defect, he or she cannot later assert the defect as a defense if it is one that could have been cured [UCC 2–605, 2A–514].

3. Substitution of Carriers
If, through no fault of either party an agreed manner of delivery is not available, a substitute is sufficient [UCC 2–614(1)].

4. Installment Contracts

a. Substantial Nonconformity
A buyer or lessee can reject an installment only if a nonconformity substantially impairs the value of the installment and cannot be cured [UCC 2–612(2), 2–307, 2A–510(1)].

b. Breach of the Entire Contract
A breach occurs if one or more nonconforming installments substantially impair the value of the whole contract. If the buyer or lessee accepts a nonconforming installment, the contract is reinstated [UCC 2–612(3), 2A–510(2)]

5. Commercial Impracticability
No breach if performance is impracticable by the occurrence of an unforeseen contingency. If the event allows for partial performance, the seller or lessor must do so, in a fair manner (with notice to the buyer or lessee) [UCC 2–615, 2A–405]

6. **Destruction of Identified Goods**
   When goods are destroyed (through no fault of a party) before risk passes to the buyer or lessee, the parties are excused from performance [UCC 2–613, 2A–221]. If goods are only partially destroyed, a buyer can treat a contract as void or accept damaged goods with a price credit.

7. **Assurance and Cooperation**
   A party with reasonable grounds to believe that the other will not perform may demand adequate assurance, suspend his or her own performance, and with no assurance within thirty days treat the contract as repudiated [UCC 2–609, 2A–401]. When required cooperation is not forthcoming, the other party can do whatever is reasonable, including holding the uncooperative party in breach [UCC 2–311(3)(b)].

III. OBLIGATIONS OF THE BUYER OR LESSEE

The buyer or lessee must make payment at the time and place he or she receives the goods unless the parties have agreed otherwise [UCC 2–310(a), 2A–516(1)].

A. PAYMENT

Payment can be by any means agreed on between the parties [UCC 2–511].

B. RIGHT OF INSPECTION

The buyer or lessee can verify, before making payment, that the goods are what were contracted for. The buyer has no duty to pay if the goods are not what were ordered [UCC 2–513(1), 2A–515(1)].

1. **Time, Place, and Manner**
   Inspection can be in any reasonable place, time and manner, determined by custom of the trade, practice of the parties, and so on [UCC 2–513(2)].

2. **C.O.D. Shipments**
   If a buyer agrees to a C.O.D. shipment or to pay for goods on presentation of a bill of lading, no right of inspection exists [UCC 2–513(3)].

3. **Payment Due—Documents of Title (C.I.F. and C.&F. Contracts)**
   Payment is required on receipt of documents of title, before inspection, and must be made unless the buyer knows the goods are nonconforming [UCC 2–310(b), 2–513(3)].

C. ACCEPTANCE

Acceptance is presumed if a buyer or lessee has a reasonable opportunity to inspect and fails to reject in a reasonable time [UCC 2–606, 2–602, 2A–515].

1. **How a Buyer or Lessee Can Accept**
   A buyer or lessee can accept by words or conduct. Under a sales contract, a buyer can accept by any act (such as using or reselling the goods) inconsistent with the seller's ownership [UCC 2–606(1)(c)].

2. **A Buyer or Lessee Can Accept Only Some of the Goods**
   But not less than a single commercial unit [UCC 2–601(c), 2A-509(1)].

IV. ANTICIPATORY REPUDIATION

The nonbreaching party can (1) treat the repudiation as a final breach by pursuing a remedy or (2) wait, hoping that the repudiating party will decide to honor the contract [UCC 2–610, 2A–402]. If the party decides to wait, the breaching party can retract the repudiation [UCC 2–611, 2A–403].

V. REMEDIES OF THE SELLER OR LESSOR

A. WHEN THE GOODS ARE IN POSSESSION OF THE SELLER OR LESSOR

1. **The Right to Cancel the Contract**
   A seller or lessor can cancel a contract (with notice to the buyer or lessee) if the other party breaches it [UCC 2–703(f), 2A–523(1)(a)].

2. **The Right to Withhold Delivery**
   A seller or lessor can withhold delivery if a buyer or lessee wrongfully rejects or revokes acceptance, fails to pay, or repudiates [UCC 2–703(a), 2A–523(1)(c)]. If a buyer or lessee is insolvent, a seller or lessor can refuse to deliver unless a buyer pays cash [UCC 2–702(1), 2A–525(1)].

3. **The Right to Resell or Dispose of the Goods**

   a. **When a Seller or Lessor Can Resell Goods**
      A seller or lessor still has the goods and the buyer or lessee wrongfully rejects or revokes acceptance, fails to pay, or repudiates the contract [UCC 2–703(d), 2–706(1), 2A–523(1)(e), 2A–527(1)].

   b. **Unfinished Goods**
      A seller or lessor can (1) resell the goods as scrap or (2) finish and resell them (buyer or lessee is liable for any difference in price). The goal is to obtain maximum value [UCC 2–704(2), 2A–524(2)].

4. **The Right to Recover the Purchase Price or Lease Payments Due**
   A seller or lessor can bring an action for the price if the buyer or lessee breaches after the goods are identified to the contract and the seller or lessor is unable to resell [UCC 2–709(1), 2A–529(1)].

5. **The Right to Recover Damages**
   If a buyer or lessee repudiates a contract or wrongfully refuses to accept, the seller or lessor can recover the difference between the contract price and the market price (at the time and place of tender), plus incidental damages. If the market price is less than the contract price, the seller or lessor gets lost profits [UCC 2–708, 2A–528].

B. **WHEN THE GOODS ARE IN TRANSIT**
   A seller or lessor can stop delivery of goods if (1) the buyer or lessee is insolvent or (2) the buyer or lessee is solvent but in breach (if the quantity shipped is a carload, a truckload, or larger) [UCC 2–705, 2A–526].

C. **WHEN THE GOODS ARE IN POSSESSION OF THE BUYER OR LESSEE**

   1. **The Right to Recover the Purchase Price or Lease Payments Due**
      A seller or lessor can bring an action for the price if the buyer or lessee accepts the goods but refuses to pay [UCC 2–709(1), 2A–529(1)].

   2. **The Right to Reclaim the Goods**

      a. **Sales Contracts—Buyer's Insolvency**
         If an insolvent buyer gets goods on credit, the seller can (within ten days) reclaim them. A seller can reclaim any time if a buyer misrepresents solvency in writing within three months before delivery [UCC 2–702(2)].

      b. **Sales Contracts—A Buyer in the Ordinary Course of Business**
         A seller cannot reclaim goods from such a buyer.

      c. **Sales Contracts—Bars the Pursuit of Other Remedies**
         A seller who reclaims gets preferential treatment over a buyer's other creditors (but cannot pursue other remedies) [UCC 2–702(3)].

      d. **Lease Contracts**
         A lessor can reclaim goods from a lessee in default [UCC 2A–525(2)].

VI.   REMEDIES OF THE BUYER OR LESSEE

A.   WHEN THE SELLER OR LESSOR REFUSES TO DELIVER THE GOODS

When a seller or lessor fails to deliver or repudiates the contract, the buyer or lessee has the following rights.

1.   The Right to Cancel the Contract

The buyer or lessee can rescind (cancel) the contract. On notice to the seller, the buyer or lessee is discharged [UCC 2–711(1), 2A–508(1)(a).

2.   The Right to Recover the Goods

A buyer or lessee who paid for goods in the hands of the seller or lessor can recover them if the seller or lessor is insolvent or becomes insolvent within ten days of receiving payment and the goods are identified to the contract. Buyer or lessee must tender any unpaid balance [UCC 2–502, 2A–522].

3.   The Right to Obtain Specific Performance

A buyer or lessee can obtain specific performance if goods are unique or damages would be inadequate [UCC 2–716(1), 2A–521(1)].

4.   The Right of Cover

The measure of damages is the difference between the cost of cover and the contract price, plus incidental and consequential damages, less expenses saved by the breach [UCC 2–712, 2–715, 2A–518, 2A–520].

5.   The Right to Replevy Goods

A buyer or lessee can use replevin if seller or lessor fails to deliver or repudiates and buyer or lessee cannot cover [UCC 2–716(3), 2A–521(3)].

6.   The Right to Recover Damages

The measure of damages is the difference between the contract price and, when the buyer or lessee learned of the breach, the market price (at the place of delivery), plus incidental and consequential damages, less expenses saved by the breach [UCC 2–713, 2A–519].

B.   WHEN THE SELLER OR LESSOR DELIVERS NONCONFORMING GOODS

1.   The Right to Reject the Goods

A buyer or lessee can reject the part of goods that fails to conform to the contract (and rescind the contract or obtain cover) [UCC 2–601, 2A–509].

   a.   Notice Required

   Notice must be timely, and a buyer or lessee must tell the seller or lessor what the defect is [UCC 2–602(1), 2–605, 2A–509(2), 2A–514].

   b.   Duties of a Merchant Buyer or Lessee

   Follow the seller or lessor's instructions about the goods [UCC 2–603, 2A–511]. Without instructions, perishable goods can be resold; otherwise they must be stored or returned.

   c.   The Right to Retain and Enforce a Security Interest

   Buyers who rightfully reject or who justifiably revoke acceptance of goods in their possession have a security interest in the goods. A buyer can recover payments made for the goods and expenses to inspect, transport, and hold the goods, or can resell, withhold delivery, or stop delivery [UCC 2–711, 2–706].

2.   The Right to Revoke Acceptance of the Goods

   a.   Substantial Impairment

   Any nonconformity must substantially impair the value of the goods *and* either not be seasonably cured or be difficult to discover [UCC 2–608, 2A–517].

    b. **Notice of a Breach Must Be within a Reasonable Time**
      Before the goods have undergone substantial change (not caused by their own defects, such as spoilage) [UCC 2–608(2), 2A–517(4)].

  3. **The Right to Recover Damages for Accepted Goods**
    Notice of a breach must be within a reasonable time. The measure of damages is the difference between value of goods as accepted and value if they had been as promised [UCC 2–714(2), 2A–519(4)].

VII. LIMITATION OF REMEDIES

Parties can provide for remedies in addition to or in lieu of those in the UCC, or they can change the measure of damages [UCC 2–719, 2A–503].

  A. LIMITATIONS ON CONSEQUENTIAL DAMAGES
    If a buyer or lessee is a consumer, limiting consequential damages for personal injuries on a breach of warranty is *prima facie* unconscionable.

  B. STATUTE OF LIMITATIONS
    An action for breach of contract under the UCC must be brought within four years of the breach. In their contract, the parties can reduce this period to not less than one year [UCC 2–725(1), 2A–506(1)]. If goods are nonconforming but the buyer accepts them, notice of the breach must be within a reasonable time or all remedies are lost [UCC 2–607(3)(a), 2A–516(3)].

TRUE-FALSE QUESTIONS

(Answers at the Back of the Book)

_____   1. The duties and obligations of the parties to a contract include those specified in the agreement.

_____   2. Generally, under a sales or lease contract, all goods must be tendered in a single delivery.

_____   3. If goods fail to conform to a contract in any way, a buyer or lessee can accept or reject the goods.

_____   4. Unless the parties agree otherwise, a buyer or lessee must pay for goods in advance.

_____   5. If a contract does not specify otherwise, the place for delivery of goods is the buyer's place of business.

_____   6. A buyer or lessee who accepts a delivery of goods cannot withdraw the acceptance.

_____   7. A seller or lessor cannot consider a buyer or lessee in breach until the time for performance has past.

_____   8. In an installment contract, a buyer can reject any installment for any reason.

_____   9. If a buyer or lessee wrongfully refuses to accept or pay for conforming goods, the seller or lessor can cancel the contract and recover damages.

_____ 10. If a seller or lessor wrongfully refuses to deliver conforming goods, the buyer or lessee can cancel the contract and recover damages.

FILL-IN QUESTIONS

(Answers at the Back of the Book)

    A seller's obligations include holding _____ (conforming/nonconforming) goods at a buyer's disposal _____ (and/or) giving notice reasonably necessary for the buyer to take delivery. Unless the parties have agreed otherwise, the _____ (seller/buyer) must provide facilities reasonably suited for _____ (delivery/receipt) of the goods. Also, unless the parties have agreed otherwise, a buyer must pay at the time and place of receipt, _____ (even if/unless) the place of shipment is the place of delivery.

MULTIPLE-CHOICE QUESTIONS

(Answers at the Back of the Book)

____   1.   First Financial Corporation (FFC) orders 100 computers from E-Electronics, Inc. For E-Electronics to tender delivery of the goods, the seller must

a.   only give notice to enable FFC to take delivery.
b.   only hold conforming goods at FFC's disposal .
c.   give notice to FFC and hold conforming goods at FFC's disposal.
d.   none of the above.

____   2.   Engineering, Inc. (EI), agrees to sell specially made parts to Precision Manufacturing Company. EI does not deliver. Due to a market shortage, Precision cannot obtain cover. The buyer's right to recover the parts from EI is

a.   novation.
b.   replevin.
c.   rescission.
d.   specific performance.

____   3.   Kay contracts to sell five laser printers to Lora under a shipment contract. Kay must

a.   only make a reasonable contract for the transport of the goods.
b.   only tender to Lora the documents needed to obtain possession of the goods.
c.   make a reasonable contract for the transport of the goods and tender the documents needed to obtain the goods.
d.   none of the above.

____   4.   Alpha Stores, Inc., refuses to buy 1,000 DVD players for $80 each from Beta Products Company under their contract, due to a drop in the market price for the players, which can be bought for $40 each. As damages, Beta can recover

a. $120,000.
b. $80,000.
c. $40,000.
d. $0.

____   5.   Delta Grocers, Inc., agrees to buy 10,000 potatoes from Eagle Farms. Only half of the shipment conforms to the contract, but conforming potatoes are in short supply in the market. Delta's best course is to

a.   accept the entire shipment.
b.   accept the conforming goods and sue Eagle for the difference between the contract price and the cost of cover.
c.   reject the entire shipment and sue Eagle for specific performance.
d.   suspend payment and wait to see if Eagle will tender conforming goods.

____   6.   Excel Corporation agrees to sell the latest version of its Go! computer game to National Retail Company. Excel delivers an outdated version of Go! (nonconforming goods). National's possible remedies may include

a.   recovering damages only.
b.   rejecting part or all of the goods, or revoking acceptance only.
c.   recovering damages, rejecting goods, or revoking acceptance.
d.   none of the above.

7. Adam contracts to buy goods from Beth. Beth wrongfully fails to deliver the goods. Adam can recover damages equal to the difference between the contract price and the market price

    a. at the time the contract was made.
    b. at the time and place of tender.
    c. when Adam learned of the breach.
    d. when Adam filed a suit against Beth.

8. Fine Poultry Corporation agrees to sell 600 frozen chickens to Fast Food, Inc., in three equal installments. In the first installment, 100 chickens are spoiled. Fast Food can

    a. cancel the contract.
    b. recover from Fine Poultry for breach of the entire contract.
    c. reject the first installment only.
    d. use the unspoiled chickens without payment.

9. Apple Farms contracts for a sale of fruit to Best Groceries, Inc. Apple can enforce its right to payment

    a. only after Best has inspected the goods.
    b. only after Best has had an opportunity to inspect the goods.
    c. only before Best has inspected the goods.
    d. whether or not Best has had the opportunity to inspect the goods.

10. Athletic Goods, Inc. (AGI), agrees to sell sports equipment to Bob's Sports Store. Before the time for performance, AGI tells Bob that it will not deliver. This is

    a. anticipatory repudiation.
    b. perfect tender.
    c. rejection of performance.
    d. revocation of acceptance.

SHORT ESSAY QUESTIONS

1. What is a seller's right to cure and how does it affect a buyer's right to reject?

2. What is a buyer's right of cover?

ISSUE SPOTTERS

(Answers at the Back of the Book)

1. Country Fruit Stand orders eighty cases of peaches from Down Home Farms. For no good reason, Down Home delivers thirty cases instead of eighty, and the delivery is late. Does Country have the right to reject the shipment?

2. Great Images, Inc. (GI), agrees to sell Catalog Corporation (CC) 5,000 posters of celebrities, to be delivered on May 1. On April 1, GI repudiates the contract. CC informs GI that it expects delivery. Can CC sue GI without waiting until May 1?

3. Pizza King agrees to buy tomatoes from Quality Farms. When Quality tenders the goods, Pizza King wrongfully refuses to accept. Quality quickly sells the tomatoes to another buyer, for a lower price. Can Quality recover from Pizza King? If so, what's the measure of recovery?

Chapter 13:
Warranties, Product Liability, and Consumer Law

WHAT THIS CHAPTER IS ABOUT

Warranties that impose duties on sellers cover most goods. A breach of a warranty is a breach of the seller's promise. Manufacturers, processors, and sellers may also be liable to consumers, users, and bystanders for physical harm or property damage caused by defective goods. This is product liability. Consumer law includes statutes, rules, and case law that protect consumers' interests.

CHAPTER OUTLINE

I. WARRANTIES

A. WARRANTIES OF TITLE

1. **Good Title**
Sellers warrant that they have good and valid title and that the transfer of title is rightful [UCC 2–312(1)(a)].

2. **No Liens**
Sellers warrant that goods are free of a security interest of which the buyer has no knowledge [UCC 2–312(1)(b)]. Lessors warrant no third party will interfere with the lessee's use of the goods [UCC 2A–211(1)].

3. **No Infringements**
Sellers warrant that the goods are free of any third person's patent, trademark, or copyright claims [UCC 2–312(3)].

   a. **Sales Contract—If the Warranty Is Breached and the Buyer Is Sued**
   The buyer must notify the seller. If the seller agrees in writing to defend and bear all costs, the buyer must let the seller do it (or lose all rights against the seller) [UCC 2–607(3)(b), (5)(b)].

   b. **Lease—If the Warranty Is Breached and the Lessee Is Sued**
   Same as above, except that a consumer who fails to notify the lessor within a reasonable time does not lose any rights against the lessor [UCC 2A–516(3)(b), (4)(b)].

4. **Disclaimer of Title Warranty**
In a sales contract, a disclaimer can be made only by specific contractual language [UCC 2–312(2)]). In a lease, the disclaimer must be specific, in writing, and conspicuous [UCC 2A–214(4)].

B. EXPRESS WARRANTIES

1. **When Express Warranties Arise**
A seller or lessor warrants that goods will conform to affirmations or promises of fact, descriptions, samples or models [UCC 2–313, 2A–210].

2. **Basis of the Bargain**

   An affirmation, promise, description, or sample must be part of the basis of the bargain: it must come at such a time that the buyer could have relied on it when agreeing to the contract [UCC 2–313, 2A–210].

3. **Statements of Opinion**

   a. **Opinions**

      A statement relating to the value of goods or a statement of opinion or recommendation about goods is not an express warranty [UCC 2–313(2), 2A–210(2)], unless the seller or lessor who makes it is an expert and gives an opinion as an expert.

   b. **Puffing**

      Whether a statement is an express warranty or puffing is not easy to determine. Factors include the reasonableness of the buyer's reliance on the statement and the specificity of the statement.

C. **IMPLIED WARRANTIES**

   An implied warranty is derived by implication or inference from the nature of a transaction or the relative situations or circumstances of the parties.

   1. **Implied Warranty of Merchantability**

      A warranty automatically arises in every sale or lease of goods by a merchant who deals in such goods that the goods are merchantable [UCC 2–314, 2A–212].

      a. **Reasonably Fit for Ordinary Purposes**

         Goods that are merchantable are "reasonably fit for the ordinary purposes for which such goods are used."

      b. **Characteristics of Merchantable Goods**

         Average, fair, or medium-grade quality; pass without objection in the market for goods of the same description; adequate package and label, as provided by the agreement; and conform to the promises or affirmations of fact made on the container or label.

   2. **Implied Warranty of Fitness for a Particular Purpose**

      Arises when seller or lessor (merchant or nonmerchant) knows or has reason to know the purpose for which buyer or lessee will use goods and knows he or she is relying on seller to select suitable goods [UCC 2–315, 2A–213]. Goods can be merchantable but unfit for a particular purpose.

   3. **Implied Warranty from Dealing, Performance, or Trade Usage**

      When the parties know a well-recognized trade custom, it is inferred that they intended it to apply to their contract [UCC 2–314, 2A–212].

D. **WARRANTY DISCLAIMERS**

   1. **Express Warranties**

      A seller can avoid making express warranties by not promising or affirming anything, describing the goods, or using of a sample or model.

      a. **Oral Warranties**

         Oral warranties made during bargaining cannot be modified later.

      b. **Negating or Limiting Express Warranties**

         A written disclaimer—clear and conspicuous—can negate all warranties not in the written contract [UCC 2–316(1), 2A–214(1)].

   2. **Implied Warranties**

a. General Language

Implied warranties can be disclaimed by the expression "as is" or a similar phrase [UCC 2–316(3)(a), 2A–214(3)(a)].

b. Specific Language

Implied warranty of fitness for a particular purpose: disclaimer must be in writing and be conspicuous (the word *fitness* is not required). Implied warranty of merchantability: disclaimer must mention merchantability; if it is in writing, it must be conspicuous.

3. Buyer's Inspection of the Goods

If a buyer examines the goods before entering a contract, there is no implied warranty with respect to defects that a reasonable examination would reveal [UCC 2–316(3)(b), 2A–214(2)(b)]. The same is true if the buyer refuses to examine over the seller or lessor's demand.

4. Unconscionability

Courts view disclaimers with disfavor, especially when consumers are involved, and have sometimes held disclaimers unconscionable [UCC 2–302, 2A–108].

E. MAGNUSON–MOSS WARRANTY ACT

No seller is required to give a written warranty for consumer goods, but if a seller chooses to do so and the cost of the goods is more than—

1. $10

The warranty must be clearly labeled full or limited. A full warranty requires free repair or replacement of defective parts (there is no time limit). A limited warranty is any warranty that is not full.

2. $15

The seller must state (fully and conspicuously in a single document in "readily understood language") the seller's name and address, what is warranted, procedures for enforcing the warranty, any limitations on relief, and that the buyer has legal rights.

II. PRODUCT LIABILITY

A. NEGLIGENCE

If the failure to exercise reasonable care in the making or marketing of a product causes an injury, the basis of liability is negligence.

1. Privity of Contract between Plaintiff and Defendant Is Not Required

2. Manufacturer's Duty of Care

Due care must be exercised in designing, assembling, and testing a product; selecting materials; inspecting and testing products bought for use in the final product; and placing warnings on the label to inform users of dangers of which an ordinary person might not be aware.

B. MISREPRESENTATION

If a misrepresentation (such as intentionally concealing product defects) results in an injury, there may liability for fraud.

C. STRICT LIABILITY

Under the doctrine of strict liability, a defendant may be liable for the result of his or her act regardless of intention or exercise of reasonable care.

1. Requirements of Strict Product Liability

These requirements, under the *Restatement (Second) of Torts*, Section 402A, are—

a. Product Is in a Defective Condition when the Defendant Sells It

b. The Defendant Is Normally in the Business of Selling the Product

   c. **The Defect Makes the Product Unreasonably Dangerous**
     A product may be so defective if either—

     1) **The Product Is Dangerous beyond the Consumer's Expectation**
       There may have been a flaw in the manufacturing process that led to some defective products being marketed, or a perfectly made product may not have had adequate warning on the label.

     2) **There Is a Less Dangerous, Economically Feasible Alter-native that the Manufacturer Failed to Use**
       A manufacturer may have failed to design a safe product.

   d. **The Plaintiff Incurs Harm to Self or Property by Use of the Product**

   e. **The Defect Is the Proximate Cause of the Harm**

   f. **The Product Was Not Substantially Changed after It Was Sold**

  2. **Product Defects—*Restatement (Third) of Torts***
    The *Restatement (Third) of Torts: Products Liability* categorizes—

   a. **Manufacturing Defects**
     These occur when a product departs from its intended design even though all possible care was taken (strict liability).

   b. **Design Defects**
     These can occur when a product poses a foreseeable risk of harm that could have been reduced by use of a reasonable alternative design and the omission makes the product unreasonably unsafe. A court would consider such factors as consumer expectations and warnings.

   c. **Warning Defects**
     These exist when a product poses a foreseeable risk of harm that could have been reduced by a reasonable warning and the omission makes the product unreasonably unsafe. Factors include the content and comprehensibility of a warning, and the expected users.

  3. **Market-Share Liability**
    In some cases, some courts have not required proof as to which specific defendant manufactured a particular product that injured the plaintiff.

  4. **Other Applications of Strict Liability**
    Defendants may be liable to injured bystanders. Suppliers of component parts and lessors may be liable for injuries caused by defective products.

  5. **Statutes of Repose**
    A statute of repose limits the time in which a suit can be filed. It runs from an earlier date and for a longer time than a statute of limitations.

D. DEFENSES TO PRODUCT LIABILITY

  1. **Assumption of Risk**
    In some states, this is a defense if (1) plaintiff knew and appreciated the risk created by the defect and (2) plaintiff voluntarily engaged in the risk, event though it was unreasonable to do so.

  2. **Product Misuse**
    The use must not be the one for which the product was designed, and the misuse must not be reasonably foreseeable.

  3. **Comparative Negligence**
    Most states consider a plaintiff's actions in apportioning liability.

4. Commonly Known Dangers
Failing to warn against such a danger is not a ground for liability.

III. CONSUMER PROTECTION LAWS

A. DECEPTIVE ADVERTISING
The Federal Trade Commission Act of 1914 created the Federal Trade Commission (FTC) to prevent unfair and deceptive trade practices. Deceptive advertising: advertising that would mislead a consumer.

1. Advertising that Is Deceptive
Scientifically untrue claims; misleading half-truths; bait-and-switch ads (if a seller refuses to show an advertised item, fails to have adequate quantities on hand, fails to promise to deliver within a reasonable time, or discourages employees from selling the item.).

2. Advertising that Is Not Deceptive
Puffing (vague generalities, obvious exaggeration).

3. Online Deceptive Advertising
The same laws that apply to other forms of advertising apply to online ads.

4. FTC Actions against Deceptive Advertising
If the FTC believes that an ad is unfair or deceptive, it sends a complaint to the advertiser, who may settle. If not, the FTC can, after a hearing, issue a cease-and-desist order or require counteradvertising.

B. TELEMARKETING AND ELECTRONIC ADVERTISING

1. Telephone Consumer Protection Act (TCPA) of 1991
The TCPA prohibits (1) phone solicitation using an automatic dialing system or a prerecorded voice and (2) transmission of ads via fax without the recipient's permission. For each violation, consumers can recover actual losses or $500, whichever is greater. If a defendant willfully or knowingly violated the act, a court can award treble damages.

2. Telemarketing and Consumer Fraud and Abuse Prevention Act of 1994
This act authorized FTC to set rules for telemarketing and bring actions against fraudulent telemarketers. The FTC's Telemarketing Sales Rule of 1995 makes it illegal to misrepresent information and requires disclosure. In 2003, the FTC set up a "National Do Not Call Registry," which prohibits telemarketers from calling consumers whose names are listed.

3. State Laws
Most states also have laws regulating phone solicitation.

C. LABELING AND PACKAGING

1. Fair Packaging and Labeling Act of 1966
This act requires labels to identify: the product; net quantity of contents; quantity of servings, if the number of servings is stated; manufacturer; and packager or distributor. More can be required (such as fat content).

2. Other Federal Laws
These include the Fur Products Labeling Act of 1951, Wool Products Labeling Act of 1939, Flammable Fabrics Act of 1953, Comprehensive Smokeless Tobacco Health Education Act of 1986.

D. SALES
Federal agencies that regulate sales include the FTC and the Federal Reserve Board of Governors (Regulation Z governs credit provisions in sales contracts). All states have some form of consumer protection laws.

1. **Door-to-Door Sales**
   States' cooling-off laws permit a buyer to rescind a purchase within a certain time; the FTC has a three-day period (consumers can choose the most favorable). The FTC requires a seller to notify a buyer of the right to cancel (in Spanish, if the sale is in Spanish).

2. **Telephone and Mail-Order Sales**
   Consumers are partly protected by federal laws prohibiting mail fraud (see Chapter 6) and by state law that parallels federal law.

   a. **FTC "Mail or Telephone Order Merchandise Rule" of 1993**
      For goods bought via phone lines or through the mail, merchants must ship orders within the time promised in their ads, notify consumers when orders cannot be shipped on time, and issue a refund within a specified time if a consumer cancels an order.

   b. **Postal Reorganization Act of 1970**
      Unsolicited merchandise sent by mail may be retained, used, discarded, or disposed of, without obligation to the sender.

3. **Online Sales**
   Consumers are protected online by the same federal and state laws that apply to other media.

E. **HEALTH AND SAFETY PROTECTION**

1. **Foods and Drugs**
   The Federal Food, Drug, and Cosmetic Act (FFDCA) of 1938 sets food standards, levels of additives, classifications of food and food ads; regulates medical devices. Drugs must be shown to be effective and safe. Enforced by the Food and Drug Administration (FDA).

2. **Consumer Product Safety**
   The Consumer Product Safety Act of 1972 includes a scheme for the regulation of consumer products and safety by the Consumer Product Safety Commission (CPSC). The CPSC—

   a. Conducts research on product safety.
   b. Sets standards for consumer products and bans the manufacture and sale of a product that is potentially hazardous to consumers.
   c. Removes from the market any products imminently hazardous and requires manufacturers to report on any products already sold or intended for sale if the products have proved to be hazardous.
   d. Administers other product safety legislation.

F. **CREDIT PROTECTION**

1. **Truth-in-Lending Act (TILA)**
   The TILA, Title I of the Consumer Credit Protection Act (CCPA), was enacted in 1968, is administered by the Federal Reserve Board, and requires the disclosure of credit terms.

   a. **Who Is Subject to the TILA?**
      The TILA covers creditors who, in the ordinary course of business, lend money or sell goods on credit to consumers, or arrange for credit for consumers.

   b. **What Does the TILA Require?**
      Under Regulation Z, in any transaction involving a sales contract in which payment is to be made in more than four installments, a lender must disclose all the credit terms clearly and conspicuously.

   c. **Equal Credit Opportunity Act of 1974**
      This act prohibits (1) denial of credit on the basis of race, religion, national origin, color, sex, marital status, age and (2) credit discrimination based on whether an individual receives certain forms of income.

d. Credit-Card Rules

Liability of a cardholder is $50 per card for unauthorized charges made before the issuer is notified the card is lost. An issuer cannot bill for unauthorized charges if a card was improperly issued. If a cardholder wishes to withhold payment for a faulty product, there are specific procedures to follow.

e. Consumer Leasing Act of 1988

Those who lease consumer goods in the ordinary course of their business, if the goods are priced at $25,000 or less and the lease term exceeds four months, must disclose all material terms in writing.

2. Fair Credit Reporting Act (FCRA) of 1970

a. What Does the FCRA Provide?

Consumer credit-reporting agencies may issue credit reports only for certain purposes (extension of credit, etc.); a consumer denied credit, or charged more than others would be, on the basis of a report must be notified and told of the agency that issued the report.

b. Consumers Can Have Inaccurate Information Deleted

If a consumer learns that the report contains inaccurate information, the agency must delete it within a reasonable period of time.

3. Fair Credit and Accurate Transactions Act (FACT Act)

The FACT Act established a national "fraud alert" system so that consumers who suspect ID theft can place an alert on their credit files. Also—

a. Credit-Reporting Agencies' Responsibilities

Consumer credit-reporting agencies must provide consumers with free copies of their reports and stop reporting allegedly fraudulent information once a consumer shows that ID theft occurred.

b. Other Businesses' Responsibilities

Businesses must include shortened ("truncated") account numbers on credit card receipts and provide consumers with copies of records to help prove an account or transaction was fraudulent.

4. Fair Debt Collection Practices Act (FDCPA)

Enacted in 1977, the FDCPA applies only to debt-collection agencies that, usually for a percentage of the amount owed, attempt to collect debts on behalf of someone else. The FTC enforces the act.

a. What Does the FDCPA Prohibit?

1) Contacting the debtor at the debtor's place of employment if the employer objects.
2) Contacting the debtor during inconvenient times or at any time if an attorney represents the debtor.
3) Contacting third parties other than the debtor's parents, spouse, or financial advisor about payment unless a court agrees.
4) Using harassment, or false and misleading information.
5) Contacting the debtor any time after the debtor refuses to pay the debt, except to advise of further action to be taken.

b. What Does the FDCPA Require?

Collection agencies must notify a debtor that he or she has thirty days to dispute the debt and request written verification of it.

c. Remedies

A debt collector may be liable for actual damages, plus additional damages not to exceed $1,000 and attorneys' fees.

TRUE-FALSE QUESTIONS

(Answers at the Back of the Book)

____ 1. Promises of fact made during the bargaining process are express warranties.

____ 2. A contract cannot include both an implied warranty and an express warranty.

____ 3. An express warranty can be limited.

____ 4. Privity of contract is required to bring a product liability suit based on negligence.

____ 5. One requirement for a product liability suit based on strict liability is a failure to exercise due care.

____ 6. In many states, the plaintiff's negligence is a defense that may be raised in a product liability suit based on strict liability.

____ 7. Advertising will be deemed deceptive if a consumer would be misled by the advertising claim.

____ 8. Labels must be accurate.

____ 9. Under no circumstances can a consumer rescind a contract freely entered into.

____ 10. The TILA applies to creditors who, in the ordinary course of business, lend money or sell goods on credit to consumers.

FILL-IN QUESTIONS

(Answers at the Back of the Book)

An express warranty _____ (can/cannot) be disclaimed in writing if it is called to the buyer's attention. An implied warranty of fitness for a particular purpose _____ (can/cannot) be disclaimed in writing. An implied warranty of merchantability _____ (can/cannot) be disclaimed in writing. A disclaimer of the implied warranty of fitness for a particular purpose _____ (must/need not) use the word "fitness." A disclaimer of the implied warranty of merchantability _____ (must/need not) include the word merchantability.

MULTIPLE-CHOICE QUESTIONS

(Answers at the Back of the Book)

____ 1. Eagle Skis, Inc., makes and sells skis. In deciding whether the skis are merchantable, a court would consider whether

a. Eagle violated any government regulations.
b. the skis are a quality product.
c. the skis are fit for the ordinary purpose for which such goods are used.
d. the skis are made in an efficient manner.

____ 2. Great Furniture Company makes and sells furniture. To avoid liability for most implied warranties, their sales agreements should note that their goods are sold

a. "as is."
b. by a merchant.
c. for cash only.
d. in perfect condition.

_____   **3.** Superb Auto Sales sells cars, trucks, and other motor vehicles. A Superb salesperson tells potential customers, "This is the finest car ever made." This statement is

a. an express warranty.
b. an implied warranty.
c. a warranty of title.
d. puffing.

_____   **4.** Standard Tools, Inc., makes and sells tools. Tina is injured as a result of using a Standard tool. Tina sues Standard for product liability based on strict liability. To succeed, Tina must prove that Standard

a. did not use care with respect to the tool.
b. misrepresented a material fact regarding the tool on which Tina relied.
c. was in privity of contract with Tina.
d. none of the above.

_____   **5.** Omega, Inc., designs and manufacturers DVD players. In a product liability suit based on negligence, Omega could be liable for violating its duty of care with respect to a player's

a. design only.
b. design or manufacture.
c. manufacture only.
d. neither design nor manufacture.

_____   **6.** Tasty Foods Company advertises that its cereal, "Fiber Rich," reduces cholesterol. After an investigation and a hearing, the FTC finds no evidence to support the claim. To correct the public's impression of Fiber Rich, the most appropriate action would be

a. a cease-and-desist order.
b. a civil fine.
c. a criminal fine.
d. counteradvertising.

_____   **7.** ABC Corporation sells consumer products. Generally, the labels must use words as they are

a. normally used in the scientific community.
b. ordinarily understood by consumers.
c. reasonably approved by ABC's officers.
d. typically explained by the marketing department.

_____   **8.** Maria does not speak English. Nick comes to her home and, after a long presentation in Spanish, sells her a vacuum cleaner. He hands her a paper that contains only in English a notice of the right to cancel a sale within three days. This transaction is

a. proper, because ignorance of your rights is no defense.
b. proper, because Nick gave Maria notice of her rights.
c. not proper, because ignorance of your rights is a defense.
d. not proper, because the deal was in Spanish but the notice was in English.

_____   **9.** Ed takes out a student loan from First National Bank. After graduation, Ed goes to work, but he does not make payments on the loan. The bank agrees with Great Collection Agency that if it collects the debt, it can keep a percentage of the amount. To collect the debt, the agency can contact

a. Ed at his place of employment, even if his employer objects.
b. Ed at unusual or inconvenient times or any time if he retains an attorney.
c. Ed only to advise him of further action that the agency will take.
d. third parties, including Ed's parents, unless ordered otherwise by a court.

____ **10.** The ordinary business of Ace Credit Company is to lend money to consumers. Ace must disclose all credit terms clearly and conspicuously in

a. all credit transactions.
b. any credit transaction in which payments are to be made in more than four installments.
c. any credit transaction in which payments are to be made in more than one installment.
d. no credit transactions.

SHORT ESSAY QUESTIONS

1. How defective must a product be to support a cause of action in strict liability in a product liability suit?

2. What are some of the more common deceptive advertising techniques and the ways in which the FTC may deal with such conduct?

ISSUE SPOTTERS

(Answers at the Back of the Book)

1. Delta Corporation makes tire rims, which it sells to Eagle Vehicles, Inc., to put on its cars. One set of rims is defective, which an inspection would reveal. Eagle does not inspect the rims. The car is sold to Fast Auto Sales. Greg buys the car, which is soon in an accident caused by the defective rims and in which Greg is injured. Is Eagle liable?

2. Real Chocolate Company makes a box of candy, which it sells to Sweet Things, Inc., a distributor. Sweet sells the box to a Tasty Candy store, where Jill buys it. Jill gives it to Ken, who breaks a tooth on a stone the same size and color of a piece of the candy. If Real, Sweet, and Tasty were not negligent, can they be liable for the injury?

3. Alpha Electronics, Inc., advertises Beta computers at a low price. Alpha keeps only a few in stock and tells its sales staff to switch consumers attracted by the price to more expensive brands. Alpha tells its staff that if all else fails, refuse to show the Betas, and if a consumer insists on buying one, do not promise delivery. Has Alpha violated a law?

Chapter 14:
Negotiable Instruments

WHAT THIS CHAPTER IS ABOUT

A **negotiable instrument** is a written promise or order to pay a sum of money. It is transferred more readily than an ordinary contract, and a person who acquires it is subject to less risk than the assignee of a contract right. This chapter outlines types of negotiable instruments, the effect of indorsements, the liability on instruments, and the defenses. Article 3 of the Uniform Commercial Code (UCC) covers the requirements and process of negotiation.

CHAPTER OUTLINE

I. **TYPES OF NEGOTIABLE INSTRUMENTS**

   A. **REQUIREMENTS FOR NEGOTIABILITY**
   To be negotiable, an instrument must be [UCC 3–104(a)]—

   1. Be in writing.
   2. Be signed by the maker or drawer.
   3. Be an unconditional promise or order to pay.
   4. State a fixed amount of money.
   5. Be payable on demand or at a definite time.
   6. Be payable to order or bearer, unless it is a check.

   B. **DRAFTS AND CHECKS (ORDERS TO PAY)**
   The person who signs or makes an order to pay is the **drawer**. The person to whom the order is made is the **drawee**. The person to whom payment is ordered is the **payee**.

   1. **Draft**
   An unconditional written order by one person to another to pay money. The drawee must be obligated to the drawer either by an agreement or through a debtor-creditor relationship to honor the order.

      a. **Time Draft**
      Payable at a definite future time.

      b. **Sight Draft (Demand Draft)**
      Payable on sight (when presented for payment). A draft payable at a stated time after sight is both a time and a sight draft.

      c. **Trade Acceptance**
      A draft in which the seller is both the drawer and the payee. The draft orders the buyer to pay a specified sum of money to the seller, at a stated time in the future.

      d. **Banker's Acceptance**
      A trade acceptance that orders the buyer's bank, rather than the buyer, to pay.

   2. **Check**
   A draft drawn on a bank and payable on demand. A **cashier's check** is a draft in which the bank is both the drawer and drawee.

C. **PROMISSORY NOTES AND CERTIFICATES OF DEPOSIT (PROMISES TO PAY)**
A person who promises to pay is a **maker**. A person to whom the promise is made is a **payee**.

1. **Promissory Note**
A written promise by one party to pay money to another party.

2. **Certificate of Deposit**
A note made by a bank promising to repay a deposit of funds with interest on a certain date [UCC 3–104(j)].

II. TRANSFER OF INSTRUMENTS

A. **TRANSFER BY ASSIGNMENT**
A transfer by assignment (see Chapter 9) gives the assignee only those rights the assignor possessed. Defenses that can be raised against an assignor can normally be raised against an assignee.

B. **TRANSFER BY NEGOTIATION**
On a transfer by negotiation, the transferee becomes a holder and receives the rights of the previous possessor (and possibly more) [UCC 3–201(a), 3–202(b), 3–203(b), 3–305, 3–306]. An order instrument is negotiated by delivery with indorsement; a bearer instrument is negotiated by delivery only [UCC 3–201(b)].

III. INDORSEMENTS

An indorsement (signature with or without additional words or statements) is required to negotiate an order instrument. The person who indorses an instrument is an **indorser**; the person to whom the instrument is transferred is an **indorsee**.

A. **BLANK INDORSEMENT**
Specifies no particular indorsee and can consist of a mere signature [UCC 3–205(b)]. Converts an order instrument to a bearer instrument.

B. **SPECIAL INDORSEMENT**
Names the indorsee [UCC 3–205(a)]. No special words are needed. Converts a bearer instrument into an order instrument.

C. **QUALIFIED INDORSEMENT**
Disclaims or limits contract liability (the notation "without recourse" is commonly used) [UCC 3–415(b)]. Often used by persons acting in a representative capacity.

1. **No Payment Guarantee**
Does not guarantee payment, but does transfer title. (Most blank and special indorsements are unqualified, guaranteeing payment and transferring title).

2. **Further Negotiation**
A *special* qualified indorsement makes an instrument order paper (and requires indorsement and delivery for negotiation). A *blank* qualified indorsement creates bearer paper (and requires only delivery).

D. **RESTRICTIVE INDORSEMENTS**

1. **Conditional Indorsement**
Specifying an event on which payment depends does not affect negotiability. A person paying or taking the instrument for value can disregard the condition [UCC 3–206(b)]. (Conditional language on the face of an instrument, however, does destroy negotiability.)

2. **Indorsement Prohibiting Further Indorsement**
Does not destroy negotiability [UCC 3–206(a)]. Has the same effect as a special indorsement.

3. **Indorsement for Deposit or Collection**
Making the indorsee (usually a bank) a collecting agent of the indorser (such as "For deposit only") locks the instrument into the bank collection process [UCC 3–206(c)].

4. **Trust Indorsement (Agency Indorsement)**
An indorsement by one who is to hold or use the funds for the benefit of the indorser or a third party [UCC 3–206(d), (e)]. To the extent the original indorsee pays or applies the proceeds consistently with the indorsement, he or she is a holder and can become a holder in due course (HDC).

IV. HOLDER IN DUE COURSE (HDC)

A. HOLDER
A **holder** is a person in possession of an instrument drawn, issued, or indorsed to him or her, to his or her order, or to bearer or in blank [UCC 1–201(20)]. A holder is subject to the same defenses that could be asserted against the transferor (the party from whom the holder obtained the instrument).

B. HOLDER IN DUE COURSE
A holder who meets certain requirements becomes a **holder in due course (HDC)**, and takes an instrument free of all claims to it and most defenses against payment that could be successfully asserted against the transferor.

C. REQUIREMENTS FOR HDC STATUS
To become an HDC, a person must be a holder and take an instrument—

1. **For Value**
A holder does not give value by receiving an instrument as a gift or inheriting it. A holder gives value by [UCC 3–303(a)]—

   a. Performing a promise for which an instrument was issued or transferred.
   b. Acquiring a security interest or other lien in the instrument (other than a lien obtained by a judicial proceeding).
   c. Taking instrument in payment of, or as security for, an antecedent debt.
   d. Giving a negotiable instrument as payment.
   e. Giving an irrevocable commitment as payment.

2. **In Good Faith**
A purchaser must honestly believe that an instrument is not defective and observe reasonable commercial standards. This applies only to the holder—a person who in good faith takes an instrument from a thief may become an HDC.

3. **Without Notice**
A holder must acquire an instrument without knowing, or having reason to know, it is defective.

   a. **What Constitutes Notice?**
   (1) Actual knowledge of a defect, (2) receipt of notice about a defect, or (3) reason to know that a defect exists [UCC 1–201(25)]. Knowledge of certain facts is not notice [see UCC 3–302(b)].

   b. **Overdue Instruments—What Constitutes Notice?**
   If a holder takes a *demand* instrument knowing demand was made or takes it an unreasonable time after its issue (ninety days for a check; other instruments depend on the circumstances [UCC 3–304(a)]). If a holder takes an *order* instrument after its expressed due date [UCC 3–304(b)].

V. HOLDER THROUGH AN HDC

A. SHELTER PRINCIPLE
A person who does not qualify as an HDC but who acquires an instrument from an HDC or from someone with HDC rights receives the rights and privileges of an HDC [UCC 3–203(b)].

B. LIMITATIONS ON THE SHELTER PRINCIPLE

A holder who was a party to fraud or illegality affecting an instrument or who, as a prior holder, had notice of a claim or defense cannot improve his or her status by repurchasing it from a later HDC [UCC 3–203(b)].

VI. SIGNATURE LIABILITY

Every party (except a qualified indorser) who signs an instrument is primarily or secondarily liable to pay it when it is due.

A. PRIMARY LIABILITY

Only makers and **acceptors** (a drawee who promises to pay an instrument when it is presented later for payment) are primarily liable—they are absolutely required to pay (subject to certain defenses) [UCC 3–305].

B. SECONDARY LIABILITY

Drawers and unqualified indorsers are secondarily liable—they pay only if a party who is primarily liable does not pay. A drawer pays if a drawee does not; an indorser pays if a maker defaults. Secondary liability is triggered by proper presentment, dishonor, and notice of dishonor.

1. Proper Presentment

a. To the Proper Person
A note or CD is presented to the maker; a draft to the drawee for acceptance, payment, or both (whatever is required); a check to the drawee [UCC 3–501(a), 3–502(b)].

b. In the Proper Manner
Depending on the type of instrument [UCC 3–501(b)]: (1) any commercially reasonable means (oral, written, or electronic; but it is not effective until the demand is received); (2) a clearinghouse procedure used by banks; or (3) at the place specified in the instrument.

c. Timely
Failure to present on time is the most common reason for improper presentment [UCC 3–414(f), 3–415(e), 3–501(b)(4)].

2. Dishonor
Occurs when payment or acceptance is refused or cannot be obtained within the prescribed time, or when required presentment is excused and the instrument is not accepted or paid [UCC 3–502(e), 3–504].

3. Proper Notice
On dishonor, to hold secondary parties liable, notice must be given within thirty days following the day on which a person receives notice of the dishonor (except a bank, which must give notice before midnight of the next banking day after receipt) [UCC 3–503].

C. UNAUTHORIZED SIGNATURES

An unauthorized signature does not bind the person whose name is forged.

1. Two Exceptions
(1) An unauthorized signature is binding if the person whose name is signed ratifies it [UCC 3–403(a)]; (2) a person can be barred, on the basis of negligence, from denying liability [UCC 3–115, 3–406, 4–401(d)(2)].

2. Liability of the Signer
An unauthorized signature operates as the signature of the *signer* in favor of an HDC [UCC 3–403(a)].

D. SPECIAL RULES FOR UNAUTHORIZED INDORSEMENTS

Generally, the loss falls on the first party to take the instrument. The loss falls on the maker or drawer in cases involving—

1. Imposters

The indorsement of an **imposter** (one who induces a maker or drawer to issue an instrument in the name of an impersonated payee) can be effective against the drawer [UCC 3–404(a)].

2. Fictitious Payees

The indorsement of a **fictitious payee** (one to whom an instrument is payable but who has no right to receive payment—often, dishonest employees issue such instruments or deceive employers into doing so) can result in the employer's liability to an innocent holder [UCC 3–404(b)(2)].

VII. WARRANTY LIABILITY

A. TRANSFER WARRANTIES

1. The Warranties

Any person who transfers an instrument for consideration warrants to the transferee and, if the transfer is by indorsement, to all later transferees and holders who take the instrument in good faith [UCC 3–416]—

a. The transferor is entitled to enforce the instrument.
b. All signatures are authentic and authorized.
c. The instrument has not been altered.
d. The instrument is not subject to a defense or claim that can be asserted against the transferor.
e. The transferor has no knowledge of any insolvency proceedings against the maker, the acceptor, or the drawer of the instrument.

2. To Whom the Warranties Run

Order paper: to any subsequent holder who takes the instrument in good faith. Bearer paper: only to the immediate transferee [UCC 3–416(a)].

B. PRESENTMENT WARRANTIES

1. The Warranties

Any person who obtains payment or acceptance of an instrument warrants to any other person who in good faith pays or accepts the instrument [UCC 3–417(a), (d)]—

a. The person obtaining payment or acceptance is entitled or authorized to enforce the instrument (that is, there are no missing or unauthorized indorsements).
b. The instrument has not been altered.
c. The person obtaining payment or acceptance has no knowledge that the signature of the issuer of the instrument is unauthorized.

2. The Last Two Warranties Do Not Apply in Certain Cases

It is assumed, for example, that a drawer or a maker will recognize his or her own signature and that a maker or an acceptor will recognize whether an instrument has been materially altered.

VIII. DEFENSES TO LIABILITY

A. UNIVERSAL DEFENSES

Valid against all holders, including HDCs and holders who take by HDCs.

1. Forgery

Forgery of a maker's or drawer's signature cannot bind the person whose name is used (unless that person ratifies the signature or is precluded from denying it) [UCC 3–403(a)].

2. **Fraud in the Execution**

Defense is valid if a person is deceived into signing an instrument, believing that it is something else. Defense is not valid if a reasonable inquiry would have revealed the nature of the instrument.

3. **Material Alteration**

An alteration is material if it changes the contract terms between any two parties in any way (making any change in an unauthorized manner that relates to a party's obligation) [UCC 3–407(a)].

   a. **Complete Defense against an Ordinary Holder**

   A holder recovers nothing [UCC 3–407(a)]. (If an alteration is visible, a holder has notice and cannot be an HDC [UCC 3–302(a)(1)].)

   b. **Partial Defense against an HDC**

   If an instrument was originally incomplete and later completed in an unauthorized manner, an HDC can enforce it as completed [UCC 3–407(b)].

4. **Discharge in Bankruptcy**

Absolute defense [UCC 3–305(a)(1)].

5. **Minority**

A defense to the extent that state law recognizes it as a defense to a contract [UCC 3–305(a)(1)(i)] (see Chapter 8).

6. **Illegality**

A defense if the statute declares that an instrument executed in connection with illegal conduct is *void* [UCC 3–305(a)(1)(ii)].

7. **Mental Incapacity**

An instrument issued by a person who has been adjudicated mentally incompetent by state proceedings is void [UCC 3–305(a)(1)(ii)].

8. **Extreme Duress**

Extreme duress is an immediate threat of force or violence [UCC 3–305(a)(1)(ii)].

B. **PERSONAL DEFENSES**

Personal defenses avoid payment to an ordinary holder (but not an HDC).

1. **Breach of Contract or Breach of Warranty**

If there is a breach of a contract for which an instrument was issued or a breach of warranty (see Chapter 13), the maker or drawer may not pay.

2. **Lack or Failure of Consideration** [UCC 3–303(b), 3–305(a)(2)]

For example, when there is no consideration for the issuing of a note.

3. **Fraud in the Inducement (Ordinary Fraud)**

If one issues an instrument based on false statements by the other party.

4. **Illegality**

When a statute makes an illegal transaction *voidable*.

5. **Mental Incapacity**

If a person drafts an instrument while mentally incompetent but before a court declares him or her so, the instrument is voidable.

6. **Others**

Discharge by payment or cancellation; unauthorized completion of an incomplete instrument; non-delivery of an instrument; ordinary duress or undue influence.

TRUE-FALSE QUESTIONS

(Answers at the Back of the Book)

_____   1.   A negotiable instrument can be transferred only by negotiation.

_____   2.   A bearer instrument is negotiated by delivery alone.

_____   3.   An instrument can be negotiable even if it is not payable on demand or at a definite time.

_____   4.   An instrument payable to the order of a specific person is not negotiable.

_____   5.   A promise to give value in the future makes a holder an HDC

_____   6.   Personal defenses can be raised to avoid payment to an HDC.

_____   7.   Taking a check knowing that the drawee dishonored it prevents a holder from becoming an HDC.

_____   8.   Signature liability extends to nearly every person who signs a negotiable instrument.

_____   9.   Warranty liability does not bind parties who only present instruments for payment.

_____ 10.   An unauthorized signature usually binds the person whose name is signed.

FILL-IN QUESTIONS

(Answers at the Back of the Book)

The person to whom an order to pay is made is a _____ (drawee/payee). If the payee indorses the instrument by signing the back, the signature is _____ (a qualified indorsement/an indorsement in blank). This converts the instrument to _____ (a bearer/an order) instrument, which the payee negotiates by _____ (delivery/further indorsement and delivery). A bearer instrument that is converted to an order instrument must be negotiated as _____ (a bearer/an order) instrument.

MULTIPLE-CHOICE QUESTIONS

(Answers at the Back of the Book)

_____   1.   Alex makes out a check "Pay to the order of Beth." Beth indorses the check on the back. The check can now be negotiated by

a. delivery only.
b. indorsement only.
c. delivery and indorsement.
d. none of the above.

_____   2.   To pay for a new truck, Eagle Transport Company issues a draft in favor of Fine Motor Sales, Inc. A draft is

a. a promise to pay money.
b. a promise to deliver goods at a future date.
c. a conditional promise to pay money.
d. an unconditional written order to pay money.

_____ 3. Gail indorses a check, "Pay to Highway Equipment Corporation if they deliver the backhoe by June 1, 2006." This indorsement is

a. a blank indorsement.
b. a qualified indorsement.
c. a restrictive indorsement.
d. a special indorsement.

_____ 4. Don signs a note that states, "Payable in thirty days." Eve buys the note on the thirty-first day. Eve is on notice that the note

a. has been dishonored.
b. is no longer negotiable.
c. is overdue.
d. is payable immediately.

_____ 5. Gail writes a check on her account at First National Bank to Hal, a famous investor. The person purporting to be Hal is an imposter, however, named Ira. Ira negotiates the check to First National. Liability for the check is on

a. First National Bank.
b. Gail.
c. Hal.
d. Ira.

_____ 6. Ann, who cannot read English, signs a note after Bob tells her that it is a credit application. If later sued by an HDC, Ann's best defense would be

a. duress.
b. mistake.
c. fraud in the inducement.
d. fraud in the execution.

_____ 7. Able Company writes a check to Baker Corporation that is drawn on Able's account at City Bank. Baker presents the check to the bank for payment. If the bank accepts the check, the bank is

a. not liable for payment.
b. primarily liable for payment.
c. secondarily liable for payment.
d. simultaneously liable for payment.

_____ 8. Bill writes a check on his account at Community Bank to Donna to pay a preexisting debt. Donna negotiates the check to Ed by indorsement. Before Bill or Donna may be liable on the check, it must be

a. lost and unpaid.
b. presented for payment and dishonored, for which notice must be given.
c. presented for payment and dishonored, without notice.
d. presented for payment and paid.

_____ 9. Delta Company writes a check to Eagle Credit, Inc., that is drawn on Delta's account at First Federal Bank. If the bank does not accept the check, liability for its amount is on

a. Delta.
b. Eagle.
c. First Federal.
d. the party holding the draft.

____ **10.** Ron contracts with Sam for monthly $200 shipments of coffee to Ron's Java Stop. Ron pays in advance with a $1,200 note. One month later, Sam sells the note to Tina for $1,100. When the note is sold, Sam is

    a. an HDC for $1,200.

    b. an HDC for $200.

    c. an HDC for $100.

    d. not an HDC.

SHORT ESSAY QUESTIONS

1. What are the requirements for an instrument to be negotiable?

2. What defenses may be raised against payment of an instrument held by an HDC?

ISSUE SPOTTERS

(Answers at the Back of the Book)

1. Mark issues a $500 note to Nora due six months from the date issued. One month later, Nora negotiates the note to Owen for $250 in cash and a check for $250. To what extent is Owen an HDC of the note?

2. Pat is an accountant with Quality Corporation, but has no authority to sign corporate checks. Pat orders office furniture from Retail Company and pays with a Quality check, signing "Quality Corp. by Pat, accountant." Retail does not know that Pat has no authority to sign the check. Can Quality refuse to pay it?

3. Roy signs corporate checks for Standard Corporation. Roy makes a check payable to U-All Company, to whom Standard owes no money. Roy signs the check, forges U-All's indorsement, and cashes the check at First State Bank, the drawee. Does Standard have any recourse against the bank for the payment?

Chapter 15:
Checks, the Banking System, and E-Money

WHAT THIS CHAPTER IS ABOUT

This chapter outlines the duties and liabilities that arise when a check is issued and paid. UCC Articles 3 and 4 govern checks. If there is a conflict between the articles, Article 4 controls. This outline also covers electronic fund transfers (EFTs), e-money, and online banking.

CHAPTER OUTLINE

I. **CHECKS**
   A **check** is a draft drawn on a bank, ordering the bank to pay a fixed amount of money on demand [UCC 3–104(f)]. If a bank wrongfully dishonors any of the following special types of checks, the holder can recover expenses, interest, and consequential damages [UCC 3–411].

   A. **CASHIER'S CHECK**
      A cashier's check is a check drawn by a bank on itself; negotiable on issue [UCC 3–104(g)].

   B. **TELLER'S CHECK**
      A teller's check is a draft drawn by a bank on another bank, or if drawn on a nonbank, payable at or through a bank [UCC 3–104(h)].

   C. **TRAVELER'S CHECK**
      A traveler's check is a check on which a financial institution is both drawer and drawee. The buyer must sign it twice (buying it and using it) [UCC 3–104(i)].

   D. **CERTIFIED CHECK**
      A certified check is a check accepted by the bank on which it is drawn [UCC 3–409(d)]. When a bank certifies a check, it immediately charges the drawer's account and transfers those funds to its own account. The effect is to discharge the drawer and prior indorsers [UCC 3–414(c), 3–415(d)].

   E. **MISSING CASHIER'S, TELLER'S, AND CERTIFIED CHECKS**

      1. **Who Can Claim a Refund?**
         The remitter or payee of a cashier's check or a teller's check, or the drawer of a certified check, can claim a refund if one of these types of checks is lost, destroyed, or stolen [UCC 3–312]. The claim becomes enforceable ninety days after the date of the check.

      2. **When Is the Bank Discharged?**
         If a person entitled to enforce a check presents it for payment and the bank pays, the bank is discharged. If no one presents it for payment, the bank's refund to the claimant discharges the bank.

II. **THE BANK-CUSTOMER RELATIONSHIP**

   A. **WHAT IS A BANK?**
      A "person engaged in the business of banking, including a savings bank, savings and loan association, credit union or trust company" [UCC 4–105(1)]. Rights and duties of bank and customer are *contractual*.

B. WHAT IS A CUSTOMER?

A customer is a *creditor* of the bank (and the bank, a debtor of the customer) when the customer deposits funds in his or her account. A bank acts as an agent for the customer (*principal*) when he or she writes a check drawn on the bank or deposits a check in his or her account for the bank to collect [UCC 4–201(a)].

III. BANK'S DUTY TO HONOR CHECKS

If a bank dishonors a check for insufficient funds, it has no liability. The customer is liable to the payee or holder of the check in a civil suit. If intent to defraud is proved, the customer is also subject to criminal prosecution. If a bank wrongfully dishonors a check, however, it is liable to the customer [UCC 4–402].

A. OVERDRAFTS

If there are insufficient funds in a customer's account, the bank can pay an item drawn on it or dishonor it. If the bank pays, it can charge the customer's account (if the customer has authorized payment) [UCC 4–401(a)]. If a check "bounces," a holder can resubmit it but must notify any indorsers of the first dishonor (or they are discharged).

B. POSTDATED CHECKS

A bank can charge a postdated check against a customer's account if the customer does not give the bank enough notice. If the bank has notice but charges the check anyway, the bank is liable [UCC 4–401(c)].

C. STALE CHECKS

A bank is not obliged to pay an uncertified check presented for payment more than six months after its date [UCC 4–404]. If a bank pays in good faith, it can charge the customer's account for the amount.

D. STOP-PAYMENT ORDERS

1. **Who Can Order a Stop Payment and When Must It Be Received?**
    Only a customer or person authorized to draw on the account. Must be received in a reasonable time and manner [UCC 4–403(a), 4–405].

2. **How Can a Stop-Payment Order Be Given and How Long Is It Effective?**
    In most states, it can be given orally, but it is binding for only fourteen calendar days unless confirmed in writing. In writing, it is effective for six months, when it may be renewed [UCC 4–403(b)].

3. **What Must the Bank Do If It Pays over an Order?**
    It must recredit the customer's account for any loss, including damages for the dishonor of subsequent items [UCC 4–403(c)].

4. **What Are the Customer's Risks?**
    These risks include possible liability to a payee for the amount of an item (and damages). Defense against payment to a payee may not prevent payment to a subsequent HDC [UCC 3–305, 3–306].

E. DEATH OR INCOMPETENCE OF A CUSTOMER

Until a bank knows of the situation and has time to act, it is not liable for paying items [UCC 4–405]. If a bank knows of a death, for ten days after the date of death it can pay items drawn on or before the date of death (unless a person claiming an interest in the account orders a stop payment).

F. CHECKS BEARING FORGED DRAWER'S SIGNATURES

1. **The General Rule**
    A forged signature on a check has no legal effect as the signature of a drawer [UCC 3–403(a)]. If the bank pays, it must recredit the account.

2. **Customer Negligence**
    If the customer's negligence substantially contributed to the forgery, the bank is not obligated to recredit the account [UCC 3–406(a)].

a. Reducing a Customer's Liability
A customer's liability may be reduced by a bank's negligence (if it substantially contributed to the loss) [UCC 3–406(b)].

b. Timely Examination of Bank Statements Required
The customer must examine the bank statement and canceled checks promptly and report any forged signatures [UCC 4–406(c)].

1) When There's a Series of Forgeries by the Same Wrongdoer
To recover for all items, a customer must report the first forgery to the bank within *thirty* calendar days of receiving the statement and canceled checks [UCC 4–406(d)(2)].

2) When the Bank Is Also Negligent
If the bank fails to exercise ordinary care ("reasonable commercial standards"), which may include not examining checks for less than a certain amount, the bank may have to recredit a customer's account for part of a loss (on a comparative negligence basis) [UCC 4–406(e)].

c. Absolute Time Limit
A customer must report a forged signature within one year of the date the statement and canceled checks were available [UCC 4–406].

G. CHECKS BEARING FORGED INDORSEMENTS

1. The General Rule
If the bank pays a check with a forged indorsement, it must recredit the account (or be held liable for breach of contract) [UCC 4–401(a)].

2. Timely Examination of Bank Statements Required
The customer must examine the bank statement and canceled checks and report forged indorsements promptly. Failure to do so within three years relieves the bank of liability [UCC 4–111].

3. Parties from Whom the Bank May Recover
The bank can recover for breach of warranty from the bank that cashed the check [UCC 4–207(a)(2)]. Ultimately, the loss usually falls on the first party to take the instrument.

H. ALTERED CHECKS
If the bank fails to detect an alteration, it is liable to its customer for the loss [UCC 4–401(d)(1)].

1. Customer Negligence
If a bank traces its loss to the customer's negligence or, on successive altered checks, to the customer's failure to discover the first alteration, its liability is reduced (unless it was negligent) [UCC 4–401, 4–406].

2. Other Parties from Whom the Bank May Recover
The bank can recover from the transferor, for breach of warranty. Exceptions relate to cashier's checks, teller's checks, and certified checks [UCC 3–417(a)(2), 4–208(a)(2), 4–207(a)(2)].

IV. BANK'S DUTY TO ACCEPT DEPOSITS

A. AVAILABILITY SCHEDULE FOR DEPOSITED CHECKS
Under the Expedited Funds Availability Act of 1987 and Regulation CC—

1. Funds That Must Be Available the Next Business Day after Deposit

a. The First $100 of Any Deposit and the Next $400 of a Local Check
The first $100 must be available for withdrawal on the opening of the next business day. The next $400 of a local check must be available by no later than 5:00 P.M. the next business day.

b. Cash Deposits, Wire Transfers, and Certain Checks
Funds must be available on the next business day for cash deposits, wire transfers, government checks, the first $100 of a day's check deposits, cashier's checks, certified checks, and checks for which the depositary and payor banks are the same institution.

2. Funds That Must Be Available within Five Business Days
All nonlocal checks and nonproprietary ATM deposits, including cash.

3. Funds That Can Be Held for Eight Days or an Extra Four Days
Eight days: funds in new accounts (open less than thirty days). Four days: deposits over $5,000 (except government and cashier's checks), accounts with many overdrafts, checks of questionable collectibility (the bank must tell the depositor it suspects fraud or insolvency).

B. THE COLLECTION PROCESS

1. Designation of Banks Involved in the Collection Process
Depositary bank: first bank to receive a check for payment. **Payor bank**: bank on which a check is drawn. **Collecting bank**: bank (except payor bank) that handles a check for collection. **Intermediary bank**: any bank (except payor and depositary banks) involved in the collection process.

2. Check Collection between Customers of the Same Bank
An item payable by a depositary bank that is also the payor bank is an "on-us item." If the bank does not dishonor it by the second banking day, it is considered paid [UCC 4–215(e)(2)].

3. Check Collection between Customers of Different Banks
A depositary bank must arrange to present a check either directly or through intermediary banks to the appropriate payor bank.

a. Midnight Deadline
Each bank in the collection chain must pass a check on before midnight of the next banking day following receipt [UCC 4–202(b)].

b. Deferred Posting and the Midnight Deadline
Posting of checks received after a certain time can be deferred until the next day [UCC 4–108].

c. Electronic Check Presentment
Can be done the same day a check is deposited. The check may be kept at the place of deposit with only information about the check presented for payment under a Federal Reserve agreement, clearinghouse rule, or truncation agreement [UCC 4–110].

V. ELECTRONIC FUND TRANSFERS

A. TYPES OF ELECTRONIC FUND TRANSFER (EFT) SYSTEMS

1. Automated Teller Machines (ATMs)
Connected online to bank computers, ATMs accept deposits, dispense funds from accounts, make credit-card advances, and receive payments.

2. Point-of-Sale Systems
Connected online to bank computers, these systems allow consumers to transfer funds to pay merchants. The merchant inserts a customer's card into a terminal to read the card's coded data.

3. Direct Deposits and Withdrawals
Through a terminal, a deposit may be made directly to a customer's account. An institution at which a customer's funds are on deposit can also make payments electronically to a third party.

4. Pay-by-Internet Systems
These systems provide access to a financial institution's computer system via the Internet to direct a transfer of funds.

B. CONSUMER FUND TRANSFERS
Governed by Electronic Fund Transfer Act (EFTA) of 1978 and Regulation E.

1. **Who Is Subject to the EFTA?**
Financial institutions that offer electronic fund transfers (EFTs) involving customer asset accounts established for personal, family, or household purposes. Telephone transfers are covered only if they are made pursuant to a prearranged plan involving periodic transfers.

2. **Financial Institutions' Responsibilities**
Financial institutions must provide customers with—

   a. **Receipts**
   At the time a transaction is made through an electronic terminal.

   b. **Periodic Statements**

      1) **What Must They Include?**
      The amounts and dates of transfers, the fees, identification of the terminals, names of third parties involved, and an address and phone number for inquiries and error notices.

      2) **How Often Must They Be Provided?**
      Monthly statements are required for every month in which there is an electronic transfer of funds.

3. **Unauthorized Electronic Fund Transfers**

   a. **What Is an Unauthorized Transfer?**
   (1) A transfer is initiated by a person who has no actual authority to initiate the transfer; (2) the consumer receives no benefit from it; and (3) the consumer did not furnish the person "with the card, code, or other means of access" to his or her account.

   b. **Customer Liability**
   If a debit card is lost or stolen, and misused, a customer is liable for (1) $50—if he or she notifies the bank within two business days of learning of the loss; (2) $500—if he or she does not tell the bank until after the second day; or (3) unlimited amounts—if notice is not within sixty days after transfer appears on customer's statement.

4. **Violations and Damages**
The bank must investigate and give the customer a report or be liable for actual damages, court costs, attorneys' fees, punitive damages. Unauthorized access to an EFT system is a crime subject to a fine of up to $10,000 and imprisonment of up to ten years.

C. COMMERCIAL TRANSFERS
In most states, UCC Article 4A clarifies the rights and liabilities of parties involved in fund transfers not subject to the EFTA or other federal or state statutes. In those states that have not adopted Article 4A, contract law and tort law govern commercial fund transfers.

VI. E-MONEY AND ONLINE BANKING
E-money has the potential to replace physical cash with virtual cash (e-money) in the form of electronic impulses, or digital cash.

A. STORED-VALUE CARDS
Plastic cards embossed with magnetic stripes containing encoded data. Can be used to buy specific goods and services offered by the issuer.

B. SMART CARDS
Contain microchips that hold more information than a magnetic stripe. Less prone to error, and carry and process security programming (such as a digital signature). Debits and credits are automatic and can be immediate.

C. **ONLINE BANKING SERVICES**

These include bill consolidation and payment, transferring funds among accounts, and applying for loans. Depositing and withdrawing is not yet generally available over the Internet, but virtual banks do business through physical delivery systems.

D. **REGULATORY COMPLIANCE**

There are questions about the application of traditional banking regulations to online banks. For example, under the Community Reinvestment Act, a bank must define its market area. What is the market area of an Internet bank?

E. **PRIVACY PROTECTION**

1. **Right to Financial Privacy Act of 1978**

An issuer of e-money may be subject to this act if the issuer is deemed to be (1) a bank by virtue of its holding customer funds or (2) an entity that issues a physical card similar to a credit or debit card.

2. **Financial Services Modernization Act (Gramm-Leach-Bliley Act) of 1999**

This act proscribes the disclosure of financial institutions' customer data without notice and an opt-out opportunity.

VII. THE UNIFORM MONEY SERVICES ACT (UMSA)

The UMSA applies to traditional money services the same regulations that apply to other, traditional financial service businesses.

A. **TRADITIONAL MONEY SERVICES**

Money service businesses do not accept deposits, but issue money orders, traveler's checks, stored-value cards; exchange foreign currency; and cash checks.

B. **INTERNET-BASED MONEY SERVICES**

1. **Systems Subject to the New Law**

May include [UMSA 1–102(c)(21)]—

a. E-money and Internet payment mechanisms
b. Internet scrip
c. Stored-value products (smart, prepaid, and value-added cards)

2. **What the UMSA Requires**

Persons engaged in money transmission, check cashing, or currency exchange must obtain a license from a state, be examined by state officials, report on their activities to the state, and comply with certain record keeping requirements [UMSA 1–104].

3. **Rules That Govern Investments**

Money service businesses are covered by rules that govern investments, and must follow "safety and soundness rules," which concern the posting of bonds and annual auditing of their books [see UMSA 2–204].

TRUE-FALSE QUESTIONS

(Answers at the Back of the Book)

____ 1. A check is a draft drawn on a bank.

____ 2. If a bank fails to honor a customer's stop-payment order, it may be liable to the customer for more than the amount of the loss suffered by the drawer because of the wrongful payment.

____ 3. A bank's duty to honor its customer's checks is absolute.

____ 4. Generally, funds must be available on the next business day for cash deposits.

____ 5. A bank that fails to investigate an error and report its conclusion promptly to the customer is in violation of the Electronic Fund Transfer Act (EFTA).

____ 6. A customer must examine the statements provided by the institution handling his or her account and notify it of any errors within sixty days.

____ 7. The rights and duties of a bank and its customers are contractual.

____ 8. All funds deposited in all bank accounts must be available for withdrawal no later than the next business day.

____ 9. A bank that pays a customer's check bearing a forged indorsement must recredit the customer's account.

____ 10. A forged drawer's signature on a check is effective as the signature of the person whose name is signed.

FILL-IN QUESTIONS

(Answers at the Back of the Book)

A depositor is the _____ (drawee/drawer) of a check. The depositor is the bank's _____ (creditor/debtor) as to the amount on deposit in the depositor's account. The depositor is the bank's _____ (agent/principal) in the deposit contract. The bank is the _____ (drawee/drawer) of a check. The bank is the depositor's _____ (creditor debtor) as to the amount on deposit in the depositor's account. The bank is the depositor'_____ (agent/principal) in the handling of the account and in the collection process.

MULTIPLE-CHOICE QUESTIONS

(Answers at the Back of the Book)

____ 1. First National Bank pays a check on which has been forged the signature of the drawer, Gail, who is the bank's customer. The bank must recredit her account for the entire amount of the check if

a. Gail's negligence substantially contributed to the forgery.
b. the amount of the check was less than $50.
c. the amount of the check was more than $5,000.
d. the bank's negligence substantially contributed to the forgery.

____ 2. First County Bank's cutoff hour is 2 P.M. The bank receives a check drawn on the account of Gamma Corporation, one of its customers, at 4 P.M. Monday, presented by Holly, not a bank customer. The bank uses deferred posting. The bank may timely dishonor the check by midnight

a. Monday.
b. Tuesday.
c. Wednesday.
d. Thursday.

____ 3. Ann buys three television sets from Bob, paying with a check. When the sets prove defective, Ann orders City Bank, the drawee, to stop payment on the check. This order is valid for fourteen

a. years.
b. months.
c. weeks.
d. days.

____ 4. First State Bank mistakenly pays one of Gary's checks with a forged indorsement. Gary can recover his loss from the bank if, after receipt of the bank statement, he notifies the bank within three

a. years.
b. months.
c. weeks.
d. days.

____ 5. Eve writes a check for $600 drawn on her account at First Federal Bank and presents it to Greg. When Greg presents the check for payment, the bank dishonors it. Greg may sue

a. the bank for dishonoring the check.
b. Eve on the underlying obligation.
c. both the bank and Eve.
d. none of the above.

____ 6. Delta Company issue a payroll check to Ed drawn on its account at First Community Bank. This check will be stale if Ed presents it for payment six

a. months after it is issued.
b. months after he indorses.
c. weeks after he receives it.
d. weeks after the pay period that it covers.

____ 7. Roy issues a check to Stereo Store in payment on his account. Tina, Stereo's accountant, forges the store's indorsement and deposits the check in her bank account. United Bank, Roy's bank, pays the check. Roy can recover from

a. no one.
b. Tina, but not United Bank.
c. United Bank, which can recover from Tina.
d. United Bank, which cannot recover from Tina.

____ 8. Adam pays for a purchase at Beta Computers with a check. Burt, the cashier, steals one of Adam's checks, forges his signature, and County Bank, Adam's bank, pays the check. Adam can recover from

a. no one.
b. Burt, but not County Bank.
c. County Bank, which can recover from Burt.
d. County Bank, which cannot recover from Burt.

____ 9. Dick loses his bank access card. He realizes his loss the next day but waits a week to call Eagle Bank, his bank. Meanwhile, Erin finds and uses Dick's card to withdraw $5,000 from his account. Dick is responsible for

a. 0.
b. $50.
c. $500.
d. $5,000.

____ 10. Web Funds, Inc., an e-money issuer, may be subject to the Right to Financial Privacy Act if Web Funds

a. does not accept deposits.
b. does not hold customer funds, whether or not the funds qualify as "deposits."
c. investigates its customers' credit backgrounds.
d. issues a physical card similar to a debit card.

SHORT ESSAY QUESTIONS

1.   What are the circumstances in which a customer might be unable to recover from a bank that pays on a forged check drawn on the customer's account?

2.   What are the principal features of the Electronic Fund Transfer Act (EFTA)?

ISSUE SPOTTERS

(Answers at the Back of the Book)

1.   Lyn writes a check for $900 to Mac, who indorses the check in blank and transfers it to Nan. She presents the check to Omega Bank, the drawee bank, for payment. Omega does not honor the check. Is Lyn liable to Nan? Could Lyn be subject to criminal prosecution?

2.   Hal steals a check from Irma, forges her signature, and transfers the check to Jay for value. Unaware that the signature is not Irma's, Jay presents the check to Local Bank, the drawee, which cashes the check. Irma discovers the forgery and insists that the bank recredit her account. Can the bank refuse to recredit the account? If not, can the bank recover the amount paid?

3.   Ron writes a check for $700 to Sue. Sue indorses the check in blank and transfers it to Tim, who alters the check to read $7,000 and presents it to Union Bank, the drawee, for payment. The bank cashes it. Ron discovers the alteration and sues the bank. How much, if anything, can Ron recover? From whom can the bank recover this amount?

Chapter 16:
Creditors' Rights and Bankruptcy

WHAT THIS CHAPTER IS ABOUT

This chapter covers transactions in which the payment of a debt is secured (guaranteed) by personal property owned by the debtor or in which the debtor has a legal interest. This chapter also sets out the rights and remedies available to a creditor, when a debtor defaults, under other laws, including federal bankruptcy laws.

CHAPTER OUTLINE

I. SECURED TRANSACTIONS

A. THE TERMINOLOGY OF SECURED TRANSACTIONS
UCC Article 9 applies to secured transactions.

1. Secured Transaction
Transaction in which payment of a debt is guaranteed by personal property owned by debtor or in which the debtor has a legal interest.

2. Security Interest, Secured Party, Collateral, and Debtor
A **security interest** is the interest in the collateral that secures payment or performance of an obligation [UCC 1–201(37)]. A **secured party** is a creditor in whose favor there is a security interest in the debtor's collateral [UCC 9–102(a)(72)]. **Collateral** is the subject of a security interest [UCC 9–102(a)(12)]. **Debtor** is the party who owes payment [UCC 9–102(a)(28)].

3. A Creditor's Main Concerns
A creditor's two main concerns are, if a debtor fails to pay, (1) satisfaction of the debt through possession or sale of the collateral and (2) priority over other creditors to the collateral.

B. CREATING A SECURITY INTEREST
A creditor's rights attach to collateral, creating an enforceable security interest against a debtor if the following requirements are met [UCC 9–203].

1. Written Security Agreement
(1) It must be written or authenticated (which includes electronic media, or records), (2) describe the collateral, and (3) be signed or authenticated by the debtor [UCC 9–102, 9–108]. Or the secured party must possess the collateral.

2. Secured Party Must Give Value
Value is any consideration that supports a contract [UCC 1–201(44)].

3. Debtor Must Have Rights in the Collateral
The debtor must have an ownership interest or right (current or future legal interest) to obtain possession of the collateral.

C. PERFECTING A SECURITY INTEREST
Perfection is the process by which secured parties protect themselves against the claims of others who wish to satisfy their debts out of the same collateral.

1. Perfection by Filing
Filing is the most common means of perfecting a security interest.

a. **What a Financing Statement Must Contain**
It must contain (1) the names of the debtor and the creditor (a trade name is not sufficient), and (3) a description of the collateral [UCC 9–502, 9–503, 9–506, 9–521].

b. **Where to File a Financing Statement**
Filing is local with a county (timber, fixtures, etc.) or central with a state (other collateral) in the state in which the debtor is located [UCC 9–301(3), 9–502(b)].

2. **Perfection Without Filing**

a. **Perfection by Possession**
A creditor can possess collateral and return it when a debt is paid [UCC 9–310, 9–312(b), 9–313].

b. **Perfection by Attachment**

1) **Purchase-Money Security Interest (PMSI)**
A PMSI is (1) retained in, or taken by the seller of, goods to secure part or all of the price, or (2) taken by a lender, such as a bank, as part of a loan to enable a debtor to buy the collateral [UCC 9–103(a)(2)].

2) **Perfection of a PMSI**
A PMSI in consumer goods is perfected automatically when it is created. The seller need do nothing more.

3) **Exception**
Security interests subject to other federal or state laws that require additional steps are excepted. For example, to perfect a PMSI in a car requires filing a certificate of title.

3. **Effective Time Duration of Perfection**
A financing statement is effective for five years [UCC 9–515]. A continuation statement filed within six months before the expiration date continues the effectiveness for five more years (and so on) [UCC 9–515(d), (e)].

D. **THE SCOPE OF A SECURITY INTEREST**

1. **Proceeds**
Proceeds include whatever is received when collateral is sold or otherwise disposed of. A secured party has an interest in proceeds that perfects automatically on perfection of the security interest and remains perfected for twenty days after the debtor receives the proceeds.

2. **After-Acquired Property**
A security agreement may provide for coverage of **after-acquired property** [UCC 9–204(a)]—collateral acquired by a debtor after execution of a security agreement.

3. **Future Advances**
A security agreement may provide that future advances against a line of credit are subject to a security interest in the collateral [UCC 9–204(c)].

4. **The Floating-Lien Concept**
A **floating lien** is a security agreement that provides for the creation of a security interest in any (or all) of the above. The lien can start with raw materials and follow them as they become finished goods and inventories and as they are sold, turning into accounts receivable or cash.

E. **PRIORITIES AMONG SECURITY INTERESTS**
When several creditors claim security interests in the same collateral of a debtor, which interest has priority?

1. **Secured Parties v. Unsecured Parties**
    Secured parties (perfected or not) prevail over unsecured creditors and creditors who have obtained judgments against the debtor but who have not begun the legal process to collect on those judgments [UCC 9–201(a)].

2. **Secured Parties v. Other Secured Parties**

    a. **The General Rule**
        The first interest to be filed or perfected has priority over other filed or perfected security interests. If none of the interests has been perfected, the first to attach has priority [UCC 9–322(a)(1), (3)].

    b. **Exception—Commingled or Processed Goods**
        When goods have lost their identity into a product or mass, security interests attach in a ratio of the cost of the goods to which each interest originally attached to the cost of the total product or mass [UCC 9–336].

3. **Secured Parties v. Buyers**

    a. **The General Rule**
        A security interest in collateral continues even after the collateral has been sold unless the secured party authorized the sale.

    b. **Exception—Buyer in the Ordinary Course of Business**
        Takes goods free of any security interest (unless the buyer knows that the purchase violates a third party's rights) [UCC 9–320(a)].

    c. **Exception—Buyers of Consumer Goods Purchased outside the Ordinary Course of Business**
        The buyer must give value and not know of the security interest; the purchase must occur before the secured party perfects by filing [UCC 9–320(b)].

    d. **Exception—Buyers of Instruments, Documents, or Securities**
        A holder in due course, a holder to whom a negotiable instrument has been negotiated, and a bona fide purchaser of securities have priority over a previously perfected security interest [UCC 9–330(d), 9–331(a)].

    e. **Exception—Buyers of Farm Products**
        A buyer from a farmer has priority over a perfected security interest unless, in some states, the secured party has filed centrally an effective financing statement or the buyer has notice before the sale.

F. **DEFAULT**
    Default occurs most often when debtors fail to make payments or go bankrupt.

1. **Basic Remedies**

    a. **Repossession of the Collateral—The Self-Help Remedy**
        A secured party can take possession of the collateral without a court order if it can be done without a breach of the peace [UCC 9–609(b)] (generally, this means not trespassing). The creditor can then retain the collateral for satisfaction of the debt [UCC 9–620] or resell it and apply the proceeds toward the debt [UCC 9–610] (see below).

    b. **Judicial Remedies**
        A secured party can give up the security interest and proceed to judgment on the debt (this is done if the value of the collateral is less than the debt and the debtor has other assets) [UCC 9–601(a)].

2. **Disposition of Collateral**
   On default, a secured party can take possession of the collateral and retain it in satisfaction of the debt, or sell, lease, or otherwise dispose of it in any commercially reasonable manner [UCC 9–602(7), 9–603, 9–610(a), 9–620].

   a. **Proceeds from Disposition**
      Must be applied to (1) expenses stemming from retaking, storing, or reselling, (2) balance of the debt, (3) junior lienholders, and (4) surplus to the debtor [UCC 9–608(a); 9–615(a), (e)].

   b. **Deficiency Judgment**
      In most cases, if a sale of collateral does not repay the debt, the debtor is liable for any deficiency. A creditor can obtain a judgment to collect.

   c. **Redemption Rights**
      Before the secured party retains or disposes of the collateral, the debtor or any other secured party can take the collateral by tendering performance of all secured obligations and paying the secured party's expenses [UCC 9–623].

II. ADDITIONAL LAWS ASSISTING CREDITORS

A. LIENS
A **lien** is an encumbrance on property to satisfy a debt or protect a claim for payment of a debt.

1. **Mechanic's Lien**
   Can be placed by a creditor on real property when a person contracts for labor, services, or materials to improve the property but does not pay.

2. **Artisan's Lien**
   A security device by which a creditor can recover from a debtor for labor and materials furnished in the repair of personal property.

   a. **The Creditor Must Possess the Property**
      Lien terminates if possession is voluntarily surrendered, unless the lienholder records notice of the lien in accord with state statutes.

   b. **What If the Owner Does Not Pay?**
      The property can be sold to satisfy the debt. Notice of the foreclosure and sale must be given to the debtor in advance.

3. **Innkeeper's Lien**
   This is a security device placed on the baggage of guests for hotel charges that are not paid. The lien terminates when the charges are paid, or the baggage is returned or sold to satisfy the debt.

4. **Judicial Liens**

   a. **Attachment**
      Attachment is a court-ordered seizure and taking into custody of property before the securing of a judgment for a past-due debt. A sheriff or other officer seizes nonexempt property. If the creditor prevails at trial, the property can be sold to satisfy the judgment.

   b. **Writ of Execution**
      A **writ of execution** is an order, usually issued by the clerk of court, directing the sheriff to seize and sell any of the debtor's nonexempt property within the court's geographical jurisdiction. Proceeds of the sale pay the debt.

B. GARNISHMENT
Garnishment occurs when a creditor collects a debt by seizing property of the debtor (such as wages or money in a bank account) that a third party (such as an employer or a bank) holds. The creditor obtains

a judgment against the debtor and serves it on the third party (known as the garnishee). There are limits on amounts that can be garnished and on the discharge of an employee for a garnishment order.

C. MORTGAGE FORECLOSURE

A **mortgagor** (creditor) can foreclose on mortgaged property if the **mortgagee** (debtor) defaults. Usual method is a judicial sale. Proceeds are applied to the debt. If proceeds do not cover the costs and the debt, the mortgagee can recover the difference from the mortgagor with a deficiency judgment.

D. SURETYSHIP AND GUARANTY

1. Suretyship
A promise by a third person to be responsible for a debtor's obligation. Does not have to be in writing. A surety is *primarily* liable—a creditor can demand payment from the surety the moment the debt is due.

2. Guaranty
A promise to be *secondarily* liable for the debt or default of another. A guarantor pays only after the debtor defaults and the creditor has made an attempt to collect from the debtor. A guaranty must be in writing unless the main-purpose exception applies (see Chapter 11).

3. Defenses of the Surety and the Guarantor
To avoid payment, a surety (guarantor) may use the following defenses.

a. Material Change to the Contract between Debtor and Creditor
Without obtaining the consent of the surety (guarantor), a surety is discharged completely or to the extent the surety suffers a loss.

b. Principal Obligation Is Paid or Valid Tender Is Made
The surety (guarantor) is discharged from the obligation.

c. Most of the Principal Debtor's Defenses
Defenses that cannot be used: debtor's incapacity, bankruptcy, and statute of limitations.

d. Surety or Guarantor's Own Defenses

e. Surrender or Impairment of Collateral
Without the surety's (guarantor's) consent, this action on the part of the creditor releases the surety to the extent of any loss suffered.

4. Rights of the Surety and the Guarantor
If the surety (guarantor) pays the debt—

a. Right of Subrogation
The surety (guarantor) has available any remedies that were available to the creditor against the debtor.

b. Right of Reimbursement
The surety (guarantor) is entitled to receive from the debtor all outlays made on behalf of the suretyship arrangement.

c. Right of Contribution
A surety who pays more than his or her proportionate share on a debtor's default is entitled to recover from co-sureties.

III. ADDITIONAL LAWS ASSISTING DEBTORS

A. HOMESTEAD EXEMPTION
Each state allows a debtor to keep the family home (in some states only if the debtor has a family) in its entirety or up to a specified amount.

B. EXEMPT PERSONAL PROPERTY
This includes household furniture up to a specified dollar amount; clothing and other possessions; a vehicle (or vehicles); certain animals; and equipment that the debtor uses in a business or trade.

IV. BANKRUPTCY AND REORGANIZATION
Bankruptcy law (1) protects a debtor by giving him or her a fresh start and (2) ensures equitable treatment to creditors competing for a debtor's assets. Current law is based on the Bankruptcy Reform Act of 1978 (the Bankruptcy Code).

A. CHAPTER 7—LIQUIDATION
This is the most familiar type of bankruptcy proceeding. A debtor declares his or her debts and gives all assets to a trustee, who sells the nonexempt assets and distributes the proceeds to creditors.

1. **Who Can File for a Liquidation?**
Any "person"—individuals, partnerships, and corporations (spouses can file jointly)—except railroads, insurance companies, banks, savings and loan associations, certain investment companies, and credit unions.

2. **Filing the Petition**

   a. **Voluntary Bankruptcy**

   1) **Debtor Files a Petition with the Court**
   Includes a list of (1) creditors and debts, (2) debtor's financial affairs, (3) debtor's property, (4) current income and expenses.

   2) **Filing of the Petition Constitutes an Order for Relief**
   The clerk of the court must give the trustee and creditors notice of the order within not more than twenty days.

   3) **Substantial Abuse**
   A court can dismiss a petition if granting it would constitute "substantial abuse" [11 U.S.C. Section 707(b)].

   b. **Involuntary Bankruptcy**
   Creditors can force a debtor into a bankruptcy proceeding.

   1) **Who Can Be Forced into Involuntary Proceedings?**
   Debtor with twelve or more creditors, three or more of whom (with unsecured claims of at least $12,300) file a petition. Debtor with fewer than twelve creditors, one or more of whom (with a claim of $12,300) files.

   2) **When Will an Order for Relief Be Entered?**
   If the debtor does not challenge the petition, the debtor is generally not paying debts as they come due, or a receiver, assignee, or custodian took possession of the debtor's property within 120 days before the petition was filed.

3. **Automatic Stay**
When a petition is filed, an **automatic stay** suspends all action by creditors against the debtor. A court may grant some relief. A stay does not apply to paternity, alimony, or maintenance and support claims.

4. **Creditors' Meeting and Claims**
Within "not less than ten days or more than thirty days," the court calls a meeting of creditors, at which the debtor answers questions. Within ninety days of the meeting, a creditor must file a proof of claim.

5. **Property of the Estate**

a. **What Property Is Included in the Debtor's Estate?**
Interests in property presently held; jointly owned property; property transferred in transactions voidable by the trustee; proceeds and profits; after-acquired property; interests in gifts, inheritances, property settlements, and life insurance death proceeds to which debtor is entitled within 180 days after filing.

b. **What Property Is Not Included?**
Property acquired after the filing of the petition, except as noted.

6. **Exempted Property**

a. **Federal Law**
Exempts such property as interest in a residence to $18,450, motor vehicle to $2,950, household goods to $9,850, tools of a trade to $1,850, and the rights to receive Social Security and other benefits.

b. **State Law**
Most states preclude the use of federal exemptions; others allow a debtor to choose between state and federal. State exemptions may include different value limitations and exempt different property.

7. **The Trustee's Role**

a. **Trustee's Duty**
To collect and reduce to money the property of the estate and distribute the proceeds.

b. **Trustee's Powers**
A trustee can require persons holding a debtor's property to turn it over to the trustee. The trustee can use any reason that a debtor can use to obtain the return of property (fraud, duress, etc.).

8. **Property Distribution**

a. **Secured Creditors**
Within thirty days of the petition or before the first creditors' meeting (whichever is first), a debtor must state whether he or she will retain secured collateral (or claim it as exempt, etc.).

b. **Unsecured Creditors**
Paid in the order of priority. The order of priority is—

1) Administrative expenses (court costs, trustee and attorney fees).
2) In an involuntary bankruptcy, expenses incurred by the debtor in the ordinary course of business from the filing of the petition to the appointment of the trustee or the issuance of an order for relief.
3) Unpaid wages, salaries, and commissions earned within ninety days of the petition, to $4,925 per claimant. A claim in excess is a claim of a general creditor (no. i below).
4) Unsecured claims for contributions to employee benefit plans, limited to services performed within 180 days before the petition and $4,925 per employee.
5) Claims by farmers and fishers, to $4,925, against storage or processing facilities.
6) Consumer deposits to $2,225 given to the debtor before the petition to buy, lease, or rent property or services that were not received.
7) Claims for paternity, alimony, maintenance, and support.
8) Taxes and penalties due to the government.
9) Claims of general creditors.

9. **Discharge**
A discharge voids any judgment on a discharged debt and bars action to collect a discharged debt. A co-debtor's liability is not affected.

a. Exceptions—What Debts May Not Be Discharged?
Claims for back taxes, amounts borrowed to pay back taxes, goods obtained by fraud, debts not listed in the petition, alimony, child support, student loans, certain cash advances, and others.

b. Objections—What Debtors Who May Not Receive a Discharge?
Those who conceal property with the intent to hinder, delay, or defraud a creditor; who fail to explain a loss of assets; or who have been granted a discharge within six years of filing of the petition.

c. Reaffirmation of Debt
A reaffirmation of debt is a debtor's agreement to pay an otherwise dischargeable debt. The agreement must be made before a discharge is granted and must be approved by the court. Can be rescinded within sixty days or before the discharge is granted.

B. CHAPTER 11—REORGANIZATION
In a Chapter 11 reorganization, the creditors and the debtor formulate a plan under which the debtor pays a portion of the debts, is discharged of the rest, and continues in business.

1. Who Is Eligible for Relief under Chapter 11?
Any debtor (except a stockbroker or a commodities broker) who is eligible for Chapter 7 relief. Used most commonly by corporate debtors. The same principles apply that govern liquidation (automatic stay, etc.).

2. Debtor in Possession
On entry of an order for relief, the debtor continues to operate his or her business as a debtor in possession (DIP).

a. If Gross Mismanagement Is Shown
Court may appoint a trustee (or receiver) to operate the business. This may also be done if it is in the best interests of the estate.

b. DIP's Role Is Similar to That of a Trustee in a Liquidation
The DIP can avoid pre-petition preferential payments and fraudulent transfers and decide whether to cancel pre-petition executory contracts.

3. The Reorganization Plan

a. What Must the Plan Do?
Administer the debtor's assets in the hope of a return to solvency; designate classes of claims and interests; specify the treatment to be afforded the classes; and provide an adequate means for execution.

b. Who Can File a Plan?
Only the debtor within the first 120 days (100 days in some cases) after the date of the order for relief. Any other party, if the debtor does not meet the deadline or fails to obtain creditor consent within 180 days.

c. The Plan Is Submitted to Creditors for Acceptance
Each class adversely affected by a plan must accept it (two-thirds of the total claims must approve). If only one class accepts, court may confirm it if it "does not discriminate unfairly" against any creditors. Debtor is given a discharge from all claims not within the plan (except those that would be denied in a liquidation).

C. INDIVIDUALS' REPAYMENT PLAN—CHAPTER 13

1. Who Is Eligible?
Individuals (not partnerships or corporations) with regular income and unsecured debts of less than $307,675 or secured debts of less than $922,975.

2. **Voluntary Filing Only**
    A Chapter 13 case can be initiated by the filing of a voluntary petition only. A trustee is appointed. The automatic stay takes effect (on consumer debts, not business debts).

3. **Repayment Plan**
    The plan must provide for turnover to trustee of debtor's future income.

    a. **Filing and Confirming the Plan**
        Only the debtor can file a plan, which the court will confirm if (1) the secured creditors accept it, (2) it provides that creditors retain their liens and the value of the property to be distributed to them is not less than the secured portion of their claims, or (3) the debtor surrenders the property securing the claim to the creditors.

    b. **Payments under the Plan**
        The time for payment must be less than three years (five years, with court approval). The payments must be timely, or the court can convert the case to a liquidation or dismiss the petition.

    c. **Objection to the Plan**
        Over the objection of the trustee or an unsecured creditor, the court may approve a plan only if (1) the value of property to be distributed is equal to the amount of claims, or (2) all the debtor's disposable income during the plan will be used to make payments.

4. **Discharge**
    After completion of all payments, all debts provided for by the plan are discharged. A discharge obtained by fraud can be revoked within one year.

D. **FAMILY FARMERS—CHAPTER 12**
    Chapter 12 is nearly identical to Chapter 13. Eligible debtors include a family farmer whose gross income is at least 50 percent farm dependent and whose debts are at least 80 percent farm related (total debt must not exceed $1.5 million), and a partnership or closely held corporation (at least 50 percent owned by a farm family).

TRUE-FALSE QUESTIONS

(Answers at the Back of the Book)

____   1. Attachment gives a creditor an enforceable security interest in collateral.

____   2. To be valid, a financing statement does not need to contain a description of the collateral.

____   3. After a default, and before a secured party disposes of the collateral, a debtor cannot exercise the right of redemption.

____   4. When two secured parties have perfected security interests in the same collateral, generally the last to perfect has priority.

____   5. A mechanic's lien involves real property.

____   6. A writ of attachment is a court order to seize a debtor's property *before* the entry of a final judgment in a creditor's suit against the debtor.

____   7. A surety cannot use defenses available to the debtor to avoid liability on an obligation to a creditor.

____   8. A debtor must be insolvent to file a voluntary petition under Chapter 7.

____   9. The filing of a petition for bankruptcy will not stay most creditors' actions against the debtor.

____   10. When a business debtor files for Chapter 11 protection, the debtor is not allowed to continue in business.

FILL-IN QUESTIONS

(Answers at the Back of the Book)

Liquidation is the purpose of Chapter _____ (7/11/13). Reorganization is the purpose of Chapter _____ (7/11/13). Adjustment is the purpose of Chapter _____ (7/11/13). Under Chapter _____ (7/11/13), nonexempt property is sold, with proceeds distributed in a certain priority to classes of creditors, and dischargeable debts are terminated. Under Chapter _____ (7/11/13), a plan for reorganization is submitted, and if it is approved and followed, debts are discharged. Under Chapter _____ (7/11/13), a plan must be approved if the debtor turns over all disposable income for a three-year period, after which debts are discharged. The advantages of Chapter _____ (7/11/13) include the debtor's opportunity for a fresh start. The advantages of Chapter _____ (7/11/13) include the debtor's continuation in business under a plan that allows for reorganization of debts. The advantages of Chapter _____ (7/11/13) include the debtor's continuation in business and discharge of most debts.

MULTIPLE-CHOICE QUESTIONS

(Answers at the Back of the Book)

____   1.   Alpha Credit Corporation files a financing statement regarding a transaction with Beta Company. To be valid, the financing statement must contain all of the following *except*

   a.   a description of the collateral.
   b.   the debtor's name.
   c.   the debtor's signature.
   d.   the secured party's name.

____   2.   Nick borrows $5,000 from Modern Financial Corporation (MFC), which files a financing statement on May 1, but does not sign a security agreement until he receives the funds on May 5. He also borrows $5,000 from Omega Bank, which advances funds, files a financing statement, and signs a security agreement on May 2. He uses the same property as collateral for both loans. On his default, in a dispute over the collateral, MFC will

   a.   lose because Omega perfected first.
   b.   lose because Omega's interest attached first.
   c.   win because it filed first.
   d.   win because its interest attached first.

____   3.   Safe Loans, Inc., wants to perfect its security interest in collateral owned by Tech Corporation. Most likely, Safe should file a financing statement with

   a.   a federal loan officer.
   b.   the city managers of the cities in which Safe and Tech are located.
   c.   the county clerk of the county in which Safe is located.
   d.   the secretary of state in the state in which Tech is located.

____   4.   Carol borrows $500 from Delta Loan Corporation. Carol defaults. Delta obtains a garnishment order from a court. To satisfy the judgment, the order will likely be served on

   a.   Carol.
   b.   Carol's employer.
   c.   Delta Loan Corporation.
   d.   the sheriff or other public officer.

_____ 5. Eve owes Fred $200,000. A court awards Fred a judgment in the amount of the debt. To satisfy the judgment, Eve's home is sold at public auction for $150,000. The state homestead exemption is $50,000. Fred gets

    a. $0.
    b. $50,000.
    c. $100,000.
    d. $150,000.

_____ 6. Good Company wants to borrow money from First State Bank. The bank insists that Holly, Good Company's president, agree to be personally liable for payment if Good defaults. Holly agrees. She is

    a. a guarantor only.
    b. a guarantor and a surety.
    c. a surety only.
    d. neither a guarantor nor a surety.

_____ 7. Cora is the sole proprietor of Diners Cafe, which owes debts in an amount more than Cora believes she and the cafe can repay. The creditors agree that liquidating the business would not be in their best interests. To stay in business, Cora could file for bankruptcy under

    a. Chapter 7 only.
    b. Chapter 11 only.
    c. Chapter 11 or Chapter 13.
    d. Chapter 13 only.

_____ 8. Mike's monthly income is $2,500, his monthly expenses are $2,100, and his debts are nearly $15,000. If he applied the difference between his income and expenses to pay off the debts, they could be eliminated within three years. The provision in the Bankruptcy Code that covers this type of plan is

    a. Chapter 7.
    b. Chapter 11.
    c. Chapter 12.
    d. Chapter 13.

_____ 9. National Corporation has not paid any of its fifteen creditors, six of whom have unsecured claims of more than $12,000. The creditors can force National into bankruptcy under

    a. Chapter 7 only.
    b. Chapter 7 or Chapter 11.
    c. Chapter 11 only.
    d. Chapter 13 only.

_____ 10. Owen files a bankruptcy petition under Chapter 7 to have his debts discharged. The debts most likely to be discharged include claims for

    a. alimony and child support.
    b. back taxes accruing within three years before the petition was filed.
    c. certain fines and penalties payable to the government.
    d. student loans, if the payment would impose undue hardship on Owen.

SHORT ESSAY QUESTIONS

1. What is the floating lien concept?

2. What are the differences between contracts of suretyship and guaranty contracts?

ISSUE SPOTTERS

(Answers at the Back of the Book)

1. Adam needs $500 to buy textbooks, and other supplies. Beth agrees to loan Adam $500, accepting as collateral Adam's computer. They put their agreement in writing. How can Beth let other creditors know of her interest in the computer?

2. Pat wants to borrow $10,000 from Quality Loan Company to buy a new car, but Quality refuses to lend the money unless Ron cosigns the note. Ron cosigns and makes three of the payments when Pat fails to do so. Can Ron get this money from Pat?

3. Star Company's creditors include Town Bank with a perfected security interest in Star's building and equipment, United Construction with a mechanic's lien on the building that predates Town Bank's interest, and Variety Suppliers, Inc., with an unperfected security interest. Star files a petition for a Chapter 7 liquidation. In what order will the creditors be paid?

Chapter 17:
Agency

WHAT THIS CHAPTER IS ABOUT

This chapter covers agency relationships, including how they are formed and the duties involved. An agency relationship involves two parties: the principal and the agent. Agency relationships are essential to a corporation, which can function and enter into contracts only through its agents.

CHAPTER OUTLINE

I. AGENCY RELATIONSHIPS
In an agency relationship, the parties agree that the agent will act on behalf and instead of the principal in negotiating and transacting business with third persons.

A. EMPLOYER-EMPLOYEE RELATIONSHIPS
Normally, all employees who deal with third parties are deemed to be agents. Statutes covering workers' compensation and so on apply only to employer-employee relationships.

B. EMPLOYER–INDEPENDENT CONTRACTOR RELATIONSHIPS
Those who hire independent contractors have no control over the details of their physical performance. Independent contractors can be agents.

C. CRITERIA FOR DETERMINING EMPLOYEE STATUS
The greater an employer's control over the work, the more likely it is that the worker is an employee. Another key factor is whether the employer withholds taxes from payments to the worker and pays unemployment and Social Security taxes covering the worker.

II. HOW AGENCY RELATIONSHIPS ARE FORMED
Consideration is not required. A principal must have capacity to contract; anyone can be an agent. An agency can be created for any legal purpose.

A. AGENCY BY AGREEMENT
Normally, an agency must be based on an agreement that the agent will act for the principal. Such an agreement can be an express written contract, can be implied by conduct, or can be oral.

B. AGENCY BY RATIFICATION
A person who is not an agent (or who is an agent acting outside the scope of his or her authority) may make a contract on behalf of another (a principal). If the principal approves or affirms that contract by word or by action, an agency relationship is created by ratification.

C. AGENCY BY ESTOPPEL

1. Principal's Actions
When a principal causes a third person to believe that another person is his or her agent, and the third person deals with the supposed agent, the principal is estopped to deny the agency relationship.

2. **Third Party's Reasonable Belief**
   The third person must prove that he or she reasonably believed that an agency relationship existed and that the agent had authority—that an ordinary, prudent person familiar with business practice and custom would have been justified in concluding that the agent had authority.

D. **AGENCY BY OPERATION OF LAW**
   An agency relationship in the absence of a formal agreement may occur in family relationships or in an emergency, if the agent's failure to act outside the scope of his or her authority would cause the principal substantial loss.

III. DUTIES OF AGENTS AND PRINCIPALS
The principal-agent relationship is fiduciary.

A. **AGENT'S DUTIES TO THE PRINCIPAL**

1. **Performance**
   An agent must perform with reasonable diligence and skill.

2. **Notification**
   An agent must notify the principal of all matters concerning the agency.

3. **Loyalty**
   An agent must act solely for the benefit of the principal.

4. **Obedience**
   An agent must follow all lawful instructions of the principal.

5. **Accounting**
   An agent must keep and make available to the principal an account of everything received and paid out on behalf of the principal.

B. **PRINCIPAL'S DUTIES TO THE AGENT**

1. **Compensation**
   A principal must pay the agent for services rendered.

2. **Reimbursement and Indemnification**
   A principal must (1) reimburse the agent for money paid at the principal's request or for necessary expenses and (2) indemnify an agent for liability incurred because of authorized acts.

3. **Cooperation**
   A principal must cooperate with his or her agent.

4. **Safe Working Conditions**
   A principal must provide safe working conditions.

IV. AGENT'S AUTHORITY

A. **ACTUAL AUTHORITY**
   Express authority may be oral or in writing. Implied authority may be conferred by custom, can be inferred from the position an agent occupies, or is implied as reasonably necessary to carry out express authority.

1. **Equal Dignity Rule**
   In most states, if a contract is or must be in writing, an agent's authority to enter into the contract must also be in writing.

2. **Power of Attorney**
   A power of attorney can be special or general. An ordinary power terminates on the incapacity or death of the person giving it. A durable power is not affected by the principal's incapacity.

B. **APPARENT AUTHORITY**
An agent has apparent authority when a principal, by word or action, causes a third party reasonably to believe that an agent has authority, though the agent has no authority. The principal may be estopped from denying it if the third party changes position in reliance.

C. **RATIFICATION**
A principal can ratify an unauthorized contract or act, if he or she is aware of all material facts. Ratification can be done expressly or impliedly (by accepting the benefits of a transaction). An entire transaction must be ratified; a principal cannot affirm only part.

V. LIABILITY IN AGENCY RELATIONSHIPS

A. **LIABILITY FOR CONTRACTS**
Who is liable to third parties for contracts formed by an agent?

1. **If an Agent Acts within the Scope of His or Her Authority**

   a. **Disclosed Principal**
   If a principal's identity is known to a third party when an agent makes a contract, the principal is liable. The agent is not liable.

   b. **Partially Disclosed Principal**
   If a principal's identity is not known to a third party when an agent makes a contract but the third party knows the agent is acting for a principal, the principal is liable. In most states, the agent is also liable.

   c. **Undisclosed Principal**
   If the principal's identity is not known to a third party when an agent makes a contract, the principal *and* the agent are liable. Exceptions—

   1) The principal is expressly excluded as a party in the contract.
   2) The contract is a negotiable instrument (check or note).
   3) The performance of the agent is personal to the contract.

2. **If the Agent Has No Authority**
   The principal is not liable to a third party. The agent is liable (for breach of an implied warranty that the agent had authority), unless the third party knew the agent did not have authority.

3. **If the Agent Is an E-agent**
   E-agents include semi-autonomous computer programs capable of executing specific tasks. How much authority do e-agents have? Generally, a party who uses an e-agent is bound by the e-agent's acts.

B. **LIABILITY FOR TORTS AND CRIMES**
An agent is liable to third parties for his or her torts and crimes. Is the principal also liable?

1. **Liability for Agent's Negligence**

   a. **The Doctrine of *Respondeat Superior***
   An employer is liable for harm caused (negligently or intentionally) to a third party by an employee acting within the scope of employment, without regard to the fault of the employer.

   b. **Scope of Employment**
   Factors for determining whether an act is within the scope of employment are—

1) the time, place, and purpose of the act.
2) whether the act was authorized by the employer.
3) whether the act is one commonly performed by employees on behalf of their employers.
4) whether the employer's interest was advanced by the act.
5) whether the private interests of the employee were involved.
6) whether the employer furnished the means by which an injury was inflicted.
7) whether the employer had reason to know that the employee would do the act in question.
8) whether the act involved the commission of a serious crime.

2. **Liability for Agent's Intentional Torts**
   The doctrine of *respondeat superior* applies in these cases. Also, a principal is responsible for an agent's misrepresentation made within the scope of the agent's authority.

3. **Liability for Independent Contractor's Torts**
   An employer is not liable for physical harm caused to a third person by an independent contractor's tort (except for hazardous activities, such as blasting operations, transportation of volatile chemicals, and use of poisonous gases, in which strict liability is imposed).

4. **Liability for Agent's Crimes**
   A principal is not liable for an agent's crime, unless the principal participated. In some states, a principal may be liable for an agent's violating, in the course and scope of employment, such regulations as those governing sanitation, prices, weights, and the sale of liquor.

VI.   HOW AGENCY RELATIONSHIPS ARE TERMINATED

A.   TERMINATION BY ACT OF THE PARTIES
An agency ends when the time specified in the agreement expires, its purpose is achieved, a specified event occurs, or by mutual agreement. Both parties have the *power* to terminate an agency, but they may not have the *right* and may therefore be liable for breach of contract.

B.   TERMINATION BY OPERATION OF LAW
Circumstances under which an agency terminates by operation of law include death or insanity of either party, destruction of the subject matter of the agency, changed circumstances, bankruptcy of either party, and war between the principal's and agent's countries.

C.   NOTICE OF TERMINATION
If an agency terminates by operation of law because of death, insanity, or some other unforeseen circumstance, there is no duty to notify third persons, unless the agent's authority is coupled with an interest. If the parties themselves terminate the agency, the principal must inform any third parties who know of the agency that it has ended.

TRUE-FALSE QUESTIONS

(Answers at the Back of the Book)

____   1.   Employees who deal with third parties are agents of their employers.

____   2.   An agent owes his or her principal a duty to act in good faith.

____   3.   An agent who fails to use reasonable diligence and skill in acting on behalf of his or her principal may be liable for breaching a duty of performance.

____   4.   A *disclosed* principal is liable to a third party for contracts made by the agent acting within the scope of authority.

_____ 5. A principal is not liable for harm caused to a third party by an agent acting in the scope of employment.

_____ 6. An _undisclosed_ principal is liable to a third party for contracts made by an agent acting within the scope of authority.

_____ 7. Both parties to an agency have the right to terminate the agency at any time.

_____ 8. If a principal does not ratify an otherwise unauthorized contract, the principal is not bound.

_____ 9. An e-agent is a person.

_____ 10. When an agent enters into a contract on behalf of a principal, the principal must ratify the contract to be bound.

FILL-IN QUESTIONS

(Answers at the Back of the Book)

An agent's use of reasonable diligence and skill is part of the agent's duty of _____ (obedience/performance). Informing a principal of all material matters that come to the agent's attention concerning the subject matter of the agency is an aspect of the agent's duty of _____ (accounting/notification). Acting solely for the benefit of the principal and not in the interest of the agent or a third party is part of the agent's duty of _____(loyalty/performance). Following all lawful and clearly stated instructions of the principal is an aspect of the agent's duty of _____ (loyalty/obedience). If an agent is required to keep and make available to the principal a record of all property and money received and paid out on behalf of the principal, this is part of the agent's duty of _____ (accounting/notification).

MULTIPLE-CHOICE QUESTIONS

(Answers at the Back of the Book)

_____ 1. Andy is an officer for Beta Corporation. When acting for Beta in ordinary business situations, Andy is

   a. an agent.
   b. an agent and a principal.
   c. a principal.
   d. neither an agent nor a principal.

_____ 2. Carol is a salesperson for Delta Products, Inc. In determining whether Carol is Delta's employee or an independent contractor, the most important factor is

   a. the degree of control that Delta exercises over Carol.
   b. the distinction between Delta's business and Carol's occupation.
   c. the length of the working relationship between Delta and Carol.
   d. the method of payment.

_____ 3. Eagle Company hires Fran, who holds herself out as possessing special accounting skills, to act as its agent. As an agent, Fran must use the degree of skill or care expected of

   a. an average, unskilled person.
   b. a person having those special skills.
   c. a reasonable person.
   d. Eagle Company.

____ 4. Greg, a salesperson at Home Electronics Company, tells Irma, a customer, "Buy your computer here, and I'll set it up for less than what Home would charge." Irma buys the computer, Greg sets it up, and Irma pays Greg, who keeps the money. Greg has breached the duty of

   a. loyalty.
   b. notification.
   c. obedience.
   d. performance.

____ 5. Java Company hires Keith to manage one of its stores. Although their employment agreement says nothing about Keith being able to hire employees to work in the store, Ken has this authority. This is

   a. apparent authority.
   b. express authority.
   c. imaginary authority.
   d. implied authority.

____ 6. Macro Company employs Nora as an agent. To terminate her authority, Macro must notify

   a. Nora and third parties who know of the agency relationship.
   b. only Nora.
   c. only third parties who know of the agency relationship.
   d. the public generally.

____ 7. Midwest Mining, Inc., employs Nick as an agent. Nick enters into a contract with Omega Resources Company within the scope of his authority but without disclosing that he is acting as Midwest's agent. Midwest does not perform. Omega can recover from

   a. Midwest only.
   b. Midwest or Nick.
   c. Nick only.
   d. no one.

____ 8. Quality Products Company requires its customers to pay by check. Ray, a Quality agent, tells customers that they can pay him with cash. Quality learns of Ray's collections, but takes no action to stop them. Ray steals some of the cash. Quality may be liable for the loss under the doctrine of

   a. apparent authority.
   b. express authority.
   c. imaginary authority.
   d. implied authority.

____ 9. Standard Delivery Company employs Tina as a driver. While acting within the scope of employment, Tina causes an accident in which Vic is injured. Vic can recover from

   a. neither Standard nor Tina.
   b. Standard only.
   c. Standard or Tina.
   d. Tina only.

____ 10. Wendy contracts with Zip Enterprises, Inc., to act as Zip's agent in a fraudulent scheme. Wendy does not successfully complete the scheme. Zip can recover from Wendy for breach of

   a. contract.
   b. implied warranty.
   c. performance.
   d. none of the above.

SHORT ESSAY QUESTIONS

1.   What are the essential differences among the relationships of principal and agent, employer and employee, and employer and independent contractor? What factors indicate whether an individual is an employee or an independent contractor?

2.   In what situations is a principal liable for an agent's torts?

ISSUE SPOTTERS

(Answers at the Back of the Book)

1.   Ann, owner of Best Goods Company, employs Cathy as an administrative assistant. In Ann's absence, and without authority, Cathy represents herself as Ann and signs a promissory note in Ann's name. In what circumstance is Ann liable on the note?

2.   Don contracts with Eve to buy a certain horse for Eve, who asks Don not to reveal her identity. Don makes a deal with Farm Stables, the owner of the horse, and makes a down payment. Eve fails to pay the rest of the price. Farm Stables sues Don for breach of contract. Can Don hold Eve liable for whatever damages he has to pay?

3.   Great Bank encourages its depositors to ask its advice concerning their investments. Holly, one of the bank's investment counselors, tells Ira to invest in Jiffy Corporation, although Holly knows its financial situation is precarious. If Ira loses money on the deal, can the bank be held liable?

Chapter 18:
Employment Law

WHAT THIS CHAPTER IS ABOUT

This chapter outlines the most significant laws regulating employment relationships, including those prohibiting employment discrimination.

CHAPTER OUTLINE

I. EMPLOYMENT AT WILL
Under the employment-at-will doctrine, either the employer or the employee may terminate an employment relationship at any time and for any reason (unless a contract or the law provides to the contrary).

A. EXCEPTIONS TO THE EMPLOYMENT-AT-WILL DOCTRINE

1. Exceptions Based on Contract Theory
Some courts have held that an implied contract exists between an employer and an employee (if, for example, a personnel manual states that no employee will be fired without good cause). A few states have held all employment contracts contain an implied covenant of good faith.

2. Exceptions Based on Tort Theory
Discharge may give rise to a tort action (based on fraud, for example) for wrongful discharge.

3. Exceptions Based on Public Policy
An employer may not fire a worker for reasons that violate a public policy of the jurisdiction (for example, for refusing to violate the law). This policy must be expressed clearly in statutory law. Some state and federal statutes protect whistleblowers from retaliation. The False Claims Reform Act of 1986 gives a whistleblower 15 to 25 percent of proceeds recovered from fraud.

B. WRONGFUL DISCHARGE
An employer cannot fire an employee in violation of an employment contract or a federal or state statute. If so, the employee may bring an action for wrongful discharge.

II. WAGE-HOUR LAWS
Davis-Bacon Act of 1931 requires "prevailing wages" for employees of some government contractors. Walsh-Healey Act of 1936 requires minimum wage and overtime for employees of some government contractors. Fair Labor Standards Act of 1938 (FLSA) covers all employees and regulates—

A. CHILD LABOR
Children under fourteen can deliver newspapers, work for their parents, and work in entertainment and agriculture. Children fourteen and older cannot work in hazardous occupations.

B. MAXIMUM HOURS
Employees who work more than forty hours per week must be paid no less than one and a half times their regular pay for all hours over forty. Executives, administrative employees, professional employees, computer employees, and outside salespersons are exempt if they meet certain requirements.

C. MINIMUM WAGE
A specified amount (periodically revised) must be paid to employees in covered industries. Wages include the reasonable cost to furnish employees with board, lodging, and other facilities.

III. WORKER HEALTH AND SAFETY

A. OCCUPATIONAL SAFETY AND HEALTH ACT OF 1970
Attempts to ensure safe and healthful work conditions for most employees.

1. Enforcement Agencies

a. Occupational Safety and Health Administration (OSHA)
Inspects workplaces and issues safety standards, including standards covering employee exposure to harmful substances.

b. National Institute for Occupational Safety and Health
Researches safety and health problems and recommends standards for OSHA to adopt.

c. Occupational Safety and Health Review Commission
Hears appeals from actions taken by OSHA administrators.

2. Procedures and Violations
Employees file complaints of OSHA violations (employers cannot retaliate); employers must keep injury and illness records; employers must file accident reports directly to OSHA. Penalties are limited.

B. STATE WORKERS' COMPENSATION LAWS
State laws establish procedure for compensating workers injured on the job.

1. No State Covers All Employees
Often excluded are domestic workers, agricultural workers, temporary employees, and employees of common carriers.

2. Requirements for Recovery
There must be an employment relationship, and the injury must be accidental and occur on the job or in the course of employment.

3. Filing a Claim
An employee must notify the employer of an injury (usually within thirty days), and file a claim with a state agency within a certain period (sixty days to two years) from the time the injury is first noticed.

4. Acceptance of Workers' Compensation Benefits Bars Suits
An employee's acceptance of benefits bars the employee from suing for injuries caused by the employer's negligence.

IV. INCOME SECURITY

A. SOCIAL SECURITY
The Social Security Act of 1935 provides for payments to persons who are retired, widowed, disabled, etc. Employers and employees must contribute under the Federal Insurance Contributions Act (FICA).

B. MEDICARE
A health insurance program administered by the Social Security Administration for people sixty-five years of age and older and for some under sixty-five who are disabled.

C. PRIVATE PENSION PLANS
The Employee Retirement Income Security Act (ERISA) of 1974 empowers the Labor Management Services Administration of the U.S. Department of Labor to oversee those who operate private pension funds.

1. Vesting
Generally, employee contributions to pension plans vest immediately; employee rights to employer contributions vest after five years.

2. Investing
Pension-fund managers must be cautious in investing and refrain from investing more than 10 percent of the fund in securities of the employer.

D. UNEMPLOYMENT INSURANCE
The Federal Unemployment Tax Act of 1935 created a state system that provides unemployment compensation to eligible individuals.

E. COBRA
The Consolidated Omnibus Budget Reconciliation Act (COBRA) of 1985 prohibits the elimination of most workers' medical, optical, or dental insurance on the termination of their employment. Coverage must continue for up to 18 months (29 months in some cases). A worker pays the premium plus 2 percent.

F. FAMILY AND MEDICAL LEAVE
Employers with fifty or more employees must provide them with up to twelve weeks of family or medical leave during any twelve-month period, continue health-care coverage during the leave, and guarantee employment in the same, or a comparable, position when the employee returns to work.

V.   EMPLOYEE PRIVACY RIGHTS

A right to privacy has been inferred from constitutional guarantees provided by the First, Third, Fourth, Fifth, and Ninth Amendments to the Constitution. Tort law, state constitutions, and some federal and state statutes also provide some privacy rights.

A. ELECTRONIC MONITORING IN THE WORKPLACE

1. Laws Protecting Employee Privacy Rights
The Electronic Communications Privacy Act (ECPA) of 1986 bars the interception of any wire or electronic communication or the disclosure or use of information obtained by interception. Excepted is employers' monitoring of *business* telephone conversations.

2. Factors Considered by the Courts in Employee Privacy Cases
If an employee sues for invasion of privacy, a court may weigh the employee's reasonable expectation of privacy against the employer's need for surveillance. This may depend on whether the employee was aware of the monitoring.

3. Privacy Expectations and E-Mail Systems
In cases involving e-mail, it has not seemed to matter whether employees were aware of being monitored.

B. OTHER TYPES OF MONITORING

1. Lie-Detector Tests
Under the Employee Polygraph Protection Act of 1988, most employers cannot, among other things, require, request, or suggest that employees or applicants take lie-detector tests, except when investigating theft, including theft of trade secrets.

2. Drug Testing

a. Protection for the Privacy Rights of Private Employees
Some state constitutions may prohibit private employers from testing for drugs. State statutes may restrict drug testing by private employers. Other sources of protection include collective bargaining agreements and tort actions for invasion of privacy (see Chapter 4).

b. Protection for Government Employees
Constitutional limitations (the Fourth Amendment) apply. Drug tests have been upheld when there was a reasonable basis for suspecting employees of using drugs, or when drug use could threaten public safety.

3. **AIDS Testing**

    Some state laws restrict AIDS testing. The federal Americans with Disabilities Act of 1990 and other statutes protect employees or applicants who have tested positive from discrimination.

4. **Genetic Testing**

    This may violate the Americans with Disabilities Act of 1990 or other privacy provisions.

5. **Screening Procedures**

    A key factor in determining whether preemployment screening tests violate privacy rights is whether there is a connection between the questions and the job for which an applicant is applying.

VI.   EMPLOYMENT DISCRIMINATION

Discrimination on the basis of race, color, religion, national origin, gender, age, or disability is prohibited. A class of persons defined by one or more of these criteria is known as a **protected class**.

A.   TITLE VII OF THE CIVIL RIGHTS ACT OF 1964

Prohibits discrimination against employees, applicants, and union members on the basis of race, color, national origin, religion, and gender.

1. **Who Is Subject to Title VII?**

    Employers with fifteen or more employees, labor unions with fifteen or more members, labor unions that operate hiring halls, employment agencies, and federal, state, and local agencies.

2. **Procedures under Title VII**

    (1) Victim files a claim with the Equal Employment Opportunity Commission (EEOC); (2) EEOC investigates and seeks a voluntary settlement; (3) if no settlement is reached, EEOC may sue the employer; (4) if EEOC chooses not to sue, victim may file a lawsuit.

3. **Intentional and Unintentional Discrimination**

    Title VII prohibits both intentional and unintentional discrimination.

    a. **Disparate-Treatment Discrimination**

        This is intentional discrimination by an employer against an employee.

        1) *Prima Facie* **Case—Plaintiff's Side of the Case**

            Plaintiff must show (1) he or she is member of a protected class, (2) he or she applied and was qualified for the job, (3) he or she was rejected by the employer, (4) employer continued to seek applicants or filled position with person not in protected class.

        2) **Defense—Employer's Side of the Case**

            Employer must articulate a legal reason for not hiring plaintiff. To prevail, plaintiff must show that employer's reason is a pretext and that discriminatory intent motivated the decision.

    b. **Disparate-Impact Discrimination**

        1) **Types of Disparate-Impact Discrimination**

            Because of a requirement or hiring practice, (1) an employer's work force does not reflect the percentage of members of protected classes that characterizes qualified individuals in the local labor market, or (2) members of a protected class are excluded from the employer's work force at a substantially higher rate than nonmembers.

        2) *Prima Facie* **Case—Plaintiff's Side of the Case**

            Plaintiff must show connection between requirement or practice and disparity; no evidence of discriminatory intent is needed.

4. **Discrimination Based on Race, Color, and National Origin**
    Employers cannot discriminate against employees on the basis of race, color, national origin, or religion (absent a substantial, demonstrable relationship between the trait and the job, etc.).

5. **Discrimination Based on Religion**
    Title VII prohibits employers and unions from discriminating against persons because of their religion.

6. **Discrimination Based on Gender**
    Employers cannot discriminate against employees on the basis of gender (unless the gender of the applicant can be proved essential to the job, etc.). The Pregnancy Discrimination Act of 1978 amended Title VII to include employees affected by pregnancy or related conditions.

7. **Sexual Harassment**

    a. **Forms of Harassment**
        (1) *Quid pro quo* harassment: when promotions, etc., are doled out on the basis of sexual favors; (2) hostile-environment harassment: when an employee is subjected to offensive sexual comments, etc. (Courts are split as to whether plaintiffs can sue for same-gender harassment.)

    b. **Harassment by Supervisors, Co-Workers, or Non-employees**

        1) **When Is an Employer Liable?**
           If someone harasses an employee, and the employer knew, or should have known, and failed to take immediate corrective action, the employer may be liable.

        2) **Employer's Defense**
           (1) Employer took "reasonable care to prevent and correct promptly any sexually harassing behavior," and (2) employee suing for harassment failed to follow policies and procedures.

8. **Remedies under Title VII**
    Reinstatement, back pay, retroactive promotions, damages.

    a. **Compensatory Damages**
        These are available only in cases of intentional discrimination, and do not include back pay, interest on back pay, or other Title VII relief.

    b. **Punitive Damages**
        These are available only if an employer acted with malice or reckless indifference.

    c. **Limitations**
        Total damages are limited to specific amounts against specific employers (from $50,000 against those with one hundred or fewer employees to $300,000 against those with more than five hundred employees).

B. **EQUAL PAY ACT OF 1963**
    This act prohibits gender-based discrimination in wages for equal work (work requiring equal skill, effort, responsibility under similar conditions) in the same workplace. Different wages are acceptable because of any factor but gender (seniority, merit, etc.).

C. **DISCRIMINATION BASED ON AGE**

    1. **Age Discrimination in Employment Act (ADEA) of 1967**
        Prohibits employment discrimination on the basis of age (including mandatory retirement), by employers with twenty or more employees, against individuals forty years of age or older.

2. **Principles Are Similar to Title VII**
   Requires the establishment of a *prima facie* case: plaintiff must show that he or she was (1) forty or older, (2) qualified for a position, and (3) rejected in circumstances that infer discrimination. The employer must articulate a legal reason; the plaintiff may show it is a pretext.

3. **State Employers**
   Suits against state agencies by state employees for age discrimination are often dismissed because, under the Eleventh Amendment, a state is immune from a suit brought by a private individual in federal court unless the state consents to the suit.

D. DISCRIMINATION BASED ON DISABILITY
Under the Americans with Disabilities Act (ADA) of 1990, an employer cannot refuse to hire a person who is qualified but disabled.

1. **Procedures under the ADA**
   A plaintiff must show he or she (1) has a disability, (2) is otherwise qualified for a job and (3) was excluded solely because of the disability. A suit may be filed only after a claim is pursued through the EEOC.

2. **Remedies under the ADA**
   These include reinstatement, back pay, some compensatory and punitive damages (for intentional discrimination), and certain other relief. Repeat violators may be fined up to $100,000.

3. **What is a Disability?**
   "(1) [A] physical or mental impairment that substantially limits one or more of the major life activities . . . ; (2) a record of such impairment; or (3) being regarded as having such an impairment." Includes AIDS, morbid obesity, etc.; not homosexuality or kleptomania.

4. **Reasonable Accommodation**
   For person with a disability, employer may have to make a reasonable accommodation (more flexible hours, new job assignment, different training materials or procedures)—but not an accommodation that will cause **undue hardship** (impose "significant difficulty or expense").

VII. DEFENSES TO EMPLOYMENT DISCRIMINATION
The first defense is to assert that the plaintiff did not prove discrimination. If discrimination is proved, an employer may attempt to justify it as—

A. BUSINESS NECESSITY
An employer may show that there is a legitimate connection between a job requirement that discriminates and job performance.

B. BONA FIDE OCCUPATIONAL QUALIFICATION (BFOQ)
Another defense applies when discrimination against a protected class is essential to a job—that is, when a particular trait is a BFOQ. Generally restricted to cases in which gender is essential. Race can never be a BFOQ.

C. SENIORITY SYSTEMS
An employer with a history of discrimination may have no members of protected classes or disabled workers in upper-level positions. If no present intent to discriminate is shown, and promotions, etc., are distributed according to a fair seniority system, the employer has a good defense.

D. AFTER-ACQUIRED EVIDENCE
Evidence of an employee's prior misconduct acquired after a lawsuit is filed may limit damages but is not otherwise a defense.

TRUE-FALSE QUESTIONS

(Answers at the Back of the Book)

____ 1. Drug testing by private employers is permitted.

____ 2. Employers are required to establish retirement plans for their employees.

____ 3. Federal wage-hour laws cover all employers engaged in interstate commerce.

____ 4. Whistleblower statutes protect employers from workers' disclosure of the employer's wrongdoing.

____ 5. Under federal law, employers can monitor employees' personal communications.

____ 6. In a sexual harassment case, an employer cannot be held liable if a nonemployee did the harassing.

____ 7. Women affected by pregnancy must be treated for all job-related purposes the same as persons not so affected but similar in ability to work.

____ 8. Employment discrimination against persons with a physical or mental impairment that substantially limits their everyday activities is prohibited.

____ 9. All employers are subject to Title VII of the Civil Rights Act of 1964.

____ 10. Disparate-treatment discrimination occurs when an employer intentionally discriminates against an employee.

FILL-IN QUESTIONS

(Answers at the Back of the Book)

Under the employment-at-will doctrine, _____ (either/neither) party may terminate an employment relationship at any time and for any reason _____ (unless/even if) a contract provides to the contrary. An employee who is fired in violation of a federal or state statute _____ (may/may not) bring an action for wrongful discharge. _____ (Some/No) courts have held that an implied contract exists between an employer and an employee. _____ (All/A few states) have held that all employment contracts contain an implied covenant of good faith. An employer _____ (may/may not) fire a worker for reasons that violate a public policy of the jurisdiction.

MULTIPLE-CHOICE QUESTIONS

(Answers at the Back of the Book)

____ 1. Wholesale Distributors, Inc., is investigating losses due to theft. Without violating employees' rights of privacy, Wholesale may

a. require employees to take polygraph tests only.
b. monitor all employee phone conversations only.
c. require employees to take polygraph tests and monitor all employee phone conversations.
d. none of the above.

____ 2. Eve, an employee of First Bank, is injured. For Eve to receive *workers' compensation*, the injury must be

a. accidental and arise out of a preexisting disease or condition.
b. accidental and occur on the job or in the course of employment.
c. intentional and arise out of a preexisting disease or condition.
d. intentional and occur on the job or in the course of employment.

____ 3. ABC Corporation provides health insurance for its 150 employees, including Dian. When Dian takes twelve weeks' leave to care for her child, she

a. can collect "leave pay" equal to twelve weeks' of health insurance coverage.
b. can continue her heath insurance at ABC's expense.
c. can continue her heath insurance at her expense.
d. loses her heath insurance immediately on taking leave.

____ 4. Mega Corporation provides health insurance for its employees. When Mega closes one of its offices and terminates the employees, the employees

a. can collect "severance pay" equal to twelve weeks' of health insurance coverage.
b. can continue their heath insurance at Mega's expense.
c. can continue their heath insurance at their expense.
d. lose their heath insurance immediately on termination of employment.

____ 5. Ann is an employee of Beta Communications Corporation. Ann attempts to resolve a gender-based discrimination claim with Beta, whose representative denies the claim. Ann's next best step is to

a. ask the Equal Opportunity Employment Commission whether a claim is justified.
b. file a lawsuit.
c. forget about the matter.
d. secretly sabotage company operations for revenge.

____ 6. Bob and Carol work for Delta Company. Bob is Carol's supervisor. During work, Bob touches Carol in ways that she perceives as sexually offensive. Carol resists the advances. Bob cuts her pay. Delta is

a. liable, because Bob's conduct constituted sexual harassment.
b. liable, because Carol resisted Bob's advances.
c. not liable, because Bob's conduct was not job-related.
d. not liable, because Carol resisted Bob's advances.

____ 7. Kay, who is hearing impaired, applies for a position with Local Company. Kay is qualified but is refused the job and sues Local. To succeed under the Americans with Disabilities Act, Kay must show that

a. Kay was willing to make a "reasonable accommodation" for Local.
b. Kay would not have to accept "significant additional costs" to work for Local.
c. Local refused to make a "reasonable accommodation" for Kay.
d. Local would not have to accept "significant additional costs" to hire Kay.

____ 8. Curt, personnel director for Digital Products, Inc., prefers to hire Asian Americans, because "they're smarter and work harder" than other minorities. This is prohibited by

a. the Age Discrimination in Employment Act of 1967.
b. the Americans with Disabilities Act of 1990.
c. Title VII of the Civil Rights Act of 1964 .
d. none of the above.

____   9. Standard Corporation terminates Tom, who sues on the basis of age discrimination. To succeed under the Age Discrimination in Employment Act, Tom must show that at the time of the discharge, he was

    a. forty or older.
    b. forty or younger.
    c. replaced with someone forty or older.
    d. replaced with someone forty or younger.

____   10. National Company requires job applicants to pass certain physical tests. Only a few female applicants can pass the tests, but it they pass, they are hired. To successfully defend against a suit on this basis under Title VII, National must show that

    a. any discrimination is not intentional.
    b. being a male is a BFOQ.
    c. passing the tests is a business necessity.
    d. some men cannot pass the tests.

SHORT ESSAY QUESTIONS

1. What is the employment-at-will doctrine? What are its exceptions?

2. Compare and contrast disparate-treatment discrimination and disparate-impact discrimination, and Title VII's response to each in the context of employment.

ISSUE SPOTTERS

(Answers at the Back of the Book)

1. Associated Services Company (ASC) issues an employee handbook that states employees will be discharged only for good cause. One day, Bob, an ASC supervisor, says to Carl, "I don't like your looks. You're fired." Is ASC liable for breach of contract?

2. Workers' compensation laws establish a procedure for compensating workers who are injured on the job. Instead of suing, an injured worker files a claim with the appropriate state agency. For the employee to obtain compensation, does the injury have to have been caused by the employer's negligence?

3. Paula, a disabled person, applies for a job at Quantity Corporation for which she is well qualified, but for which she is rejected. Quantity continues to seek applicants and eventually fills the position with a person who is not disabled. Could Paula succeed in a suit against Quantity for discrimination?

Chapter 19:
The Entrepreneur's Options

WHAT THIS CHAPTER IS ABOUT

This chapter sets out the basic features of sole proprietorships, partnerships, limited liability companies, and other forms for doing business. The chapter also discusses private franchises.

CHAPTER OUTLINE

I. MAJOR BUSINESS FORMS

A. SOLE PROPRIETORSHIPS
The simplest form of business—the owner is the business.

1. Advantages of the Sole Proprietorship
The proprietor takes all the profits. Easier to start than other kinds of businesses (few legal forms involved); has more flexibility (proprietor is free to make all decisions); owner pays only personal income tax on profits.

2. Disadvantages of the Sole Proprietorship
The proprietor has all the risk (unlimited liability for all debts); limited opportunity to raise capital; the business dissolves when the owner dies.

B. PARTNERSHIPS
Arises from an agreement between two or more persons to carry on a business for profit.

1. The Law Governing Partnerships
A partnership arises from an agreement between two or more persons to carry on a business for profit. The partnership is governed by this agreement, the principles of agency law, and the Uniform Partnership Act (UPA) or the Revised Uniform Partnership Act (RUPA).

2. Features of Partnerships
General partners jointly and equally control the operation and share the profits (and losses). No particular form of agreement is necessary to create a general partnership; partners may agree to any terms. Each partner may be held fully liable for all of the partnership's debts.

3. Advantages and Disadvantages
Partners are subject to personal liability for partnership obligations; a partnership is not subject to federal income tax (profit is taxed as individual income to the partners).

C. LIMITED PARTNERSHIPS
Consist of at least one general partner and one or more limited partners. General partners run the firm and are subject to personal liability for its obligations. Limited partners have limited liability.

D. CORPORATIONS
Corporations consist of shareholders, who own the business; a board of directors, who are elected by the shareholders to manage the business; and officers, who oversee day-to-day operations (see Chapter 20). An advantage of this form is that the liability of the owners (shareholders) is usually limited to their investment. A disadvantage is that corporate income is taxed twice—once as income to the corporation, and once when distributed to shareholders.

E. LIMITED LIABILITY COMPANIES

A limited liability company (LLC) is a business form that offers the limited liability of a corporation with the tax advantages of a partnership. To form an LLC, articles of organization are filed with a state, which issues a charter.

1. The LLC Operating Agreement

Provisions relate to management, division of profits, transfer of membership, what events trigger dissolution, and so on. In the absence of an agreement, state statutes govern. If there is no statute, the principles of partnership law apply.

2. Advantages of an LLC

Taxed as a partnership; liability of members is limited to the amount of their investment; members can participate in management; no limit on the number of members (in many states, one is enough).

F. LIMITED LIABILITY PARTNERSHIPS

Professionals may organize as a limited liability partnership (LLP) to enjoy the tax advantages of a partnership, while avoiding personal liability for the wrongdoing of other partners.

II. SPECIAL BUSINESS FORMS

A. JOINT VENTURES

A joint venture is a relationship in which two or more persons combine their interests for a single transaction or project, or a related series of transactions or projects.

1. Characteristics of a Joint Venture

A joint venture is not a legal entity and cannot be sued as such (members can be sued individually). Taxed like partnerships.

2. Members' Power and Profit

Members have limited power to bind other members. Unless otherwise agreed, members share profits and losses equally.

B. SYNDICATES

A group of individuals financing a project; may exist as a corporation, a partnership, or no legally recognized form.

C. JOINT STOCK COMPANIES

Usually treated like a partnership (formed by agreement, members have personal liability, etc.), but members are not agents of one another, and has many characteristics of a corporation: (1) ownership by shares of stock, (2) managed by directors and officers, and (3) perpetual existence.

D. BUSINESS TRUSTS

Legal ownership and management of the property of the business is in one or more trustees; profits are distributed to beneficiaries, who are not personally responsible for the debts of the trust. Resembles a corporation.

E. COOPERATIVES

This is an association that is organized to provide an economic service to its members (or shareholders).

1. Incorporated Cooperative

Subject to state laws governing nonprofit corporations. Distributes profits to owners on the basis of their transactions with the cooperative rather than on the basis of the amount of capital they contributed.

2. Unincorporated Cooperatives

Often treated like partnerships. The members have joint liability for the cooperative's acts.

III.   PRIVATE FRANCHISES

A **franchise** is any arrangement in which the owner of a trademark, a trade name, or a copyright has licensed others to use it in selling goods or services.

A.   TYPES OF FRANCHISES

1.   **Distributorship**
A distributorship occurs when a manufacturer licenses a dealer to sell its product (such as an automobile dealer). Often covers an exclusive territory.

2.   **Chain-Style Business Operation**
This is when a franchise operates under a franchisor's trade name and is identified as a member of a group of dealers engaged in the franchisor's business (such as most fast-food chains). The franchisee must follow standardized or prescribed methods of operations, and may be obligated to obtain supplies exclusively from the franchisor.

3.   **Manufacturing or Processing-Plant Arrangement**
This arises when a franchisor transmits to the franchisee the essential ingredients or formula to make a product (such as Coca-Cola), which the franchisee makes and markets according to the franchisor's standards.

B.   THE FRANCHISE CONTRACT

A franchise relationship is created by a contract between the franchisor and the franchisee.

1.   **Payment for the Franchise**
A franchisee pays (1) a fee for a franchise license, (2) fees for products bought from or through the franchisor, (3) a percentage of sales, and (4) a percentage of marketing and administrative costs.

2.   **Business Premises**
The agreement may specify whether the premises for the business are leased or purchased and who is to supply equipment and furnishings.

3.   **Location of the Franchise**
The franchisor determines the territory to be served and its exclusivity.

4.   **Business Organization of the Franchisee**
A franchisor may specify requirements for the form and capital structure of the business.

5.   **Quality Controls**
A franchisor may specify standards of operation (such as quality standards) and personnel training methods. Too much control may result in a franchisor's liability for torts of a franchisee's employees.

6.   **Price Controls**
A franchisor may require a franchisee to buy supplies from the franchisor at a set price and may set prices for the goods the franchisee sells, but this price-setting may violate antitrust laws.

7.   **Termination of the Franchise**
Determined by the parties. Usually, termination must be "for cause" (such as breach of the agreement, etc.) and notice must be given. A franchisee must be given reasonable time to wind up the business.

TRUE-FALSE QUESTIONS

(Answers at the Back of the Book)

_____   **1.**   In a sole proprietorship, the owner and the business are entirely separate.

_____   **2.**   A partnership is an association of two or more persons to carry on, as co-owners, a business for profit.

_____ 3. A general partner is not personally liable for partnership debts if its assets are insufficient to pay its creditors.

_____ 4. A limited liability company must be formed and operated in compliance with federal law.

_____ 5. A limited liability company does not offer the limited liability of a corporation.

_____ 6. In a limited liability partnership, no partner is exempt from personal liability for partnership obligations.

_____ 7. In a limited partnership, the liability of a *limited* partner is limited to the amount of capital he or she invests in the partnership.

_____ 8. A joint venture can be sued as an entity.

_____ 9. A franchise is an arrangement in which the owner of a trademark, a trade name, or a copyright has licensed others to use it in selling goods or services.

_____ 10. A franchisee is not subject to the franchisor's control in the area of product quality.

FILL-IN QUESTIONS

(Answers at the Back of the Book)

Unless the participants agree otherwise, all of the _____ (members/limited partners) of a _____ (limited liability company/limited partnership) may participate in management without assuming liability for the obligations of the firm. In contrast, the _____ (members/limited partners) of a _____ (limited liability company/limited partnership) who participate in management may be personally liable for the debts of the firm.

MULTIPLE-CHOICE QUESTIONS

(Answers at the Back of the Book)

_____ 1. Ann owns Beta Enterprises, a sole proprietorship. Ann's liability for the obligations of the business is

a. limited by state statute.
b. limited to the amount of his original investment.
c. limited to the total amount of capital Ann invests in the business.
d. unlimited.

_____ 2. Holly owns International Imports. She hires Jay as a salesperson, agreeing to pay $10.00 per hour, plus a commission of 10 percent of his sales. The term is one year. Holly and Jay are

a. not partners, because Jay does not have an ownership interest or management rights in the business.
b. not partners, because the pay includes an hourly wage.
c. not partners, because the pay includes only a 10-percent commission.
d. partners for one year.

_____ 3. Jay is a limited partner in Kappa Sales, a limited partnership. Jay is liable for the firm's debts

a. in no way.
b. in proportion to the total number of partners in the firm.
c. to the extent of his capital contribution.
d. to the full extent of the debts.

____   4. Adam and Beth form A&B, LLC, a limited liability company (LLC). One advantage of an LLC is that it may be taxed as

    a. a corporation.
    b. a partnership.
    c. a sole proprietorship.
    d. a syndicate.

____   5. Carol and Don form E-Stuff as a limited liability company. They can participate in the firm's management

    a. only to the extent that they assume personal liability for the firm's debts.
    b. only to the extent of the amount of their investment in the firm.
    c. to any extent.
    d. to no extent.

____   6. Kay and Lyle are partners in a medical clinic, which is organized as a limited liability partnership. Kay manages the clinic. A court holds Lyle liable in a malpractice suit. Kay is liable

    a. in no way.
    b. in proportion to the total number of partners in the firm.
    c. to the extent of her capital contribution.
    d. to the full extent of the liability.

____   7. Alpha Corporation and Beta, Inc., form a joint venture to develop and market molecular-based computer chips. A joint venture is similar to

    a. a corporation.
    b. a partnership.
    c. a sole proprietorship.
    d. a syndicate.

____   8. Adam invests in a franchise with Best Gas Stations, Inc. Best requires Adam to buy Best products for every phase of the operation. Adam's best argument to challenge this requirement is that it violates

    a. an implied covenant of good faith and fair dealing.
    b. antitrust laws.
    c. the Federal Trade Commission's Franchise Rule.
    d. the U.S. Franchise Agency's Purchase and Sale Regulations.

____   9. Dan wants the exclusive right to sell Excel Corporation software in a specific area. If Excel agrees, it may require Dan to pay

    a. a fee for a license and a percentage of the receipts.
    b. neither a fee for a license nor a percentage of the receipts.
    c. only a fee for a license to sell the software.
    d. only a percentage of the receipts from sales of the software.

____   10. Ron buys a franchise from Sports Club Corporation. If their agreement is like most franchise agreements, it will allow Sports Club to terminate the franchise

    a. for any reason only with notice.
    b. for any reason without notice.
    c. for cause only.
    d. under no circumstances.

SHORT ESSAY QUESTIONS

1.   What are the principal characteristics of a sole proprietorship, a partnership, and a corporation?

2.   How do franchise agreements generally deal with the following: (1) payment for the franchise, (2) location, (3) price controls, (4) quality control, and (5) termination?

ISSUE SPOTTERS

(Answers at the Back of the Book)

1.   Frank plans to open a sporting goods store, and to hire Gail and Hal. Frank will invest only his own money. He does not expect to make a profit for at least eighteen months and to make little profit for the first three years. He hopes to expand eventually. Which form of business organization would be most appropriate?

2.   Great Delivery Company and Highway Trucking, Inc., form a business trust. Interstate Equipment Company and Jiffy Supply Corporation form a joint stock company. Kappa Resources, Inc., and Local Storage, Inc., form an incorporated cooperative. What do these forms of business organization have in common?

3.   Fine Dining Cafes, Inc. (FDC), sells franchises. FDC imposes on its franchisees standards of operation and personnel training methods. What is the potential pitfall if FDC exercises too much control over its franchisees?

Chapter 20:
Corporations

What this Chapter Is About

This chapter covers the basic features of corporations. Most corporations are formed under state law, and a majority of states follow some version of the Revised Model Business Corporation Act (RMBCA).

Chapter Outline

I. THE NATURE OF THE CORPORATION

A. THE CONSTITUTIONAL RIGHTS OF CORPORATIONS
A corporation is recognized by the law as a "person" and, under the Bill of Rights, has the same rights as a natural person (see Chapter 1). Only officers and employees have the right against self-incrimination, however, and the privileges and immunities clause does not protect corporations.

B. THE LIMITED LIABILITY OF SHAREHOLDERS
Shareholders elect a board of directors, which is responsible for overall management and hires corporate officers to run daily operations. Shareholders normally are not liable for corporate obligations beyond the extent of their investments.

C. CORPORATE TAXATION
Corporate profits are taxed twice: as income to the corporation and, when distributed as dividends, as income to the shareholders.

D. TORTS AND CRIMINAL ACTS
A corporation is liable for the torts committed by its agents within the course and scope of employment. A corporation may be held liable for the crimes of its employees and agents if the punishment for the crimes can be applied to a corporation.

E. CORPORATE POWERS
Express powers are in (in order of priority) the U.S. Constitution, state constitution, state statutes, articles of incorporation, bylaws, and board resolutions. A corporation has the *implied* power to perform all acts reasonably appropriate and necessary to accomplish its purposes.

II. CLASSIFICATION OF CORPORATIONS

A. DOMESTIC, FOREIGN, AND ALIEN CORPORATIONS
A corporation is a **domestic corporation** in the state in which it incorporated, a **foreign corporation** in other states, and an **alien corporation** in other countries. A foreign corporation normally must obtain a certificate of authority to do business in any state except its home state.

B. CLOSE CORPORATIONS
To qualify as a **close corporation**, a firm must have a limited number of shareholders, and restrict its issue and transfer of stock.

C. S CORPORATIONS
An S corporation is a close corporation that meets certain requirements and thus qualifies for special tax treatment (taxed same as a partnership).

D. PROFESSIONAL CORPORATIONS
A shareholder in a professional corporation is normally protected from liability for torts (except malpractice) committed by other members.

III.   CORPORATE FORMATION

A. PROMOTIONAL ACTIVITIES
Promoters take the first steps in organizing a corporation: issue a prospectus (see Chapter 21) and secure the corporate charter.

B. INCORPORATION PROCEDURES
Some states have more advantageous tax or incorporation law. The articles of incorporation include basic information about the corporation and serve as a primary source of authority for its organization and functions.

IV.   CORPORATE MANAGEMENT—DIRECTORS AND OFFICERS
The board of directors governs a corporation. Officers handle daily business.

A. ELECTION OF DIRECTORS

1. Number of Directors
Set in a corporation's articles or bylaws. Corporations with fewer than fifty shareholders can eliminate the board of directors [RMBCA 8.01].

2. How Directors Are Chosen
The first board (appointed by the incorporators or named in the articles) serves until the first shareholders' meeting. Subsequent directors are elected by a majority vote of the shareholders (see below).

3. Removal of Directors
A director can be removed for cause by shareholder action (or the board may have the power). In most states, a director cannot be removed without cause, unless the shareholders have reserved the right.

B. DIRECTORS' QUALIFICATIONS AND COMPENSATION
A few states have minimum age and residency requirements. Compensation for directors is ordinarily specified in the articles or bylaws.

C. BOARD OF DIRECTORS' MEETINGS

1. Formal Minutes and Notice
A board conducts business by holding formal meetings with recorded minutes. The dates for regular meetings are set in the articles and bylaws or by board resolution. Special meetings require special notice.

2. Quorum Requirements and Voting
Quorum requirements vary. If the firm specifies none, in most states a quorum is a majority of the number of directors authorized in the articles or bylaws. Voting is done in person, one vote per director.

D. DIRECTORS' MANAGEMENT RESPONSIBILITIES

1. Areas of Responsibility
Major policy and financial decisions; appointment, supervision, pay, and removal of officers and other managerial employees.

2. Executive Committee
Most states permit a board to elect an executive committee from among the directors to handle management between board meetings. The committee is limited to ordinary business matters.

E. ROLE OF CORPORATE OFFICERS AND EXECUTIVES
The board of directors hires officers and other executive employees. Officers act as agents of the corporation (see Chapter 17).

1. Qualifications
At the discretion of the firm; included in the articles or bylaws. A person can hold more than one office and also be a director.

2. Rights and Duties
The rights of corporate officers and other high-level managers are defined by employment contracts. Normally, the board can remove officers at any time (but the corporation could be liable for breach of contract). Officers' duties are the same as those of directors.

F. DUTIES OF DIRECTORS AND OFFICERS
Directors and officers are fiduciaries of the corporation.

1. Duty of Care
Directors and officers must act in good faith, in what they consider to be the best interests of the corporation, and with the care that an ordinarily prudent person would exercise in similar circumstances.

a. Duty to Make Informed and Reasonable Decisions
Directors must be informed on corporate matters and act in accord with their knowledge and training. A director can rely on information furnished by competent officers, or others, without being accused of acting in bad faith or failing to use due care [RMBCA 8.30].

b. Duty to Exercise Reasonable Supervision
When directors delegate work to others.

2. Duty of Loyalty
Directors and officers cannot use corporate funds or confidential information for personal advantage. Specifically, they cannot—

a. Compete with the corporation.
b. Usurp a corporate opportunity.
c. Have an interest that conflicts with the interest of the corporation.
d. Engage in insider trading (see Chapter 21).
e. Authorize a corporate transaction that is detrimental to minority shareholders.

3. Conflicts of Interest
Directors and officers must disclose fully any conflict of interest that might occur in a deal involving the corporation. A contract may be upheld if it is fair and reasonable to the firm when it is made, there is full disclosure of the interest of the officers or directors involved, and it is approved by a majority of disinterested directors or shareholders.

4. The Business Judgment Rule
Honest mistakes of judgment and poor business decisions do not make directors and officers liable to the firm for poor results, if the decision complies with management's fiduciary duties, has a reasonable basis, and is within managerial authority and the power of the corporation.

V. CORPORATE OWNERSHIP—SHAREHOLDERS

A. SHAREHOLDERS' POWERS
Shareholders own the corporation, approve fundamental corporate changes, and elect and remove directors.

B. SHAREHOLDERS' MEETINGS

Regular meetings must occur annually; special meetings can be called to handle urgent matters. Rather than attend a meeting, shareholders normally authorize third parties to vote their shares. This authorization is called a **proxy**.

C. SHAREHOLDER VOTING

1. Quorum Requirements

At the meeting, a quorum must be present. A majority vote of the shares present is required to pass resolutions. Fundamental changes require a higher percentage.

2. Cumulative Voting

Each common shareholder has one vote per share. The number of board members to be elected is multiplied by the number of voting shares. This is the number of votes a shareholder has and, through cumulative voting, can be cast for one or more nominees.

D. SHAREHOLDERS' RIGHTS

1. Stock Certificates

Notice of shareholder meetings, dividends, and corporate reports are distributed to owners listed in the corporate books, not on the basis of possession of stock certificates (which most states do not require).

2. Preemptive Rights

Usually apply only to additional, newly issued stock sold for cash and must be exercised within a specified time (usually thirty days).

3. Dividends

Dividends can be paid in cash, property, or stock. Once declared, a cash dividend is a corporate debt. Dividends are payable only from (1) retained earnings, (2) current net profits, or (3) any surplus.

a. Illegal Dividends

A dividend paid when a corporation is insolvent is illegal and must be repaid. A dividend paid from an unauthorized account or causing a corporation to become insolvent may have to be repaid. In any case, the directors can be held personally liable.

b. If the Directors Fail to Declare a Dividend

Shareholders can ask a court to compel a declaration of a dividend, but the directors' conduct must be an abuse of discretion.

4. Inspection Rights

Shareholders (or their attorney, accountant, or agent) can inspect and copy corporate books and records for a proper purpose, if the request is made in advance [RMBCA 16.02].

5. Transfer of Shares

Any restrictions on transferability must be noted on the face of a stock certificate. Restrictions must be reasonable—for example, a right of first refusal remains with the corporation or the shareholders for only a specified time or a reasonable time.

6. Rights on Dissolution

Shareholders can petition a court to dissolve a firm if [RMBCA 14.30]—

a. The directors are deadlocked, shareholders are unable to break the deadlock, and there is or could be irreparable injury to the firm.
b. The acts of the directors or those in control of the corporation are illegal, oppressive, or fraudulent.
c. Corporate assets are being misapplied or wasted.

   d. Shareholders are deadlocked in voting power and have failed, for a specified period (usually two annual meetings), to elect directors.

   7. Shareholder's Derivative Suit
   If directors fail to sue in the corporate name to redress a wrong suffered by the firm, shareholders can do so (after complaining to the board). Any recovery normally goes into the corporate treasury.

VI. MERGER AND CONSOLIDATION

Whether a combination is a merger or a consolidation, the rights and liabilities of shareholders, the corporation, and its creditors are the same.

A. MERGER

1. What a Merger Is
The combination of two or more corporations, often by one absorbing the other. After a merger, only one of the corporations exists.

2. The Results of a Merger
The surviving corporation has all of the rights, assets, liabilities, and debts of itself and the other corporation. Its articles of incorporation are deemed amended to include changes stated in the articles of merger.

B. CONSOLIDATION
In a **consolidation**, two or more corporations combine so that each corporation ceases to exist and a new one emerges. The results of a consolidation are essentially the same as the results of a merger.

VII. PURCHASE OF ASSETS

A. IS SHAREHOLDER APPROVAL REQUIRED?
A corporation that buys all or substantially all of the assets of another corporation does not need shareholder approval. The corporation whose assets are acquired must obtain approval of its board and shareholders.

B. ASSUMPTION OF LIABILITY
An acquiring corporation is not responsible for the seller's liabilities, unless there is (1) an implied or express assumption, (2) a sale amounting to a merger or consolidation, (3) a buyer retaining the seller's personnel and continuing the business, or (4) a sale executed in fraud to avoid liability.

VIII. PURCHASE OF STOCK

A purchase of a substantial number of the voting shares of a corporation's stock enables an acquiring corporation to control a target corporation. The acquiring corporation deals directly with shareholders to buy shares.

A. TENDER OFFERS
A tender offer is a public offer. The offer can turn on the receipt of a specified number of shares by a specified date.

1. The Price Offered for the Target's Stock
Generally higher than the stock's market price before the tender offer. May involve an exchange of stock or cash for stock in the target.

2. Federal and State Securities Laws
Federal laws control the terms, duration, and circumstances in which most tender offers are made. Most states also impose regulations.

B. **TARGET RESPONSES**

The directors of a target must make a good faith decision as to whether the shareholders' acceptance or rejection of the offer would be most beneficial. Directors must fully disclose all material facts. To resist a takeover, among other tactics, a target may make a self-tender.

IX. TERMINATION

A. **DISSOLUTION**

Dissolution may be brought about by—

1. **An Act of the Legislature in the State of Incorporation**

2. **Expiration of the Time in the Certificate of Incorporation**

3. **Voluntary Approval of the Shareholders and the Board**

4. **Unanimous Approval of the Shareholders**

5. **Court Decree**

   a. In an action brought by the secretary of state or the state attorney general, a corporation may be dissolved for [RMBCA 14.20]—

      1) Failing to comply with corporate formalities or other administrative requirements.
      2) Procuring a charter through fraud or misrepresentation.
      3) Abusing corporate powers (*ultra vires* acts).
      4) Violating the state criminal code after a demand to discontinue the violation has been made by the secretary of state.
      5) Failing to commence business operations.
      6) Abandoning operations before starting up.

   b. In an action by shareholders, a court may dissolve a corporation when a board is deadlocked or for mismanagement [RMBCA 14.30].

B. **LIQUIDATION**

Corporate assets are converted into cash and distributed among creditors and shareholders according to specific rules.

1. **Board Supervision**

   If dissolution is by voluntary action, the members of the board act as trustees of the assets, and wind up the affairs of the corporation for the benefit of corporate creditors and shareholders.

2. **Court Supervision**

   If dissolution is involuntary, the board does not wish to act as trustee, or shareholders or creditors can show why the board should not act as trustee, a court will appoint a receiver to wind up the corporate affairs.

TRUE-FALSE QUESTIONS

(Answers at the Back of the Book)

_____ 1. A shareholder can sue a corporation, and a corporation can sue a shareholder.

_____ 2. A foreign corporation is a corporation formed in another country but doing business in the United States.

_____ 3. State corporate laws are completely uniform.

____ 4. Damages recovered in a shareholder's derivative suit are paid to the shareholder who filed the suit.

____ 5. Generally, shareholders are not personally responsible for the debts of the corporation.

____ 6. Directors, but not officers, owe a duty of loyalty to the corporation.

____ 7. The business judgment rule makes a director liable for losses to the firm in most cases.

____ 8. A self-tender is a corporation's offer to buy stock from its own shareholders.

____ 9. Dissolution of a corporation cannot occur without the unanimous approval of its shareholders.

____ 10. In a consolidation, the new corporation inherits all of the rights of the consolidating corporations.

FILL-IN QUESTIONS

(Answers at the Back of the Book)

A stock certificate may be lost or destroyed, _____(and ownership is/but ownership is not) destroyed with it. A new certificate _____ (can/cannot) be issued to replace one that has been lost or destroyed. Notice of meetings, dividends, and operational and financial reports are all distributed according to the individual _____ (in possession of the certificate/recorded as the owner in the corporation's books).

MULTIPLE-CHOICE QUESTIONS

(Answers at the Back of the Book)

____ 1. Adam and Beth want to incorporate to sell computers. The first step in the incorporation procedure is to

a. file the articles of incorporation.
b. hold the first organizational meeting.
c. obtain a corporate charter.
d. select a state in which to incorporate.

____ 2. Alpha Company is a corporation. Alpha has the implied power to

a. amend the corporate charter.
b. declare dividends.
c. file a derivative suit.
d. perform all acts reasonably appropriate and necessary to accomplish its corporate purposes.

____ 3. Responsibility for the overall management of Beta, Inc., a corporation, is entrusted to

a. the board of directors.
b. the corporate officers and managers.
c. the owners of the corporation.
d. the promoters of the corporation.

____ 4. Fred is a director of Great Sales, Inc. As a director, Fred owes Great Sales a duty of

a. care and loyalty.
b. care only.
c. loyalty only.
d. neither care nor loyalty.

___ 5. Holly is a shareholder of Interstate Products, Inc. When the directors fail to act to redress a wrong suffered by Interstate, Holly may file

a. a derivative suit.
b. a preemptive right suit.
c. a proxy suit.
d. a suit of first refusal.

___ 6. Local Business Corporation invests in intrastate businesses. In Local's state, as in most states, the minimum number of directors that must be present before its board can transact business is

a. all of the directors authorized in the articles.
b. a majority of the number authorized in the articles or bylaws.
c. any odd number.
d. one.

___ 7. Micro Company makes and sells computer chips. Like most corporations, Micro's officers are hired by its

a. directors.
b. incorporators.
c. officers.
d. shareholders.

___ 8. Alpha Corporation and Beta Company consolidate to form AB, Inc. AB assumes Alpha and Beta's

a. assets and liabilities.
b. assets only.
c. liabilities only.
d. neither assets nor liabilities.

___ 9. Gamma, Inc., is unprofitable. In a suit against Gamma, a court might order dissolution if the firm does not

a. buy its stock from its shareholders.
b. declare a dividend.
c. make a profit this year.
d. pay its taxes.

___ 10. Carl files a suit against Diners Company. While the suit is pending, Eats, Inc., merges with Diners. Eats absorbs Diners. After the merger, liability in the suit rests with

a. Carl.
b. Diners.
c. Eats.
d. the court.

SHORT ESSAY QUESTIONS

1. How do the duty of care and the duty of loyalty govern the conduct of directors and officers in a corporation?

2. What is the process by which a corporation is dissolved and liquidated?

ISSUE SPOTTERS

(Answers at the Back of the Book)

1.   Alpha Corporation's board of directors, who include Beth and Carl (officers of the firm), is deadlocked over whether to market a new product. Dan, a minority shareholder, suspects that Beth and Carl are taking advantage of the deadlock to use corporate assets (offices, equipment, supplies, staff time) to initiate a competing enterprise. Can Dan intervene?

2.   Beta Corporation has an opportunity to buy stock in Gamma, Inc. The directors decide that, instead of Beta buying the stock, the directors will buy it. Frank, a Beta shareholder, learns of the purchase and wants to sue the directors on Beta's behalf. Can he do it?

3.   Gail is Omega Corporation's majority shareholder. She owns enough stock in Omega that if she were to sell it, the sale would be a transfer of control of the firm. Does she owe a duty to Omega or the minority shareholders in selling her shares?

Chapter 21:
Financing, Investor Protection, and Online Securities Offerings

WHAT THIS CHAPTER IS ABOUT

The general purpose of securities laws is to provide sufficient, accurate information to investors to enable them to make informed buying and selling decisions about securities. This chapter provides an outline of corporate financing and federal securities laws.

CHAPTER OUTLINE

I. **CORPORATE FINANCING**

    A. **BONDS**
    Bonds are issued as evidence of funds that business firms borrow from investors. A lending agreement, or bond indenture, specifies the terms (maturity date, interest). A trustee ensures the terms are met.

    B. **STOCKS**
    The most important characteristics of stocks are (1) they need not be paid back, (2) stockholders receive dividends only when voted by the directors, (3) stockholders are the last investors to be paid on dissolution, and (4) stockholders vote for management and on major issues.

II. **THE SECURITIES AND EXCHANGE COMMISSION (SEC)**
    The SEC administers the federal securities laws and regulates the sale and purchase of securities.

    A. **THE SEC'S BASIC FUNCTIONS**

        1. Require disclosure of facts concerning offerings of certain securities.

        2. Regulate national securities trading.

        3. Investigate securities fraud.

        4. Regulate securities brokers, dealers, and investment advisers.

        5. Supervise mutual funds.

        6. Recommend sanctions in cases involving violations of securities laws. (The U.S. Department of Justice prosecutes violations.)

    B. **THE SEC'S EXPANDING REGULATORY POWERS**
    The SEC's powers include the power to seek sanctions against those who violate foreign securities laws; to suspend trading if prices rise and fall in short periods of time; to exempt persons, securities, and transactions from securities law requirements; and to require more corporate disclosure.

III. **SARBANES-OXLEY ACT OF 2002**
    Imposes strict disclosure requirements and harsh penalties for violations of securities laws.

A. RESPONSIBLE PARTIES
Chief corporate executives (CEOs and CFOs) are responsible for the accuracy and completeness of financial statements and reports filed with the SEC [Sections 302 and 906]. Penalties for knowingly certifying a report or statement that does not meet statutory requirements include up to $1 million in fines and ten years imprisonment ($5 million and twenty years for "willful" certification). Altering or destroying documents is also subject to fines and imprisonment.

B. PUBLIC COMPANY ACCOUNTING OVERSIGHT BOARD
The SEC oversees this entity, which regulates and oversees public accounting firms.

C. LIMITATIONS ON PRIVATE ACTIONS
A private action for securities fraud must be brought within two years of the discovery of the violation or five years after the violation, whichever is earlier [Section 804].

IV. SECURITIES ACT OF 1933
Requires that all essential information concerning the issuance (sales) of new securities be disclosed to investors.

A. WHAT IS A SECURITY?

1. Courts' Interpretation of the Securities Act
Securities includes investment contracts, which exist in any transaction in which a person (1) invests (2) in a common enterprise (3) reasonably expecting profits (4) derived *primarily* or *substantially* from others' managerial or entrepreneurial efforts.

2. A Security Is an Investment
Examples: stocks, bonds, investment contracts in condominiums, franchises, limited partnerships, and oil or gas or other mineral rights.

B. REGISTRATION STATEMENT
Before offering securities for sale, issuing corporations must (1) file a registration statement with the Securities and Exchange Commission (SEC) and (2) provide investors with a prospectus that describes the security being sold, the issuing corporation, and the investment or risk. These documents must be written in "plain English."

1. Contents of a Registration Statement

a. Description of the significant provisions of the security and how the registrant intends to use the proceeds of the sale.
b. Description of the registrant's properties and business.
c. Description of the management of the registrant; its security holdings; its remuneration and other benefits, including pensions and stock options; and any interests of directors or officers in any material transactions with the corporation.
d. Financial statement certified by an independent public accountant.
e. Description of pending lawsuits.

2. Twenty-Day Waiting Period after Registration
Securities cannot be sold for twenty days (oral offers can be made).

3. Advertising
During the waiting period, very limited written advertising is allowed. After the period, no written advertising is allowed, except a tombstone ad, which simply tells how to obtain a prospectus.

C. EXEMPT SECURITIES
Securities that can be sold (and resold) without being registered include—

1. **Small Offerings under Regulation A**
   An issuer's offer of up to $5 million in securities in any twelve-month period (including up to $1.5 million in nonissuer resales). The issuer must file with the SEC a notice of the issue and an offering circular (also provided to investors before the sale). A company can "test the waters" (determine potential interest) before preparing the circular.

2. **Other Exempt Securities**

   a. All bank securities sold prior to July 27, 1933.
   b. Commercial paper if maturity does not exceed nine months.
   c. Securities of charitable organizations.
   d. Securities resulting from a reorganization issued in exchange for the issuer's existing securities and certificates issued by trustees, receivers, or debtors in possession in bankruptcy (see Chapter 16).
   e. Securities issued exclusively in exchange for the issuer's existing securities, provided no commission is paid (such as stock splits).
   f. Securities issued to finance the acquisition of railroad equipment.
   g. Any insurance, endowment, or annuity contract issued by a state-regulated insurance company.
   h. Government-issued securities.
   i. Securities issued by banks, savings and loan associations, farmers' cooperatives, and similar institutions.

D. **EXEMPT TRANSACTIONS**
   Securities that can be sold without being registered include those sold in transactions that consist of—

   1. **Limited Offers (Regulation D)**
      Offers that involve a small amount of money or are not made publicly.

      a. **Small Offerings**
         Noninvestment company offerings up to $1 million in a twelve-month period [Rule 504].

      b. **Blank-Check Company Offerings**
         Offerings up to $500,000 in any one year by companies with no specific business plans are exempt if (1) no general solicitation or advertising is used, (2) the SEC is notified of the sales, and (3) precaution is taken against nonexempt, unregistered resales [Rule 504a].

      c. **Small Offerings**
         Private, noninvestment company offerings up to $5 million in a twelve-month period if (1) no general solicitation or advertising is used; (2) the SEC is notified of the sales; (3) precaution is taken against nonexempt, unregistered resales; and (4) there are no more than thirty-five unaccredited investors. If the sale involves any unaccredited investors, all investors must be given material information about the company, its business, the securities [Rule 505].

      d. **Private Offerings**
         Essentially the same requirements as Rule 505, except (1) there is no limit on the amount of the offering and (2) the issuer must believe that each unaccredited investor has sufficient knowledge or experience to evaluate the investment [Rule 506].

   2. **Small Offerings to Accredited Investors Only**
      An offer up to $5 million is exempt if (1) no general solicitation or advertising is used; (2) the SEC is notified of the sales; (3) precaution is taken against nonexempt, unregistered resales; and (4) there are no unaccredited investors [Section 4(6)].

   3. **Intrastate Issues**
      Offerings in the state in which the issuer is organized and doing business are exempt [Rule 147] if, for nine months after the sale, no resale is made to a nonresident.

4. Resales—"Safe Harbors"

Most securities can be resold without registration. Resales of blank-check company offerings [Rule 504a], small offerings [Rule 505], private offerings [Rule 506], and offers to accredited investors only [Section 4(6)] are exempt from registration if—

a. The Securities Have Been Owned for Three Years or More

If seller is not an affiliate (in control with the issuer) [Rule 144].

b. The Securities Have Been Owned for at Least Two Years

There must be adequate public information about the issuer, the securities must be sold in limited amounts in unsolicited brokers' transactions, and the SEC must be notified of the resale [Rule 144].

c. The Securities Are Sold Only to an Institutional Investor

The securities, on issue, must not have been of the same class as securities listed on a national securities exchange or a U.S. automated interdealer quotation system, and the seller on resale must take steps to tell the buyer they are exempt [Rule 144A].

E. VIOLATIONS AND PENALTIES

The SEC can bring civil actions. The U.S. Department of Justice enforces the criminal provisions. Private parties can also sue. Penalties include fines to $10,000, imprisonment for five years, or both.

V. SECURITIES EXCHANGE ACT OF 1934

Regulates the markets in which securities are traded by requiring disclosure by Section 12 companies (corporations with securities on the exchanges and firms with assets in excess of $5 million and five hundred or more shareholders).

A. INSIDER TRADING—SECTION 10(b) AND SEC RULE 10b-5

Section 10(b) proscribes the use of "any manipulative or deceptive device or contrivance in contravention of such rules and regulations as the [SEC] may prescribe." Rule 10b-5 prohibits the commission of fraud in connection with the purchase or sale of any security (registered or unregistered).

1. What Triggers Liability?

Any material omission or misrepresentation of material facts in connection with the purchase or sale of any security triggers liability.

2. What Does Not Trigger Liability?

Under the Private Securities Litigation Reform Act of 1995, financial forecasts and other forward-looking statements do not trigger liability if they include "meaningful cautionary statements identifying factors that could cause actual results to differ materially."

3. Who Can Be Liable?

Those who take advantage of inside information when they know it is unavailable to the person with whom they are dealing.

a. Insiders

These include officers, directors, majority shareholders, and persons having access to or receiving information of a nonpublic nature on which trading is based (accountants, attorneys).

b. Outsiders

1) Tipper/Tippee Theory

One who acquires inside information as a result of an insider's breach of fiduciary duty to the firm whose shares are traded can be liable, if he or she knows or should know of the breach.

        2) Misappropriation Theory
One who wrongfully obtains inside information and trades on it to his or her gain can be liable, if a duty to the lawful possessor of information was violated and harm to another results.

B. INSIDER REPORTING AND TRADING—SECTION 16(b)
Officers, directors, and shareholders owning 10 percent of the securities registered under Section 12 are required to file reports with the SEC concerning their ownership and trading of the securities.

    1. Corporation Is Entitled to All Profits
A firm can recapture *all* profits realized by an insider on *any* purchase and sale or sale and purchase of its stock in any six-month period.

    2. Applicability of Section 16(b)
Applies to stock, warrants, options, securities convertible into stock.

C. PROXY STATEMENTS—SECTION 14(a)
Regulates the solicitation of proxies from shareholders of Section 12 companies. Whoever solicits a proxy must disclose, in the proxy statement, all of the pertinent facts.

D. VIOLATIONS OF THE 1934 ACT

    1. Criminal Penalties
Maximum jail term is five years; fines up to $5 million for individuals and $2.5 million for partnerships and corporations.

    2. Civil Sanctions

        a. Insider Trading Sanctions Act of 1984
SEC can bring suit in federal court against anyone violating or aiding in a violation of the 1934 act or SEC rules. Penalties include triple the profits gained or the loss avoided by the guilty party.

        b. Insider Trading and Securities Fraud Enforcement Act of 1988
Enlarged the class of persons subject to civil liability for insider-trading violations, increased criminal penalties, and gave the SEC authority to (1) reward persons providing information and (2) make rules to prevent insider trading.

VI. REGULATION OF INVESTMENT COMPANIES
The SEC regulates investment companies and mutual funds under the Investment Company Act of 1940, the Investment Company Act Amendments of 1970, the Securities Act Amendments of 1975, and later amendments.

A. WHAT IS AN INVESTMENT COMPANY?
Any entity that (1) is engaged primarily "in the business of investing, reinvesting, or trading in securities" or (2) is engaged in such business and has more than 40 percent of the company's assets in investment securities. (Does not include banks, finance companies, and others).

B. WHAT MUST AN INVESTMENT COMPANY DO?
Register with the SEC by filing a notification of registration and, each year, file reports with the SEC. All securities must be in the custody of a bank or stock-exchange member.

C. WHAT MUST AN INVESTMENT COMPANY NOT DO?
No dividends may be paid from any source other than accumulated, undistributed net income. There are restrictions on investment activities.

VII. STATE SECURITIES LAWS

Each state regulates the offer and sale of securities within its borders. Exemptions from federal law are not exemptions from state laws, which have their own exemptions. Under the National Market Securities Improvement Act of 1996, the SEC regulates most national securities activities. The National Conference of Commissioners on Uniform State Laws recommends that the states adopt the revised Uniform Securities Act, which is designed to coordinate state and federal securities regulation and enforcement efforts.

VIII. ONLINE SECURITIES OFFERINGS AND DISCLOSURES

Federal and state laws set out the requirements for online initial public offerings. Under SEC interpretations, there is no difference in the disclosure requirements, only in the medium of disclosure, for which there may be new avenues of liability. Also, an online prospectus may not qualify for a Regulation D exemption.

IX. ONLINE SECURITIES FRAUD

Issues include the use of chat rooms to affect the price of securities, fictitious press releases, and illegal offerings. The First Amendment protects the use of chat rooms. Also, there is a distinction between statements of fact and opinion.

TRUE-FALSE QUESTIONS

(Answers at the Back of the Book)

_____ 1. A security that does not qualify for an exemption must be registered before it is offered to the public.

_____ 2. Before a security can be sold to the public, prospective investors must be provided with a prospectus.

_____ 3. Stock splits are exempt from the registration requirements of the Securities Act of 1933, if no commission is paid.

_____ 4. Sales of securities may not occur until twenty days after registration.

_____ 5. Private offerings of securities in unlimited amounts that are not generally solicited or advertised must be registered before they can be sold.

_____ 6. A proxy statement must fully and accurately disclose all of the facts that are pertinent to the matter on which shareholders are being asked to vote.

_____ 7. All states have disclosure requirements and antifraud provisions that cover securities.

_____ 8. *Scienter* is not a requirement for liability under Section 10(b) of the Securities Exchange Act of 1934.

_____ 9. No one who receives inside information as a result of another's breach of his or her fiduciary duty can be liable under SEC Rule 10b-5.

_____ 10. No security can be resold without registration.

FILL-IN QUESTIONS

(Answers at the Back of the Book)

The SEC can award "bounty" payments to persons providing information leading to the _____ (conviction/prosecution) of insider-trading violations. Civil penalties include _____ (double/triple) the profits gained or the loss avoided. Criminal penalties include maximum jail terms of _____ (five/ ten) years. Individuals and corporations _____ (may/may not) also be subject to million dollar fines.

MULTIPLE-CHOICE QUESTIONS

(Answers at the Back of the Book)

_____ 1. Beth, a director of Alpha Company, learns that an Alpha engineer has developed a new, improved product. Over the next six months, Beth buys and sells Alpha stock for a profit. Of Beth's profit, Alpha may recapture

   a. all.
   b. half.
   c. 10 percent.
   d. none.

_____ 2. Central Brokerage Associates sells securities, which include investment contracts. The definition of an investment contract does *not* include, as an element,

   a. an investment.
   b. a common enterprise.
   c. a reasonable expectation of profits.
   d. profits derived entirely from the efforts of the investor.

_____ 3. Superior, Inc., is a private, noninvestment company. In one year, Superior advertises a $300,000 offering. Concerning registration, this offering is

   a. exempt because of the low amount of the issue.
   b. exempt because it was advertised.
   c. exempt because the issuer is a private company.
   d. not exempt.

_____ 4. Huron, Inc., makes a $6 million private offering to twenty accredited investors and less than thirty unaccredited investors. Huron advertises the offering and believes that the unaccredited investors are sophisticated enough to evaluate the investment. Huron gives material information about itself, its business, and the securities to all investors. Concerning registration, this offering is

   a. exempt because of the low amount of the issue.
   b. exempt because it was advertised.
   c. exempt because the issuer believed that the unaccredited investors were sophisticated enough to evaluate the investment.
   d. not exempt.

_____ 5. Frank, an officer of Gamma, Inc., learns that Gamma has developed a new source of energy. Frank tells Gail, an outsider. They each buy Gamma stock. When the development is announced, the stock price increases, and they each immediately sell their stock. Subject to liability for insider trading is

   a. Frank and Gail.
   b. Frank only.
   c. Gail only
   d. neither Frank nor Gail.

_____ 6. Erie, Inc., is a noninvestment company. In one year, Erie advertises two $1.75 million offerings. Buying the issues are sixty accredited investors and twenty unaccredited investors. Erie gives information about itself, its business, and the securities to unaccredited investors only. Concerning registration, this offering is

   a. exempt because of the low amount of the issue.
   b. exempt because it was advertised.
   c. exempt because the unaccredited investors were informed.
   d. not exempt.

_____ 7. Ontario, Inc., in one year, advertises two $2.25 million offerings. Buying the stock are twelve accredited investors. Concerning registration, this offering is

    a. exempt because of the low amount of the issue.
    b. exempt because it was advertised.
    c. exempt from registration because only accredited investors bought stock.
    d. not exempt from registration.

_____ 8. Omega Corporation's registration statement must include

    a. a description of the accounting firm that audits Omega.
    b. a description of the security being offered for sale.
    c. a financial forecast for Omega's nest five years.
    d. all of the above.

_____ 9. National Sales, Inc., wants to make an offering of securities to the public. The offer is not exempt from registration. Before National sells these securities, it must provide _investors_ with

    a. a prospectus.
    b. a registration statement.
    c. a tombstone ad.
    d. all of the above.

_____ 10. Great Lakes Company is a private, noninvestment company. Last year, as part of a $250,000 advertised offering, Great Lakes sold stock to John, a private investor. John would now like to sell the shares. Concerning registration, this resale is

    a. exempt because of the low amount of the original issue.
    b. exempt because the offering was advertised.
    c. exempt because all resales are exempt.
    d. not exempt.

SHORT ESSAY QUESTIONS

1. What is the process by which a company sells securities to the public?

2. How is insider trading regulated by Section 10(b), SEC Rule 10b-5, and Section 16(b)?

ISSUE SPOTTERS

(Answers at the Back of the Book)

1. When a corporation wants to issue certain securities, it must provide sufficient information for an unsophisticated investor to evaluate the financial risk involved. Specifically, the law imposes liability for making a false statement or omission that is "material." What sort of information would an investor consider material?

2. Lee is an officer of Macro Oil, Inc. Lee knows that a Macro geologist has just discovered a new deposit of oil. Can Lee take advantage of this information to buy and sell Macro stock?

3. The Securities Act of 1933, the Securities Exchange Act of 1934, and other securities regulation is federal law. In-State Corporation incorporated in one state, does business exclusively in that state, and offers its securities for sale only in that state. Are there securities laws to regulate this offering?

Chapter 22:
Antitrust Law

WHAT THIS CHAPTER IS ABOUT

This chapter outlines aspects of the major antitrust statutes, including the Sherman Act and the Clayton Act. Keep in mind that the basis of the antitrust laws is a desire to foster competition (to result in lower prices and so on) by limiting restraints on trade (agreements that have the effect of reducing competition).

CHAPTER OUTLINE

I. THE SHERMAN ANTITRUST ACT
Enacted in 1890, the Sherman Act is one of the government's most powerful weapons to maintain a competitive economy.

    A. MAJOR PROVISIONS OF THE SHERMAN ACT
Section 1 requires two or more persons; cases often concern agreements (written or oral) that have a wrongful purpose and lead to a restraint of trade. Section 2 cases deal with monopolies that already exist.

    B. JURISDICTIONAL REQUIREMENTS
The Sherman Act applies to restraints that substantially affect interstate commerce. The act also covers activities by nationals that have an effect on U.S. foreign commerce.

II. SECTION 1 OF THE SHERMAN ACT

    A. *PER SE* VIOLATIONS VERSUS THE RULE OF REASON
Some trade restraints are deemed *per se* violations. Others are subject to analysis under the rule of reason.

        1. *Per Se* Violations
Agreements that are blatantly anticompetitive are illegal *per se*.

        2. Rule of Reason
A court considers the purpose of an agreement, the power of the parties, the effect of the action on trade, and in some cases, whether there are less restrictive alternatives to achieve the same goals. If the competitive benefits outweigh the anticompetitive effects, the agreement is held lawful.

    B. HORIZONTAL RESTRAINTS
Agreements that restrain competition between rivals in the same market.

        1. Price Fixing
Any agreement among competitors to fix prices is a *per se* violation.

        2. Group Boycotts
An agreement by two or more sellers to refuse to deal with a particular person or firm is a *per se* violation, if it is intended to eliminate competition or prevent entry into a given market.

        3. Horizontal Market Division
An agreement between competitors to divide up territories or customers is a *per se* violation.

    4. Trade Associations
    Businesses within the same industry or profession organized to pursue common interests. The rule of reason is applied.

C. VERTICAL RESTRAINTS
A vertical restraint is a restraint of trade that results from an agreement between firms at different levels in the manufacturing and distribution process.

    1. Territorial or Customer Restrictions
    This is an agreement between a manufacturer and a distributor or retailer to restrict sales to certain areas or customers. Judged under a rule of reason.

    2. Resale Price Maintenance Agreements
    This is an agreement between a manufacturer and a distributor or retailer in which the manufacturer specifies the retail prices of its products. Subject to the rule of reason.

    3. Refusals to Deal
    A firm is free to deal, or not, unilaterally, with whomever it wishes.

III. SECTION 2 OF THE SHERMAN ACT
This section of the Sherman Act applies to individuals and to several people; cases concern the structure of a monopoly in the marketplace and the misuse of monopoly power. Covers two distinct types of behavior: monopolization and attempts to monopolize.

A. MONOPOLIZATION
This requires two elements: (1) the possession of monopoly power in the relevant market and (2) the willful acquisition or maintenance of that power.

    1. Monopoly Power
    Monopoly power is sufficient market power to control prices and exclude competition.

        a. Market-Share Test
        A firm has monopoly power if its share of the relevant market is 70 percent or more.

        b. The Relevant Market Has Two Elements—

            1) Relevant Product Market
            All products with identical attributes and those that are sufficient substitutes for each other are included.

            2) Relevant Geographical Market
            If competitors sell in only a limited area, the geographical market is limited to that area.

    2. The Intent Requirement
    If a firm has market power as a result of a purposeful act to acquire or maintain that power through anticompetitive means, it is a violation of Section 2. Intent may be inferred from evidence that the firm had monopoly power and engaged in anticompetitive behavior.

B. ATTEMPTS TO MONOPOLIZE
Any action challenged as an attempt to monopolize must (1) be intended to exclude competitors and garner monopoly power and (2) have a dangerous probability of success.

IV. THE CLAYTON ACT
Enacted in 1914, the Clayton Act is aimed at practices not covered by the Sherman Act. Conduct is illegal only if it substantially tends to lessen competition or create monopoly power.

A. **SECTION 2—PRICE DISCRIMINATION**
Price discrimination occurs when a seller charges different prices to competitive buyers for identical goods.

1. **Elements**
(1) The seller must be engaged in interstate commerce, (2) the effect of the price discrimination must be to substantially lessen competition or create a competitive injury, and (3) a seller's pricing policies must include a reasonable prospect of the seller's recouping its losses.

2. **Exception**
When a lower price is charged temporarily and in good faith to meet another seller's equally low price to the buyer's competitor.

B. **SECTION 3—EXCLUSIONARY PRACTICES**

1. **Exclusive-Dealing Contracts**
This is a contract in which a seller forbids the buyer to buy products from the seller's competitors. Prohibited if the effect is "to substantially lessen competition or tend to create a monopoly."

2. **Tying Arrangements**
These exist when a seller conditions the sale of a product on the buyer's agreement to buy another product produced or distributed by the same seller. Legality depends on the agreement's purpose and its likely effect on competition in the relevant markets.

C. **SECTION 7—MERGERS**
A person or firm cannot hold stock or assets in another firm if the effect may be to substantially lessen competition. A crucial consideration in most cases is **market concentration** (percentage of market shares of firms in the relevant market).

1. **Horizontal Mergers**
These are mergers between firms that compete with each other in the same market. If a merger creates an entity with more than a small percentage market share, it is presumed illegal. Factors include—

a. The degree of concentration in the relevant market.
b. The ease of entry into the relevant market.
c. Economic efficiency.
d. The financial condition of the merging firms.
e. The nature and prices of the products.

2. **Vertical Mergers**
This occurs when a company at one stage of production acquires a company at a higher or lower stage of production. Legality depends on market concentration, barriers to entry into that market, and the parties' intent.

D. **SECTION 8—INTERLOCKING DIRECTORATES**
No person may be a director in two or more corporations at the same time if either firm has capital, surplus, or undivided profits of more than $20,090,000 or if a firm's competitive sales are $2,009,000 or more (as of 2004).

V.   ENFORCEMENT OF ANTITRUST LAWS

A. **U.S. DEPARTMENT OF JUSTICE (DOJ)**
The DOJ prosecutes violations of the Sherman Act as criminal or civil violations. Violations of the Clayton Act are not crimes; the DOJ can enforce it only through civil proceedings. Remedies include divestiture and dissolution.

B. FEDERAL TRADE COMMISSION (FTC)
The FTC enforces the Clayton Act; has the sole authority to enforce the Federal Trade Commission Act of 1914 (Section 5 condemns all forms of anticompetitive behavior that are not covered by other federal antitrust laws); issues administrative orders; can seek court sanctions.

C. PRIVATE PARTIES

1. **Treble Damages and Attorneys' Fees**
   Private parties can sue for treble damages and attorneys' fees under the Clayton Act if they are injured by a violation of any federal antitrust law (except the FTC Act).

2. **Injunctions**
   Private parties may seek an injunction to prevent an antitrust violation if it will injure business activities protected by the antitrust laws.

VI. EXEMPTIONS FROM ANTITRUST LAWS

A. LABOR ACTIVITIES
A labor union can lose its exemption if it combines with a nonlabor group.

B. AGRICULTURAL ASSOCIATIONS AND FISHERIES
Except exclusionary practices or restraints of trade against competitors.

C. INSURANCE COMPANIES
Exempt in most cases when state regulation exists.

D. FOREIGN TRADE
U.S. exporters may cooperate to compete with similar foreign associations (if it does not restrain trade in the United States or injure other U.S. exporters).

E. PROFESSIONAL BASEBALL
Players may sue team owners for anticompetitive practices. Other professional sports are not exempt.

F. OIL MARKETING
States set quotas on oil to be marketed in interstate commerce.

G. COOPERATIVE RESEARCH AND PRODUCTION
Cooperative research among small business firms is exempt.

H. JOINT EFFORTS TO OBTAIN LEGISLATIVE OR EXECUTIVE ACTION
Joint efforts by businesspersons to obtain executive or legislative action are exempt (*Noerr-Pennington* doctrine). Exception: an action is not protected if "no reasonable [person] could reasonably expect success on the merits" and it is an attempt to make anticompetitive use of government processes.

I. OTHER EXEMPTIONS

1. Activities approved by the president in furtherance of defense.
2. State actions, when the state policy is clearly articulated and the policy is actively supervised by the state.
3. Activities of regulated industries when federal commissions, boards, or agencies have primary regulatory authority.

TRUE-FALSE QUESTIONS

(Answers at the Back of the Book)

____ 1. A horizontal restraint results from an agreement between firms at different levels in the manufacturing and distribution process.

____ 2. An agreement that restrains competition between rivals in the same market is a vertical restraint.

____ 3. Monopoly power is market power sufficient to control prices and exclude competition.

____ 4. An exclusive dealing contract is a contract under which competitors agree to divide up customers.

____ 5. Price discrimination occurs when a seller forbids a buyer to buy products from the seller's competitors.

____ 6. A horizontal merger results when a company at one stage of production acquires another company at a higher or lower stage in the chain of production and distribution.

____ 7. A merger between firms that compete with each other in the same market is a vertical merger.

____ 8. A relevant product market consists of all products with identical attributes and those that are sufficient substitutes for each other.

____ 9. An agreement that is inherently anticompetitive is illegal *per se*.

____ 10. An agreement between competitors to fix prices is a *per se* violation.

FILL-IN QUESTIONS

(Answers at the Back of the Book)

_____ (Monopoly power / Restraint of trade) is any agreement that has the effect of reducing competition in the marketplace. _____ (Monopoly power / Restraint of trade) is an extreme amount of market power. A firm that can raise its prices somewhat without too much concern for its competitors' response has some degree of market power. Whether such power is sufficient to call it _____ (monopoly power / a restraint of trade) is one of the most difficult tasks in antitrust law.

MULTIPLE-CHOICE QUESTIONS

(Answers at the Back of the Book)

____ 1. National Coal Association (NCA) is a group of independent coal mining companies. Demand for coal falls. The price drops. Coal Refiners Association, a group of coal refining companies, agrees to buy NCA's coal and sell it according to a schedule that will increase the price. This agreement is

   a. a *per se* violation of the Sherman Act.
   b. exempt from the antitrust laws.
   c. subject to continuing review by the appropriate federal agency.
   d. subject to the rule of reason.

____ 2. International Sales, Inc. (ISI), is charged with a violation of antitrust law. ISI's conduct is a *per se* violation

   a. if the anticompetitive harm outweighs the competitive benefits.
   b. if the competitive benefits outweigh the anticompetitive harm.
   c. if the conduct is blatantly anticompetitive.
   d. only if it qualifies as an exemption.

____ 3. Techno, Inc., sells its brand-name computer equipment directly to its franchised retailers. Depending on how existing franchisees do, Techno may limit the number of franchisees in a given area to reduce intrabrand competition. Techno's restrictions on the number of dealers is

a. a *per se* violation of the Sherman Act.
b. exempt from the antitrust laws.
c. subject to continuing review by the appropriate federal agency.
d. subject to the rule of reason.

____ 4. Gamma Corporation is charged with a violation of antitrust law that requires evaluation under the rule of reason. The court will consider

a. only the purpose of the conduct.
b. only the effect of the conduct on trade.
c. only the power of the parties to accomplish what they intend.
d. the purpose of the conduct, the effect of the conduct on trade, and the power of the parties to accomplish what they intend.

____ 5. Omega, Inc., controls 80 percent of the market for telecommunications equipment in the southeastern United States. To show that Omega is monopolizing that market in violation of the Sherman Act requires proof of

a. only the possession of monopoly power in the relevant market.
b. only the willful acquisition or maintenance of monopoly power.
c. the possession of monopoly power in the relevant market and the willful acquisition or maintenance of that power.
d. none of the above.

____ 6. Handy Tools, Inc., charges Jack's Hardware five cents per item and Irma's Home Store ten cents per item for the same product. The two stores are competitors. If this substantially lessens competition, it constitutes

a. a market division.
b. an exclusionary practice.
c. a tying arrangement.
d. price discrimination.

____ 7. ABC Company is charged with a violation of antitrust law subject to evaluation under the rule of reason. ABC's conduct is unlawful

a. only if it qualifies as an exemption.
b. if the competitive benefits outweigh the anticompetitive harms.
c. if the anticompetitive harms outweigh the competitive benefits.
d. if the conduct is blatantly anticompetitive.

____ 8. Central Data Corporation and Digital, Inc., are competitors. They form a joint venture to research, develop, and produce new software for a particular line of computers. This joint venture is

a. a *per se* violation of the Sherman Act.
b. exempt from the antitrust laws.
c. subject to continuing review by the appropriate federal agency.
d. subject to the rule of reason.

____ 9. The Sherman and Clayton Acts can be enforced through civil proceedings by

  a. the U.S. Department of Justice (DOJ) only.
  b. the Federal Trade Commission (FTC) only.
  c. private parties only.
  d. the DOJ, the FTC, and private parties.

____ 10. Alpha, Inc., and Beta Corporation are competitors. They merge, and after the merger, Alpha is the surviving firm. To assess whether this is in violation of the Clayton Act requires a look at the market

  a. concentration.
  b. discrimination.
  c. division.
  d. power.

SHORT ESSAY QUESTIONS

1. How does Section 1 of the Sherman Act deal with horizontal restraints?

2. How does the Clayton Act deal with exclusionary practices?

ISSUE SPOTTERS

(Answers at the Back of the Book)

1. Able Company, a bicycle manufacturer, refuses to deal with Baker Bikes, a retailer. In what circumstances might Able's refusal to deal with Baker violate antitrust law?

2. Under what circumstances would Pop's Market, a small store in a small, isolated town, be considered a monopolist? If Pop's is a monopolist, is it in violation of Section 2 of the Sherman Act?

3. Maple Corporation conditions the sale of its syrup on the buyer's agreement to buy Maple's pancake mix. What factors would a court consider to decide whether this arrangement violates the Clayton Act?

Chapter 23:
Personal Property, Bailments, and Insurance

WHAT THIS CHAPTER IS ABOUT

This chapter covers the nature of personal property, forms of property ownership, the acquisition of personal property, bailments, and insurance. Note that personal property can be tangible (such as a car) or intangible (such as stocks, bonds, patents, or copyrights).

CHAPTER OUTLINE

I. PROPERTY OWNERSHIP
Ownership can be viewed as the rights to possess property and to dispose of it.

A. FEE SIMPLE
A person who holds all of the rights is an owner in fee simple. On death, the owner's interest descends to his or her heirs.

B. CONCURRENT OWNERSHIP
Persons who share ownership rights simultaneously are concurrent owners.

1. Tenancy in Common
A tenancy in common exists when each of two or more persons owns an undivided interest (each has rights in the whole—if each had rights in specific items, the interests would be divided). On death, a tenant's interest passes to his or her heirs.

2. Joint Tenancy
This occurs when each of two or more persons owns an undivided interest in the property; a deceased joint tenant's interest passes to the surviving joint tenant or tenants. Can be terminated at any time before a joint tenant's death by gift or by sale.

3. Tenancy by the Entirety
A transfer of real property to a husband and wife can create a tenancy by the entirety; neither spouse can transfer separately his or her interest during his or her life.

4. Community Property
Each spouse owns an undivided half interest in property that either spouse acquired during the marriage. This is recognized in only some states.

II. ACQUIRING OWNERSHIP OF PERSONAL PROPERTY

A. POSSESSION
An example of acquiring ownership by possession is the capture of wild animals. (Exceptions: (1) wild animals captured by a trespasser are the property of the landowner, and (2) wild animals captured or killed in violation of statutes are the property of the state.)

B. PRODUCTION
Those who produce personal property have title to it. (Exception: employees do not own what they produce for their employers.)

C. GIFTS
A **gift** is a voluntary transfer of property ownership not supported by consideration.

1. Requirements for an Effective Gift
There are three requirements for an effective gift—

a. Donative Intent
Determined from the language of the donor and the surrounding circumstances (relationship between the parties and the size of the gift in relation to the donor's other assets).

b. Delivery

1) Constructive Delivery
If a physical object cannot be delivered, an act that the law holds to be equivalent to an act of real delivery is sufficient (a key to a safe-deposit box for the contents of the box, for example).

2) Delivery by a Third Person
If the person is the donor's agent, the gift is effective when the agent delivers the property to the donee. If the person is the donee's agent, the gift is effective when the donor delivers the property to the agent.

3) Giving Up Control
Effective delivery requires giving up control over the property.

c. Acceptance
Courts assume a gift is accepted unless shown otherwise.

2. Gifts *Inter Vivos* and Gifts *Causa Mortis*
Gifts *inter vivos* are made during one's lifetime. Gifts *causa mortis* are made in contemplation of imminent death, do not become effective until the donor dies, and are automatically revoked if the donor does not die.

D. ACCESSION
Accession occurs when someone adds value to a item of personal property by labor or materials. Ownership can be at issue if—

1. Accession Occurs without Permission of the Owner
Courts tend to favor the owner over the one who improved the property (and deny the improver any compensation for the value added).

2. Accession Greatly Increases the Value or Changes the Identity
If the accession is in good faith, then the greater the increase, the more likely that ownership will pass to the improver, who must compensate the original owner for the value of the property before the accession.

E. CONFUSION
Commingling goods so that one person's cannot be distinguished from another's. Frequently involves fungible goods. If goods are confused due to a wrongful act, the innocent party acquires all. If confusion is by agreement, mistake, or a third party's act, the owners share as tenants in common.

III. MISLAID, LOST, AND ABANDONED PROPERTY

A. MISLAID PROPERTY
Mislaid property is property that has been voluntarily placed somewhere by the owner and then inadvertently forgotten. When the property is found, the owner of the place where it was mislaid (not the finder) becomes the caretaker.

B. LOST PROPERTY
Lost property is property that is involuntarily left. A finder can claim title against the whole world, except the true owner. Many states require the finder to make a reasonably diligent search to locate the true owner. *Estray statutes* allow finders, after passage of a specified time, to acquire title to the property if it remains unclaimed.

C. ABANDONED PROPERTY
Abandoned property is property that has been discarded by the true owner, who has no intention of claiming title to it. A finder acquires title good against the whole world, including the original owner. A trespasser does not acquire title, however; the owner of the real property on which it was found does.

IV. BAILMENTS
A bailment is formed by the delivery of personal property, without transfer of title, by a bailor to a bailee, usually under an agreement for a particular purpose, after which the property is returned or otherwise disposed of.

A. ELEMENTS OF A BAILMENT

1. **Personal Property**
Only personal property is bailable.

2. **Delivery of Possession (Without Title)**
A bailee must (1) be given exclusive possession and control of the property and (2) knowingly accept it. Delivery may be actual or constructive.

3. **Bailment Agreement**
The agreement must provide for the return of the property to the bailor or a third person, or for its disposal by the bailee.

B. ORDINARY BAILMENTS
The three types of ordinary bailments are: (1) bailment for the sole benefit of the bailor, (2) bailment for the sole benefit of the bailee, and (3) bailment for their mutual benefit.

1. **Rights of the Bailee**

    a. **Right to Control and Possess the Property**
    This right permits a bailee to recover damages from any third persons for damage or loss to the property.

    b. **Right to Use the Property**
    The extent to which a bailee can use property depends on the bailment agreement.

    c. **Right to Be Compensated**
    A bailee has a right to be compensated as agreed and to be reimbursed for costs and services in the keeping of the property. To enforce the right, a bailee can put a possessory lien on the property.

    d. **Right to Limit Liability**
    Bailees can limit their liability as long as—

        1) **Limitations Are Called to the Attention of the Bailor**
        Fine print on the back of a ticket stub is not sufficient.

        2) **Limitations Are Not Against Public Policy**
        If a bailee attempts to exclude liability for his or her own negligence, the clause is unenforceable.

2. **Duties of the Bailee**

a. Duty of Care

A bailment for the sole benefit of the bailor requires a slight degree of care; a bailment for the sole benefit of the bailee requires great care. A mutual-benefit bailment requires reasonable care. Failure to use the right amount of care results in tort liability.

b. Duty to Return Bailed Property

When a bailment ends, the bailee must relinquish the property. Failure to do so is a breach of contract (unless the property is destroyed, lost, or stolen through no fault of the bailee, or given to a third party with a superior claim) and could be conversion.

c. Presumption of Negligence

If a bailee has the property and damage occurs that normally results only from someone's negligence, the bailee's negligence is presumed. The bailee must prove he or she was not at fault.

3. Rights of the Bailor

The bailor's rights are essentially the same as the duties of the bailee.

4. Duties of the Bailor

A bailor has a duty to provide the bailee with goods free from defects that could injure the bailee.

a. Bailor's Duty Has Two Aspects

1) In a mutual-benefit bailment, bailor must notify bailee of all known defects and any hidden defects that the bailor knew of or could have discovered with reasonable diligence and proper inspection.

2) In a bailment for the sole benefit of the bailee, the bailor must notify the bailee of any known defects.

b. To Whom Does Liability Extend?

Liability extends to anyone who might be expected to come in contact with the goods. A bailor may also be liable under UCC Article 2A's implied warranties.

C. SPECIAL TYPES OF BAILMENTS

1. Common Carriers

Common carriers are publicly licensed to provide transportation services to the general public.

a. Strict Liability

Common carriers are absolutely liable, regardless of negligence, for all loss or damage to goods in their possession, except if it is caused by an act of God, an act of a public enemy, an order of a public authority, an act of the shipper, or the nature of the goods.

b. Limits to Liability

Common carriers can limit their liability to an amount stated on the shipment contract.

2. Warehouse Companies

Warehouse companies are liable for loss or damage to property resulting from negligence. A warehouse company can limit the dollar amount of liability, but the bailor must be given the option of paying an increased storage rate for an increase in the liability limit.

3. Innkeepers

Those who provide lodging to the public for compensation as a regular business are strictly liable for injuries to guests.

a. Hotel Safes

In many states, innkeepers can avoid strict liability for loss of guests' valuables by providing a safe. Statutes often limit the liability of innkeepers for articles that are not kept in the safe.

    b. Parking Facilities

    If an innkeeper provides parking facilities, and the guest's car is entrusted to the innkeeper, the innkeeper will be liable under the rules that pertain to parking lot bailments (ordinary bailments).

V. INSURANCE

A. RISK MANAGEMENT

Risk management consists of plans to protect personal and financial interests should some event undermine their security. The most common method is to transfer risk from a business or individual to an insurance company.

B. CLASSIFICATIONS OF INSURANCE

Insurance is classified according to the nature of the risk involved.

C. INSURANCE TERMINOLOGY

An insurance company is an *underwriter* or an insurer; the party covered by insurance is the *insured*; an insurance contract is a *policy*; consideration paid to an insurer is a *premium*; policies are obtained through an *agent* or *broker*.

D. INSURABLE INTEREST

To obtain insurance, one must have a sufficient interest in what is insured.

    1. Property Insurance

    One has an insurable interest in property if one would suffer a pecuniary loss from its destruction. This interest must exist *when the loss occurs*.

    2. Life Insurance

    One must have a reasonable expectation of benefit from the continued life of another. The benefit may be related to money or may be founded on a relationship (by blood or affinity).

        a. Key-Person Insurance

        A business (partnership, corporation) can insure the life of an employee who is important to that organization (partner, officer).

        b. When the Insurable Interest Must Exist

        An interest in someone's life must exist *when the policy is obtained*.

E. THE INSURANCE CONTRACT

    1. Application

    The application is part of the contract. Misstatements can void a policy, especially if the insurer shows that it would not have issued the policy if it had known the facts.

    2. Effective Date

    A policy is effective when (1) a binder is written, (2) the policy is issued, or (3) a certain time elapses.

        a. When a Policy Is Obtained from a Broker

        A broker is the agent of the applicant. Until the broker obtains a policy, the applicant is normally not insured.

        b. When a Policy Is Obtained from an Agent

        An agent is the agent of the insurer. One who obtains a policy from an agent can be protected from the moment the application is made (under a binder), or the parties may agree to delay coverage until a policy is issued or some condition is met (such as a physical exam).

3. **Provisions and Clauses**

An ambiguity in the policy will be interpreted against the insurer. Some important clauses include—

a. **Coinsurance Clause**

If an owner insures property up to a specified percentage (usually 80 percent) of its value, he or she will recover any loss up to the face amount of the policy. If the insurance is for less than this percentage, the owner is responsible for a proportionate share.

b. **Incontestability Clause**

After a policy has been in force for a certain time (two or three years), the insurer cannot cancel the policy or avoid a claim on the basis of statements made in the application.

4. **Cancellation**

A policy may be canceled for nonpayment of premiums, fraud or misrepresentation, conviction for a crime that increases the hazard insured against, or gross negligence that increases the hazard insured against. An insurer may be required to give advance written notice.

5. **Good Faith Obligations**

Parties must act in good faith and disclose all material facts. If there is a claim, the insurer must investigate. Insurer and insured must fulfill the terms of the policy.

6. **Defenses against Payment**

Fraud, misrepresentation, violation of warranties, and improper actions that are against public policy or that are otherwise illegal.

TRUE-FALSE QUESTIONS

(Answers at the Back of the Book)

____ 1. To constitute a gift, a voluntary transfer of property must be supported by consideration.

____ 2. If an accession is performed in good faith, the improver keeps the property as improved.

____ 3. One who finds abandoned property acquires title to it good against the original owner.

____ 4. In some ordinary bailments, bailees can limit their liability.

____ 5. Warehouse companies have the same duty of care as ordinary bailees.

____ 6. Risk management involves the transfer of certain risks from the insured to the insurer.

____ 7. Insurance is classified by the nature of the person or interest protected.

____ 8. An insurance broker is an agent of an insurance company.

____ 9. An insurance applicant is usually protected from the time an application is made, if a premium has been paid, possibly subject to certain conditions.

____ 10. A person can insure anything in which he or she has an insurable interest.

FILL-IN QUESTIONS

(Answers at the Back of the Book)

A gift made during the donor's lifetime is a gift _____ (*causa mortis/inter vivos*).
A gift _____ (*causa mortis/inter vivos*) is made in contemplation of imminent death.

Gifts _____ (*causa mortis/inter vivos*) do not become absolute until the donor dies from the contemplated illness or disease. A gift _____ (*causa mortis/inter vivos*) is revocable at any time up to the death of the donor and is automatically revoked if the donor recovers. A gift _____ (*causa mortis/inter vivos*) is revocable at any time before the donor's death.

MULTIPLE-CHOICE QUESTIONS

(Answers at the Back of the Book)

____ 1. Nan sells her boat to Owen and Pat, who are not married. The contract of sale says that the buyers each have a right of survivorship in the boat. Owen and Pat own the boat as

a. community property.
b. joint tenants.
c. tenants by the entirety.
d. tenants in common.

____ 2. Dina wants to give Edie a pair of diamond earrings that Dina has in her safe-deposit box at First City Bank. Dina gives Edie the key to the box and tells her to go to the bank and take the earrings from the box. Edie does so. Two days later, Dina dies. The earrings belong to

a. Dina's heirs.
b. Edie.
c. First City Bank.
d. the state.

____ 3. Jan, Ken, and Lee store their grain in three silos. Jan contributes half of the grain, Ken a third, and Lee a sixth. A tornado hits two of the silos and scatters the grain. Of the grain that is left

a. Jan and Ken split it equally because they lost the most.
b. Jan, Ken, and Lee share it equally.
c. Jan owns half, Ken a third, and Lee a sixth.
d. Ken owns it all because only a third is left.

____ 4. Pam parks her car in an unattended lot behind a Quik Mart store, which is closed. Pam locks the car and takes the keys. This is *not* a bailment because there is *no*

a. contract.
b. money.
c. personal property.
d. transfer of possession.

____ 5. Able Corporation ships goods via Baker Transport Company. Baker will *not* be liable for the loss of the goods if they are

a. crushed in a warehouse accident that is the fault of Baker's crane operator.
b. damaged because Able failed to package the goods properly.
c. destroyed in a traffic accident that is the fault of Baker's truck driver.
d. stolen by an unknown person.

____ 6. Ruth applies to Standard Insurance Company for a fire insurance policy for her warehouse. To obtain a lower premium, she misrepresents the age of the property. The policy is granted. After the warehouse is destroyed by fire, Standard learns the true facts. Standard can

a. not refuse to pay, because an application is not part of an insurance contract.
b. not refuse to pay, because fire destroyed the warehouse.
c. refuse to pay on the ground of fraud in the application.
d. refuse to pay on the ground that fire destroyed the warehouse.

____   7.   Carl is an executive with DigiCom, Inc. Because his death would cause a financial loss to the firm, it insures his life. Later, he resigns to work for a competitor, E-Tech Corporation. Six months later, Carl dies. Regarding payment for the loss, DigiCom can

a.   collect, because the firm's insurable interest existed when the policy was obtained.
b.   collect if the firm suffered a financial loss when Carl resigned.
c.   not collect, because the firm's insurable interest did not exist when a loss occurred.
d.   not collect, because the firm suffered no financial loss from Carl's death.

____   8.   Tom buys a house and obtains from Union Insurance Company a fire insurance policy on the property. If fire destroys the house, to collect payment under the policy, Tom's insurable interest

a.   exists only if the property is owned by Tom or a related individual.
b.   exists only if the property is owned in fee simple.
c.   must exist when the loss occurs.
d.   must exist when Union issues the policy and when the loss occurs.

____   9.   Satellite Communications, Inc., takes out an insurance policy on its plant with United Insurance, Inc. United could cancel the policy

a.   for any reason.
b.   if any of Satellite's drivers have their driver's licenses suspended.
c.   if Satellite begins using grossly careless manufacturing practices.
d.   if Satellite's president appears as a witness in a case against United.

____   10.   Tech Corporation makes computers. To insure its products to cover injuries to consumers if the products prove defective, Tech should buy

a.   group insurance.
b.   liability insurance.
c.   major medical insurance.
d.   term life insurance.

SHORT ESSAY QUESTIONS

1.   What are the principal features of the forms of concurrent property ownership: tenancies in common, joint tenancies, tenancies by the entirety, and community property?

2.   What is the concept of insurable interest, and what is its effect on insurance payments?

ISSUE SPOTTERS

1.   Alpha Corporation sends important documents to Beta, Inc., via Speedy Messenger Service. While the documents are in Speedy's care, a third party causes an accident to Speedy's delivery vehicle that results in the loss of the documents. Does Speedy have a right to recover from the third party for the loss of the documents?

2.   Ed applies to Farm Insurance Company for a life insurance policy. On the application, Ed understates his age. Ed obtains the policy, but for a lower premium than he would have had to pay had he disclosed his actual age. The policy includes an incontestability clause. Six years later, Ed dies. Can the insurer refuse payment?

3.   Adam is divorced and owns a house. He has no reasonable expectation of benefit from the life of Beth, his ex-spouse, but applies for insurance on her life anyway. He obtains a fire insurance policy on the house and then sells the house. Ten years later, Beth dies and fire destroys the house. Can Adam obtain payment for these events?

Chapter 24:
Real Property and Environmental Law

WHAT THIS CHAPTER IS ABOUT

This chapter covers ownership rights in real property, including the nature of those rights and their transfer. The chapter also outlines the right of the government to take private land for public use, zoning laws, other restrictions on ownership, including federal laws that protect the environment.

CHAPTER OUTLINE

I. THE NATURE OF REAL PROPERTY
Real property consists of land and the buildings, plants, and trees on it.

A. LAND
Includes the soil on the surface of the earth, natural products or artificial structures attached to it, the water on or under it, and the air space above.

B. AIR AND SUBSURFACE RIGHTS
Limitations on air rights or subsurface rights normally have to be indicated on the deed transferring title at the time of purchase.

1. Air Rights
Flights over private land do not normally violate the owners' rights.

2. Subsurface Rights
Ownership of the surface can be separated from ownership of the subsurface. Conflicts may arise between surface and subsurface owners' interests.

C. PLANT LIFE AND VEGETATION
A sale of land with growing crops on it includes the crops, unless otherwise agreed. When crops are sold by themselves, they are personal property.

D. FIXTURES
Personal property so closely associated with certain real property that it is viewed as part of it (such as plumbing in a building). Fixtures are included in a sale of land if the contract does not provide otherwise.

II. OWNERSHIP INTERESTS IN REAL PROPERTY

A. OWNERSHIP IN FEE SIMPLE
A fee simple owner has the most rights possible—he or she can give the property away, sell it, transfer it by will, use it for almost any purpose, and possess it to the exclusion of all the world—potentially forever.

B. LIFE ESTATES
A life estate lasts for the life of a specified individual ("to A for his life"). A life tenant can use the land (but not commit waste), mortgage the life estate, and create liens, easements, and leases (but no longer than the life estate).

C. NONPOSSESSORY INTERESTS

1. Easements and Profits
Easement: the right of a person to make limited use of another person's land without taking anything from the property. *Profit*: the right to go onto another's land and take away a part or product of the land.

2. License
This is the revocable right of a person to come onto another person's land.

III. TRANSFER OF OWNERSHIP

A. DEEDS
Possession and title to land can be passed by deed without consideration.

1. Requirements
(1) Names of the grantor and grantee, (2) words evidencing an intent to convey, (3) legally sufficient description of the land, (4) grantor's (and sometimes spouse's) signature, and (5) delivery.

2. Warranty Deed
This provides the most protection against defects of title—covenants that grantor has title to, and power to convey, the property; that the property is not subject to any outstanding interests that diminish its value; and that the buyer will not be disturbed in his or her possession.

3. Special Warranty Deed
This warrants only that the grantor held good title during his or her ownership of the property, not that there were no title defects when others owned it. If all liens and encumbrances are disclosed, the seller is not liable if a third person interferes with the buyer's ownership.

4. Quitclaim Deed
This warrants less than any other deed. It conveys to the grantee only the interest the grantor had.

5. Recording Statutes
Recording statutes require transfers to be recorded in public records (generally in the county in which the property is located) to give notice to the public that a certain person is the owner. Many states require the grantor's signature and two witnesses' signatures.

B. WILL OR INHERITANCE
Transfers by will or inheritance on the owner's death are possible.

C. ADVERSE POSSESSION
A person who possesses another's property acquires title good against the original owner if the possession is (1) actual and exclusive; (2) open, visible, and notorious; (3) continuous and peaceable for a required period of time; and (4) hostile, as against the whole world.

D. EMINENT DOMAIN
The government can take private property for public use. To obtain title, a condemnation proceeding is brought. The Fifth Amendment requires that just compensation be paid for a *taking*; thus, in a separate proceeding a court determines the land's fair value (usually market value) to pay the owner.

IV. LEASEHOLD ESTATES
Created when an owner or landlord conveys a right to possess and use property to a tenant. The tenant's interest is a leasehold estate.

A. TENANCY FOR YEARS
Created by an express contract by which property is leased for a specific period (a month, a year, a period of years). At the end of the period, the lease ends (without notice). If the tenant dies during the lease, the lease interest passes to the tenant's heirs.

B. PERIODIC TENANCY

Created by a lease that specifies only that rent is to be paid at certain intervals. Automatically renews unless terminated. Terminates, at common law, on one period's notice.

C. TENANCY AT WILL

A tenancy for as long as the landlord and tenant agree. Exists when a tenant for years retains possession after termination with the landlord's consent before payment of the next rent (when it becomes a periodic tenancy). Terminates on the death of either party or tenant's commission of waste.

D. TENANCY AT SUFFERANCE

Possession of land without right (without the owner's permission). Owner can immediately evict the tenant.

V.   LANDLORD-TENANT RELATIONSHIPS

A.   CREATING THE LANDLORD-TENANT RELATIONSHIP

1. Form of the Lease

To ensure the validity of a lease, it should be in writing and—

a. Express an intent to establish the relationship.
b. Provide for transfer of the property's possession to the tenant at the beginning of the term.
c. Provide for the landlord to retake possession at the end of the term.
d. Describe the property (include the address).
e. Indicate the length of term and the amount and due dates of rent.

2. Legal Requirements

A landlord cannot discriminate against tenants on the basis of race, color, religion, national origin, or sex. A tenant cannot promise to do something against these (or other) laws.

B.   RIGHTS AND DUTIES

1. Possession

a. Landlord's Duty to Deliver Possession

A landlord must give a tenant possession of the property at the beginning of the term.

b. Tenant's Right to Retain Possession

The tenant retains possession exclusively until the lease expires.

c. Covenant of Quiet Enjoyment

The landlord promises that during the lease term no one having superior title to the property will disturb the tenant's use and enjoyment of it. If so, the tenant can sue for damages for breach.

d. Eviction

If the landlord deprives the tenant of possession of the property or interferes with his or her use or enjoyment of it, an eviction occurs. *Constructive eviction* occurs when this results from a landlord's failure to perform adequately his or her duties under the lease.

2. Use and Maintenance of the Premises

a. Tenant's Use

Generally, a tenant may make any legal use of the property, as long as it is reasonably related to the purpose for which the property is ordinarily used and does not harm the landlord's interest. A tenant is not responsible for ordinary wear and tear.

b. Landlord's Maintenance

A landlord must comply with local building codes.

3. Implied Warranty of Habitability

In most states, a landlord must furnish residential premises that are habitable. This applies to substantial defects that the landlord knows or should know about and has had a reasonable time to repair.

4. Rent

A tenant must pay rent even if he or she moves out or refuses to move in (if the move is unjustifiable). If the landlord violates the implied warranty of habitability, a tenant may withhold rent, pay for repair and deduct the cost, cancel the lease, or sue for damages.

C. TRANSFERRING RIGHTS TO LEASED PROPERTY

1. Transferring the Landlord's Interest

A landlord can sell, give away, or otherwise transfer his or her real property. If complete title is transferred, the tenant becomes the tenant of the new owner, who must also abide by the lease.

2. Transferring the Tenant's Interest

Before a tenant can assign or sublet his or her interest, the landlord's consent may be required (it cannot be unreasonably withheld). If the assignee or sublessee later defaults, the tenant must pay the rent.

VI. ENVIRONMENTAL LAW

A. STATE AND LOCAL REGULATION

States regulate the environment through zoning or more direct regulation. Local governments regulate through zoning laws, waste removal and disposal regulations, aesthetic ordinances, and so on.

B. FEDERAL REGULATION

1. Environmental Protection Agency (EPA)

Coordinates federal environmental responsibilities and administers most federal environmental policies and statutes.

2. National Environmental Policy Act (NEPA) of 1969

Requires all federal agencies to consider environmental factors when making significant decisions.

a. When Must an Environmental Impact Statement (EIS) Be Prepared?

When a major federal action significantly affects the quality of the environment. An action is *major* if it involves substantial commitment of resources. An action is *federal* if a federal agency has the power to control it.

b. What Must an EIS Analyze?

(1) Impact on the environment that the action will have, (2) any adverse effects to the environment and alternative actions that might be taken, (3) irreversible effects the action might generate.

c. Can an Agency Decide Not to Issue an EIS?

Yes, but it must issue a statement explaining why an EIS is unnecessary.

C. AIR POLLUTION

The Clean Air Act of 1963 (and amendments) is the basis for regulation.

1. Mobile Sources

Regulations governing air pollution from automobiles and other mobile sources specify standards and time schedules. For example, under the 1990 amendments to the Clean Air Act—

a. New Automobiles' Exhaust

Manufacturers had to cut emission of nitrogen oxide by 60 percent and emission of other pollutants by 35 percent. Other sets of emission controls go into effect in 2004 and 2007.

b. EPA Action

If a vehicle does not meet the standards, the EPA can order a recall and repair or replacement of pollution-control devices.

c. Gasoline

Service stations must sell gasoline with higher oxygen content.

2. Stationary Sources

The EPA sets air quality standards for stationary sources (such as industrial plants), and the states formulate plans to achieve them. For example, under the 1990 amendments to the Clean Air Act—

a. Major New Sources

These sources must use the *maximum achievable control technology (MACT)* to reduce emissions from the combustion of fossil fuels (coal and oil).

b. Other Factories and Businesses

Industrial emissions of hazardous air pollutants must be reduced through use of the *best available technology*.

3. Hazardous Air Pollutants

Industrial emissions of 189 specific hazardous air pollutants must be reduced by 90 percent by 2000 (through MACT). Certain landfills must install air-pollution collection and control systems.

4. Penalties

Civil penalties of up to $25,000 per day, or an amount equal to a violator's economic benefits from noncompliance. Criminal fines are possible. Private citizens can sue violators.

D. WATER POLLUTION

1. Navigable Waters

The Clean Water Act of 1972 amended the Federal Water Pollution Control Act (FWPCA) of 1948 to provide—

a. Goals

(1) Make waters safe for swimming, (2) protect fish and wildlife, (3) eliminate the discharge of pollutants into the water.

b. Limits on Discharges Based on *Best Available Technology*

Time schedules (extended by amendment in 1977 and by the Water Quality Act of 1987) limit discharges of pollutants.

c. Permits

Municipal and industrial polluters must obtain permits before discharging wastes into navigable waters. Filling or dredging wetlands requires a permit from the Army Corps of Engineers.

d. Penalties and Remedies

Civil penalties from $10,000 per day (up to $25,000 per violation) to $25,000 per day. Criminal penalties from fines of $2,500 per day to $1 million total and one to fifteen years' imprisonment. Injunctions, damages, and clean-up costs can be imposed.

2. Drinking Water

The Safe Drinking Water Act of 1974 requires the EPA to set maximum levels for pollutants in public water systems. Operators must come as close as possible to the standards using the best available technology.

3. Ocean Dumping

The Marine Protection, Research, and Sanctuaries Act of 1972 (the Ocean Dumping Act) prohibits the ocean dumping of radiological, chemical, and biological-warfare agents and high-level radioactive waste. Civil penalty: $50,000. Criminal penalties: fine ($50,000) or imprisonment (up to a year).

4. Oil Spills
The Oil Pollution Act of 1990 provides that any oil facility, oil shipper, vessel owner, or vessel operator that discharges oil may be liable for clean-up costs, damages, and fines of up to $25,000 per day.

E. NOISE POLLUTION
Under the Noise Control Act of 1972, the EPA sets maximum levels for noise. The act requires use of the best available technology. Injunctions may be imposed. Penalties include fines of up to $50,000 per day and up to two years' imprisonment.

F. TOXIC CHEMICALS

1. Pesticides and Herbicides
Federal Insecticide, Fungicide, and Rodenticide Act (FIFRA) of 1947—

a. Registration, Certification, and Use
Pesticides and herbicides must be (1) registered before they can be sold, (2) certified and used only for approved applications, and (3) used in limited quantities when applied to food crops.

b. Labels
Labels must include directions for use of a pesticide or herbicide, warnings to protect human health and the environment, a statement of treatment in the case of poisoning, and a list of the ingredients.

c. Penalties
For registrants and producers: fine of up to $50,000, imprisonment up to one year. For commercial dealers: $25,000, one year. For farmers and other private users: $1,000, thirty days.

2. Toxic Substances
Under the Toxic Substances Control Act of 1976, for substances that potentially pose an imminent hazard or an unreasonable risk of injury to health or the environment, the EPA may require special labeling, set production quotas, or limit or prohibit the use of a substance.

G. HAZARDOUS WASTE DISPOSAL

1. Resource Conservation and Recovery Act (RCRA) of 1976
The EPA determines which forms of solid waste are hazardous, and sets requirements for disposal, storage, and treatment. Penalties include up to $25,000 (civil) per violation, $50,000 (criminal) per day, imprisonment up to two years (may be doubled for repeaters).

2. Superfund
The Comprehensive Environmental Response, Compensation, and Liability Act (CERCLA) of 1980 regulates the clean up of leaking hazardous waste disposal sites. If a release or a threatened release occurs, the EPA can clean up the site and recover the cost from—

a. Potentially Responsible Parties
(1) The person who generated the wastes disposed of at the site, (2) the person who transported the wastes to the site, (3) the person who owned or operated the site at the time of the disposal, or (4) the current owner or operator.

b. Joint and Several Liability
One party can be charged with the entire cost (which that party may recover in a contribution action against others).

TRUE-FALSE QUESTIONS

(Answers at the Back of the Book)

____   1.   A fee simple absolute is potentially infinite in duration and can be disposed of by deed or by will.

____   2.   The owner of a life estate has the same rights as a fee simple owner.

____   3.   An easement allows a person to use land and take something from it, but a profit allows a person only to use land.

____   4.   Deeds offer different degrees of protection against defects of title.

____   5.   The government can take private property for *public* use without just compensation.

____   6.   A covenant of quiet enjoyment guarantees that a tenant will not be disturbed in his or her possession of leased property by the landlord or any third person.

____   7.   Generally, a tenant must pay rent even if he or she moves out, if the move is unjustifiable.

____   8.   When a landlord sells leased premises to a third party, any existing leases terminate automatically.

____   9.   Under federal environmental laws, there is a single standard for all polluters and all pollutants.

____   10.   If a release of hazardous waste occurs at a hazardous waste disposal site, the Environmental Protection Agency (EPA) can clean it up and recover the entire cost from a potentially responsible party.

FILL-IN QUESTIONS

(Answers at the Back of the Book)

The deed that provides the most protection against defects of title is the _____ (warranty/special warranty/quitclaim) deed. Among other things, it covenants that the transfer is made without any unknown adverse claims of third parties. The deed that warrants only that the grantor has done nothing to lessen the value of the property is the _____ (warranty/special warranty/quitclaim) deed. Under this deed, the seller may not be liable if a third person interferes with the buyer's ownership. The deed that warrants less than any other deed is the _____ (warranty/special warranty/quitclaim) deed. This deed conveys to the grantee only whatever interest the grantor had.

MULTIPLE-CHOICE QUESTIONS

(Answers at the Back of the Book)

____   1.   Eve owns two hundred acres next to Floyd's lumber mill. Eve sells to Floyd the privilege of removing the timber from her land. This privilege is

a.   a leasehold estate.
b.   a license.
c.   an easement.
d.   a profit.

____   2.   Investors Property, Inc., sells an office building to Jill with a deed that makes the greatest number of warranties and provides the most extensive protection against defects of title. This deed is

a.   a grant deed.
b.   a quitclaim deed.
c.   a special warranty deed.
d.   a warranty deed.

____ 3. Dora owns a half-acre of land fronting Eagle Lake. Frank owns the property behind Dora's land. Dora has a right to drive across Frank's land to reach an access road. This right is

a. a leasehold estate.
b. a license.
c. an easement.
d. a profit.

____ 4. Curt operates Diners Cafe in space that he leases in East Mall, which is owned by First Property Company. First sells the mall to Great Investments, Inc. For the rest of the lease term, Curt owes rent to

a. Diners Cafe.
b. First Property.
c. Great Investments.
d. no one.

____ 5. Sue signs a lease for an apartment, agreeing to make rental payments before the fifth of each month. The lease does not specify a termination date. This is

a. a periodic tenancy.
b. a tenancy at sufferance.
c. a tenancy at will.
d. a tenancy for years.

____ 6. The U.S. Department of the Interior's approval of coal mining operations in several western states requires an environmental impact statement

a. because it affects the quality of the environment, is "federal," and is "major."
b. only because it affects the quality of the environment.
c. only because it is "federal."
d. only because it is "major."

____ 7. Red Glow Power Plant burns fossil fuels. Under the Clean Air Act and EPA regulations, as a major new source of possible pollution, to reduce emissions the plant must use

a. the best available technology (BAT).
b. the lowest common denominator (LCD).
c. the maximum achievable control technology (MACT).
d. the minimum allowable technology (MAT).

____ 8. Auto Motors Corporation (AMC) does not manufacture its cars to comply with current EPA standards for automobile exhaust emissions. The EPA can order

a. AMC's lender to pay clean-up costs.
b. AMC to recall its cars and repair or replace the exhaust controls.
c. customers to fix their AMC cars at the customers' expense.
d. the export of the cars to any non-adjacent country.

____ 9. Eagle Industries, Inc., fails to obtain a permit before discharging waste into navigable waters. Under the Clean Water Act, Eagle can be required

a. only to clean up the pollution.
b. only to pay for the cost of cleaning up the pollution.
c. to clean up the pollution or pay for the cost of doing so.
d. to do nothing.

____   **10.**   Petro, Inc., ships unlabeled containers of hazardous waste to off-site facilities for disposal. If the containers later leak, Petro could be found to have violated

    a.   neither the Comprehensive Environmental Response, Compensation, and Liability Act (CERCLA) nor the Resource Conservation and Recovery Act (RCRA).
    b.   the CERCLA and the RCRA.
    c.   the CERCLA only.
    d.   the RCRA only.

SHORT ESSAY QUESTIONS

1.   What does the implied warranty of habitability require, and when does it apply?

2.   What federal laws regulate toxic chemicals?

ISSUE SPOTTERS

(Answers at the Back of the Book)

1.   Gary owns a commercial building in fee simple. Gary transfers temporary possession of the building to Holding Corporation (HC). Can HC transfer possession for even less time to Investment Company?

2.   Charles sells his house to Dian under a warranty deed. Later, Carol appears, holding a better title to the house than Dian. Carol wants Dian off the property. What can Dian do?

3.   ChemCorp generates hazardous wastes from its operations. Central Trucking Company transports those wastes to Intrastate Disposal, Inc., which owns a hazardous waste disposal site. Intrastate sells the property on which the disposal site is located to ABC Properties, Inc. If the EPA cleans up the site, from whom can it recover the cost?

Chapter 25:
International Law in a Global Economy

WHAT THIS CHAPTER IS ABOUT

This chapter outlines some of the principles of international law, some of the ways in which international business is conducted, and some of the ways in which that business is regulated.

CHAPTER OUTLINE

I. **INTERNATIONAL PRINCIPLES AND DOCTRINES**
   The following are based on courtesy and respect and are applied in the interest of maintaining harmony among nations.

   A. **THE PRINCIPLE OF COMITY**
      One nation defers and gives effect to the laws and judicial decrees of another country, so long as those laws and judicial decrees are consistent with the law and public policy of the accommodating nation.

   B. **THE ACT OF STATE DOCTRINE**
      A judicially created doctrine under which the judicial branch of one country will not examine the validity of public acts committed by a recognized foreign government within its own territory. Often used in cases involving—

      1. **Expropriation**
         This occurs when a government seizes a privately owned business or goods for a proper public purpose and pays just compensation.

      2. **Confiscation**
         This occurs when a government seizes private property for an illegal purpose or without just compensation.

   C. **THE DOCTRINE OF SOVEREIGN IMMUNITY**
      Immunizes foreign nations from the jurisdiction of domestic courts. In the United States, the Foreign Sovereign Immunities Act (FSIA) of 1976 exclusively governs the circumstances in which an action may be brought against a foreign nation.

      1. **When Is a Foreign State Subject to U.S. Jurisdiction?**
         When the state has waived its immunity expressly or impliedly, or when the action is based on commercial activity in the United States by the foreign state [Section 1605].

      2. **What Entities Fall within the Category of Foreign State?**
         A political subdivision and an instrumentality (an agency or entity acting for the state) [Section 1603].

      3. **What Is Commercial Activity?**
         The FSIA leaves it to the courts to decide whether an activity is governmental or commercial.

II. **DOING BUSINESS INTERNATIONALLY**

A. EXPORTING

The simplest way to do business internationally is to export to foreign markets. Direct exporting: signing a sales contract with a foreign buyer. Indirect exporting: selling directly to consumers through a foreign agent or foreign distributor.

B. MANUFACTURING ABROAD

A domestic firm can establish a manufacturing plant abroad by—

1. Licensing

A domestic firm may license its intellectual property to a foreign manufacturer. The foreign firm agrees to keep the technology secret and to pay royalties for its use. Franchising (see Chapter 19) is a form of licensing.

2. Investing in a Wholly Owned Subsidiary or a Joint Venture

When a wholly owned subsidiary is established, the domestic firm retains ownership of the foreign facilities and control over the entire operation. In a joint venture, a domestic firm and one or more foreign firms share ownership, responsibilities, profits, and liabilities.

III.   COMMERCIAL CONTRACTS IN AN INTERNATIONAL SETTING

To avoid problems in international commercial contracts, special provisions are available.

A. CHOICE OF LANGUAGE

A choice-of-language clause designates the official language by which a contract will be interpreted in the event of disagreement. Clauses may also provide for translations and arbitration in certain languages.

B. CHOICE OF FORUM

A forum-selection clause designates the jurisdiction, including the specific court, in which a dispute will be litigated (if one arises). The forum may be anywhere (it does not have to be in the nations of parties to the contract).

C. CHOICE OF LAW

A choice-of-law clause designates what law to apply in a dispute. There is no limit on the parties' choice. If no law is specified, the governing law is that of the country in which the seller's place of business is located.

D. *FORCE MAJEURE* ("IMPOSSIBLE OR IRRESISTIBLE FORCE") CLAUSE

Force majeure clauses stipulate that acts of God and other eventualities (such as government orders or regulations, embargoes, or shortages of materials) may excuse a party from liability for nonperformance.

E. CIVIL DISPUTE RESOLUTION

1. Arbitration

Arbitration clauses (see Chapter 3) are often in international contracts. The arbitrator may be a neutral entity, a panel of individuals representing both parties' interests, or another group. The United Nations Convention on the Recognition and Enforcement of Foreign Arbitral Awards assists in the enforcement of arbitration clauses, as do provisions in specific treaties between nations.

2. Litigation

Litigation may be subject to forum-selection and choice-of-law clauses. If no forum and law are specified, litigation may be complex and uncertain (held simultaneously in two countries, for example, without regard of one for the other; a judgment may not be enforced).

IV.   MAKING PAYMENT ON INTERNATIONAL TRANSACTIONS

A. MONETARY SYSTEMS

Doing business abroad requires dealing with different currencies. Problems arising from this situation can be reduced by—

1. Foreign Exchange Markets

Foreign exchange markets are a worldwide system for converting (buying and selling) foreign currencies. The exchange rate is the price of a unit of one country's currency in terms of another country's currency.

2. Correspondent Banking

Correspondent banking is a means of transferring funds internationally. A domestic bank with correspondent banks in other countries can transfer funds, etc., through those banks.

B. LETTERS OF CREDIT

1. Principal Parties

The issuer (a bank) agrees to issue a letter of credit and to ascertain whether the beneficiary (seller) does certain acts. The account party (buyer) promises to reimburse the issuer for payment to the beneficiary.

2. Other Banks

An advising bank sends information; a paying bank expedites payment.

3. Issuer's Obligation

The issuer is bound to pay the beneficiary when the beneficiary has complied with the terms of the letter of credit (by presenting the required documents—typically a bill of lading).

4. The Value of a Letter of Credit

Payment is made against documents, not against what those documents represent. The issuer does not police the contract; this reduces costs.

5. Compliance with a Letter of Credit

Some courts require strict compliance with the terms of a letter; others require reasonable compliance. If the beneficiary complies as required, but the issuer refuses to pay, the beneficiary can sue to enforce payment.

V. REGULATION OF SPECIFIC BUSINESS ACTIVITIES

A. INVESTING

When a government confiscates property without just compensation, few remedies are available. Many countries guarantee compensation to foreign investors in their constitutions, statutes, or treaties. Some countries provide insurance for their citizens' investments abroad.

B. EXPORT CONTROLS

1. Restricting Exports

Under the U.S. Constitution, Congress cannot tax exports, but may set export quotas. Under the Export Administration Act of 1979, restrictions can be imposed on the flow of technologically advanced products and technical data.

2. Stimulating Exports

Devices to stimulate exports include export incentives and subsidies.

C. IMPORT CONTROLS

Laws prohibit, for example, importing illegal drugs and agricultural products that pose dangers to domestic crops or animals.

1. **Quotas and Tariffs**
   Quotas limit how much can be imported. Tariffs are taxes on imports (usually a percentage of the value, but can be a flat rate per unit).

2. **Dumping**
   A tariff may be assessed on imports to prevent *dumping* (sales of imported goods at "less than fair value," usually determined by prices in the exporting country).

3. **Minimizing Trade Barriers**

   a. **World Trade Organization (WTO)**
   This the principal instrument for regulating international trade. Each member country agrees to grant *most-favored-nation status* to other members (the most favorable treatment with regard to trade).

   b. **European Union (EU)**
   A regional trade association that minimizes trade barriers among European member nations.

   c. **North American Free Trade Agreement (NAFTA)**
   Created a regional trading unit consisting of Mexico, the United States, and Canada. The goal is to eliminate tariffs among them on substantially all goods over a period of fifteen to twenty years.

D. **BRIBING FOREIGN OFFICIALS**
   To reduce bribery of foreign officials by U.S. corporations, Congress enacted the Foreign Corrupt Practices Act (FCPA) in 1977 (see Chapter 2).

VI. U.S. LAWS IN A GLOBAL CONTEXT

A. **U.S. ANTITRUST LAWS**
   For U.S. courts to exercise jurisdiction over a foreign entity under U.S. antitrust laws, a violation must (1) have a substantial effect on U.S. commerce or (2) constitute a *per se* violation (see Chapter 22). Foreign governments and persons can also sue U.S. firms and persons for antitrust violations.

B. **DISCRIMINATION LAWS**
   U.S. employers must abide by U.S. employment discrimination laws (see Chapter 18) unless to do so would violate the laws of the country in which their workplace is located.

TRUE-FALSE QUESTIONS

(Answers at the Back of the Book)

____ 1. All nations must give effect to the laws of all other nations.

____ 2. Under the act of state doctrine, foreign nations are subject to the jurisdiction of U.S. courts.

____ 3. Under the doctrine of sovereign immunity, foreign nations are subject to the jurisdiction of U.S. courts.

____ 4. The Foreign Sovereign Immunities Act states the circumstances in which the United States can be sued in foreign courts.

____ 5. A member of the World Trade Organization must usually grant other members most-favored nation status with regard to trade.

____ 6. The Foreign Corrupt Practices Act is an attempt to stop the bribery of foreign officials by U.S. corporations.

____ 7. U.S. courts cannot exercise jurisdiction over foreign entities under U.S. antitrust laws.

____ 8. U.S. employers with workplaces abroad must generally comply with U.S. discrimination laws.

____ 9. When a seller complies with the terms of a letter of credit, the issuing bank is obliged to pay.

____ 10. Under a *force majeure* clause, a party may be excused from liability for nonperformance.

FILL-IN QUESTIONS

(Answers at the Back of the Book)

_____ (A confiscation/An expropriation) occurs when a national government seizes a privately owned business or privately owned goods for a proper public purpose. _____ (A confiscation/An expropriation) occurs when the taking is made for an illegal purpose. When _____ (a confiscation/an expropriation) occurs, the government pays just compensation. When _____ (a confiscation/an expropriation) occurs, the government does not pay just compensation.

MULTIPLE-CHOICE QUESTIONS

(Answers at the Back of the Book)

____ 1. A group of foreign manufacturers organize to control the price for digital cameras in the United States. FotoQuik Company, a U.S. firm, joins the group. If their actions have a substantial effect on U.S. commerce, a suit for violation of U.S. antitrust laws may be brought against

   a. FotoQuik and the foreign manufacturers.
   b. neither FotoQuik nor the foreign manufacturers.
   c. only FotoQuik.
   d. only the foreign manufacturers.

____ 2. To obtain a contract in Russia, Standard Company bribes a government official whose signature is needed on the contract. This may violate

   a. the act of state doctrine.
   b. the doctrine of sovereign immunity.
   c. the Foreign Corrupt Practices Act.
   d. the principle of comity.

____ 3. El Salvador issues bonds to finance the construction of an international airport. Fred, in the United States, buys some of the bonds. A terrorist group destroys the airport, and El Salvador refuses to pay interest or principal on the bonds. Fred files suit in a U.S court. The court will hear the suit

   a. if El Salvador's acts constitute a confiscation.
   b. if El Salvador's acts constitute an expropriation.
   c. if El Salvador's selling bonds is a "commercial activity."
   d. under no circumstances.

____ 4. To obtain new computers, Liberia accepts bids from U.S. firms, including Macro Corporation and Micro, Inc. Macro wins the contract. Alleging impropriety in the awarding of the contract, Micro files a suit in a U.S. court against Liberia and Macro. The court may decline to hear the suit under

   a. the act of state doctrine.
   b. the doctrine of sovereign immunity.
   c. the Foreign Corrupt Practices Act.
   d. the World Trade Organization.

____ 5. A South African seller and a U.S. buyer form a contract that the buyer breaches. The seller sues in a South African court and wins damages, but the buyer's assets are in the United States. If a U.S. court enforces the judgment, it will be because of

    a. the act of state doctrine.
    b. the doctrine of sovereign immunity.
    c. the principle of comity.
    d. the World Trade Organization.

____ 6. Global, Inc., is a U.S. firm. Holly, a U.S. citizen, works for Global in a country outside the United States. Ilsa, a citizen of a foreign country, also works for Global outside the United States. Holly and Ilsa believe that they are being harassed on the job, in violation of U.S. discrimination laws. Those laws protect

    a. Holly and Ilsa.
    b. Holly only.
    c. Ilsa only.
    d. neither Holly nor Ilsa.

____ 7. A contract between Delta, Inc., a U.S. firm, and Electronique, S.A., a French company, provides that disputes between the parties will be adjudicated in a specific British court. This clause is

    a. a choice-of-forum clause.
    b. a choice-of-law clause.
    c. a *force majeure* clause.
    d. an arbitration clause.

____ 8. Alpha, Inc., a U.S. firm, signs a contract with Beta, Ltd., a Russian company, to give Beta the right to sell Alpha's products in Russia. This is

    a. a distribution agreement.
    b. a joint venture.
    c. direct exporting.
    d. licensing.

____ 9. Digital, Inc., makes supercomputers that feature advanced technology. To inhibit Digital's export of its products to other countries, Congress can

    a. confiscate all profits on exported supercomputers.
    b. expropriate all profits on exported supercomputers.
    c. set quotas on exported supercomputers.
    d. tax exported supercomputers.

____ 10. Auto Corporation makes cars in the United States. To boost the sales of Auto Corporation and other domestic automakers, Congress can

    a. neither set quotas nor tax imports.
    b. only set quotas on imports.
    c. only tax imports.
    d. set quotas and tax imports.

SHORT ESSAY QUESTIONS

1. In what ways may a company conduct international business?

2. How does the Foreign Sovereign Immunities Act affect commercial activities by foreign governments?

ISSUE SPOTTERS

(Answers at the Back of the Book)

1. Cafe Rojo, Ltd., a Colombian firm, agrees to sell coffee beans to A.B. Coffee Company, a U.S. firm. A.B. accepts the beans, but refuses to pay. Cafe Rojo sues A.B. in a Colombian court and is awarded damages, but A.B.'s assets are in the United States. Under what circumstances would a U.S. court enforce the Colombian court's judgment?

2. Hi-Cola Corporation, a U.S. firm, markets a popular soft drink. The formula is secret, but with careful chemical analysis, its ingredients could be discovered. What can Hi-Cola do to prevent its product from being pirated abroad?

3. Gems International, Ltd., is a foreign firm that has a 12-percent share of the U.S. market for diamonds. To capture a larger share, Gems offers its products at a below-cost discount to U.S. buyers (and inflates the prices in its own country to make up the difference). How can this attempt to undersell U.S. businesses be defeated?

Answers

Chapter 1

True-False Questions

1. T
2. T
3. T
4. F. The Constitution takes precedence over any conflicting federal or state statute, local ordinance, administrative rule, or court decision.
5. T
6. T
7. T
8. F. The protections in the Bill of Rights limit the power of the federal government, but most of these protections also apply to the states through the due process clause of the Fourteenth Amendment.
9. F. Commercial speech (advertising) can be restricted as long as the restriction (1) seeks to implement a substantial government interest, (2) directly advances that interest, and (3) goes no further than necessary to accomplish its objective.
10. T

Fill-in Questions

with similar facts; precedent; permits a predictable

Multiple-Choice Questions

1. B. The use of precedent—the doctrine of *stare decisis*—permits a predictable, relatively quick, and fair resolution of cases. Under this doctrine, a court must adhere to principles of law established by higher courts.
2. D. The doctrine of *stare decisis* attempts to harmonize the results in cases with similar facts. When the facts are sufficiently similar, the same rule is applied. Cases with identical facts could serve as binding authority, but it is more practical to expect to find cases with facts that are not identical but similar—as similar as possible.
3. A. An order to do or refrain from a certain act is an injunction. An order to perform as promised is a decree for specific performance. These remedies, as well as rescission, are equitable remedies. An award of damages is a remedy at law.
4. A. Equity and law provide different remedies, and at one time, most courts could grant only one type. Today, most states do not maintain separate courts of law and equity, and a judge may grant either or both forms of relief. Equitable relief is generally granted, however, only if damages (the legal remedy) is inadequate.
5. A. State statutes that impinge on interstate commerce are not always struck down, nor are they always upheld. A court will balance a state's interest in regulating a certain matter against the burden that the

statute places on interstate commerce. If the statute does not substantially interfere, it will not be held in violation of the commerce clause.

6.   B. Commercial speech does not have as much protection under the First Amendment as noncommercial speech. Commercial speech that is misleading may be restricted, however, if the restriction (1) seeks to advance a substantial government interest, (2) directly advances that interest, and (3) goes no further than necessary.

7.   B. Aspects of the Fifth and Fourteenth Amendments that cover procedural due process concern the procedures used to make any government decision to take life, liberty, or property. These procedures must be fair, which generally mean that they give an opportunity to object.

8.   C. Substantive due process focuses on the content (substance) of a law under the Fifth and Fourteenth Amendments. Depending on which rights a law regulates, it must either promote a compelling or overriding government interest or be rationally related to a legitimate governmental end.

9.   A. Equal protection means that the government must treat similarly situated individuals in a similar manner. The equal protection clause of the Fourteenth Amendment applies to state and local governments, and the due process clause of the Fifth Amendment guarantees equal protection by the federal government. Generally, a law regulating an economic matter is considered valid if there is a "rational basis" on which the law relates to a legitimate government interest.

10.   D. A federal law takes precedence over a state law on the same subject. Also under the supremacy clause, if Congress chooses to act exclusively in an area in which the states have concurrent power, Congress is said to preempt the area.

Issue Spotters

1.   No. The U.S. Constitution is the supreme law of the land, and applies to all jurisdictions. A law in violation of the Constitution (in this question, the First Amendment to the Constitution) will be declared unconstitutional.

2.   Yes. Administrative rulemaking starts with the publication of a notice of the rulemaking in the *Federal Register*. A public hearing is held at which proponents and opponents can offer evidence and question witnesses. After the hearing, the agency considers what was presented at the hearing and drafts the final rule.

3.   No. Even if commercial speech is not related to illegal activities nor misleading, it may be restricted if a state has a substantial interest that cannot be achieved by less restrictive means. In this case, the interest in energy conservation is substantial, but it could be achieved by less restrictive means. That would be the utilities' defense against the enforcement of this state law.

Chapter 2

True-False Questions

1.   T

2.   T

3.   F. According to utilitarianism, it is the consequences of an act that determine how ethical the act is. Applying this theory requires determining who will be affected by an act, assessing the positive and negatives effects of alternatives, and choosing the alternative that will provide the greatest benefit for the most people. Utilitarianism is premised on acting so as to do the greatest good for the greatest number of people. An act that affects a minority negatively may still be morally acceptable.

4.   T

5.   F. The legality of a particular action may be unclear, in part because it can be difficult to predict how a court may rule on a particular issue. The best course is to act responsibly and in good faith. Similarly, in situations involving *ethical* decisions, a balance must sometimes be struck between equally good or equally poor courses of action, and sometimes one group—employees or shareholders for example—may be adversely affected.

6.   T

7.   F. Simply obeying the law will not meet all ethical obligations. The law does not cover all ethical requirements. An act may be unethical but not illegal. In fact, compliance with the law is at best a moral minimum. Furthermore, there is an ethical aspect to almost every decision that a business firm makes.

8.   T

9.   F. Compliance with GAAP and GAAS may be required, but it is no guarantee of freedom from liability. Also, there may be a higher standard of conduct under a state statute or judicial decision.

10.   F. Bribery is also a legal issue, regulated in the United States by the Foreign Corrupt Practices Act. Internationally, a treaty signed by the members of the Organization for Economic Cooperation and Development makes bribery of public officials a serious crime. Each member nation is expected to enact legislation implementing the treaty.

Fill-in Questions

Religious standards; Kantian ethics; the principle of rights

Multiple-Choice Questions

1.   C. Business ethics focus on the application of moral principles in a business context. Different standards are not required. Business ethics is a subset of ethics that relates specifically to what constitutes right and wrong in situations that arise in business.

2.   B. Traditionally, ethical reasoning relating to business has been characterized by two fundamental approaches—duty-based ethics and utilitarianism, or outcome-based ethics. Duty-based ethics derive from religious sources or philosophical principles. These standards may be absolute, which means that an act may not be undertaken, whatever the consequences.

3.   A. Under religious ethical standards, it is the nature of an act that determines how ethical the act is, not its consequences. This is considered an *absolute* standard. But this standard is tempered by an element of compassion (the "Golden Rule").

4.   A. In contrast to duty-based ethics, outcome-based ethics (utilitarianism) involves a consideration of the consequences of an action. Utilitarianism is premised on acting so as to do the greatest good for the greatest number of people.

5.   C. Utilitarianism requires determining who will be affected by an action, assessing the positive and negatives effects of alternatives, and choosing the alternative that will provide the greatest benefit for the most people. This approach has been criticized as tending to reduce the welfare of human beings to plus and minus signs on a cost-benefit worksheet.

6.   A. In part because it is impossible to be entirely aware of what the law requires and prohibits, the best course for a business firm is to act responsibly and in good faith. This course may provide the best defense if a transgression is discovered. Striking a balance between what is profitable and what is legal and ethical can be difficult, however. A failure to act legally or ethically can result in a reduction in profits, but a failure to act in the profitable interest of the firm can also cause profits to suffer. *Optimum* profits are the maximum profits that a firm can realize while staying within legal and ethical limits.

7.   C. Under the Securities Act of 1933, an accountant may be liable for any false statement of material fact or omission of a material fact in a registration statement. An accountant is required to exercise due diligence in preparing financial statements, which means that "using" due diligence would not result in liability for losses based on those statements. Also, financial statements should include all essential information concerning the issuance of stock, which means that if the statements contain that information, liability would not result on that basis.

8.   D. In this problem, the attorney failed to exercise reasonable care and professional judgment, thereby breaching the duty of care owed to clients. If a statute of limitations runs out, a client can no longer file a suit and loses a potential award of damages.

9.   D. The principle of rights theory of ethics follows the belief that persons have fundamental rights. This belief is implied by duty-based ethical standards and Kantian ethics. The rights are implied by the duty that forms the basis for the standard (for example, the duty not to kill implies that persons have a right to live), or

by the personal dignity implicit in the Kantian belief about the fundamental nature of human beings. Not to respect these rights would, under the principle of rights theory, be morally wrong.

10.   C. The Foreign Corrupt Practices Act prohibits any U.S. firm from bribing foreign officials to influence official acts to provide the firm with business opportunities. Such payments are allowed, however, if they would be lawful in the foreign country. Thus, to avoid violating the law, the firm in this problem should determine whether such payments are legal in the minister's country.

Issue Spotters

1.   The answer depends on which system of ethics is used. Under a duty-based ethical standard, it may not be the consequences of an act that determine how ethical the act is; it may be the nature of the act itself. Stealing would be unethical regardless of whether the fruits of the crime are given to the poor. In contrast, utilitarianism is premised on acting so as to do the greatest good for the greatest number of people. It is the consequences of an act that determine how ethical the act is.

2.   Maybe. On the one hand, it is not the company's "fault" when a product is misused. Also, keeping the product on the market is not a violation of the law, and stopping sales would hurt profits. On the other hand, suspending sales could reduce suffering and could stop potential negative publicity if sales continued.

3.   When a corporation decides to respond to what it sees as a moral obligation to correct for past discrimination by adjusting pay differences among its employees, an ethical conflict is raised between the firm and its employees and between the firm and its shareholders. This dilemma arises directly out of the effect such a decision has on the firm's profits. If satisfying this obligation increases profitability, then the dilemma is easily resolved in favor of "doing the right thing." In any case, there will likely be a conflict among the various interest groups, however, which may require a decision as to which group will receive priority.

Chapter 3

True-False Questions

1.   T
2.   T
3.   F. The decisions of a state's highest court on all questions of state law are final. The United States Supreme Court can overrule only those state court decisions that involve questions of federal law.
4.   T

5. T

6. T

7. F. A losing party may appeal an adverse judgment to a higher court, but the party in whose favor the judgment was issued may also appeal if, for example, he or she is awarded less than sought in the suit.

8. F. Most lawsuits—as many as 95 percent—are dismissed or settled before they go to trial. Courts encourage alternative dispute resolution (ADR) and sometimes order parties to submit to ADR, particularly mediation, before allowing their suits to come to trial.

9. F. In mediation, a mediator assists the parties in reaching an agreement, but not by deciding the dispute. The mediator emphasizes points of agreement, helps the parties evaluate their positions, and proposes solutions.

10. F. If an arbitration agreement covers the subject matter of a dispute, a party to the agreement can be compelled to arbitrate the dispute. A court would order the arbitration without ruling on the basic controversy.

Fill-in Questions

to dismiss; for judgment on the pleadings; summary judgment

Multiple-Choice Questions

1. A. On a "sliding scale" test, a court's exercise of personal jurisdiction depends on the amount of business that an individual or firm transacts over the Internet. Jurisdiction is most likely proper when there is substantial business, most likely improper when a Web site is no more than an ad, and may or may not be appropriate when there is some interactivity. "Any" interactivity with "any resident" of a state would likely not be enough, however.

2. A. This is part of discovery. Discovery saves time, and the trend is toward more, not less, discovery. Discovery is limited, however, to relevant materials. A party cannot obtain access to such data as another's trade secrets or, in testimony, an admission concerning unrelated matters. A party is not entitled to any privileged material either.

3. C. In the suit in this question, the court can exercise *in rem* jurisdiction. A court can exercise jurisdiction over property located within its boundaries. A corporation is also subject to the jurisdiction of the courts in any state in which it is incorporated, in which it has its main office, or in which it does business.

4. A. As noted above, a corporation is subject to the jurisdiction of the courts in any state in which it is incorporated, in which it has its main office, or in which it does business. The court may be able to exercise personal jurisdiction or *in rem* jurisdiction, or the court may reach a defendant corporation with a long arm statute. In the right circumstances, this firm might also be involved in a suit in a federal court, if the requirements for federal jurisdiction are met: a federal question is involved, or there is diversity of citizenship and the amount in controversy is $75,000 or more.

5. D. An appeals court examines the record of a case, looking mostly at questions of law for errors by the court below. If it determines that a retrial is necessary, the case is sent back to the lower court. For this reason, an appellant's best ground for an appeal focuses on the law that applied to the issues in the case, not questions concerning the credibility of the evidence or other findings of fact.

6. D. The United States Supreme Court is not required to hear any case. The Court has jurisdiction over any case decided by any of the federal courts of appeals and appellate authority over cases decided by the states' highest courts if the latter involve questions of federal law. But the Court's exercise of its jurisdiction is discretionary, not mandatory.

7. C. If a defendant's motion to dismiss is denied, the defendant must then file an answer, or another appropriate response, or a default judgment will be entered against him or her. Of course, the defendant is given more time to file this response. If the motion is granted, the plaintiff is given more time to file an amended complaint.

8. D. Negotiation is an informal means of dispute resolution. Generally, unlike mediation and arbitration, no third party is involved in resolving the dispute. In those two forms, a third party may render a binding or nonbinding decision. Arbitration is a more formal process than mediation or negotiation. Litigation involves a third party—a judge—who renders a legally binding decision.

9. C. In a summary jury trial, the jury's verdict is advisory, not binding as it would otherwise be in a court trial. In a mini-trial, the attorneys argue a case and a third party renders an opinion, but the opinion discusses how a court would decide the dispute. Early neutral case negotiation is what its name suggests, involving a third party who evaluates the disputing parties' positions.

10. C. Online dispute resolution (ODR) is a new type of alternative dispute resolution. Most ODR forums resolve disputers informally and come to nonbinding resolutions. Any party to a dispute being considered in ODR may discontinue the process and appeal to a court at any time.

Issue Spotters

1. Yes. Submission of the dispute to mediation or nonbinding arbitration is mandatory, but compliance with a decision of the mediator or arbitrator is voluntary.

2. The defendant could file a motion for a directed verdict. This motion asks the judge to direct a verdict for the defendant on the ground that the plaintiff presented no evidence that would justify granting the plaintiff relief. The judge grants the motion if there is insufficient evidence to raise an issue of fact.

3. Either a plaintiff or a defendant, or both, can appeal a judgment to a higher court. An appellate court can affirm, reverse, or remand a case, or take any of these actions in combination. To appeal successfully, it is best to appeal on the basis of an error of law, because appellate courts do not usually reverse on findings of fact.

Chapter 4

True-False Questions

1. T
2. F. A reasonable apprehension or fear of *immediate* harmful or offensive contact is an assault.
3. T
4. F. Puffery is seller's talk—the seller's *opinion* that his or her goods are, for example, the "best." For fraud to occur, there must be a misrepresentation of a *fact*.
5. T
6. F. To establish negligence, the courts apply a *reasonable person* standard to determine whether certain conduct resulted in a breach of a duty of care.
7. T
8. F. This is not misconduct, in terms of a wrongful interference tort. Bona fide competitive behavior is permissible, whether or not it results in the breaking of a contract or other business relation. In fact, it is a defense to charges of wrongful interference.
9. T
10. F. Some states have statutes prohibiting or regulating the use of spam. Also, the sending of spam may constitute trespass to personal property, and could be curtailed by private lawsuits. What the government can do to restrict spam may be limited by the First Amendment's protection for freedom of speech, however.

Fill-in Questions

1. negligence
2. assumption of risk
3. comparative

Multiple-Choice Questions

1. B. Joe committed a battery and may have committed an assault. For an intentional tort, what matters is the actor's intent regarding the consequences of an act or his or her knowledge with substantial certainty that certain consequences will result. Motive is irrelevant, and the other person's fear is not a factor in terms of the actor's intent.
2. A. To delay a customer suspected of shoplifting, a merchant must have probable cause (which requires more than a mere suspicion). A customer's concealing merchandise in his or her bag and leaving the store without paying for it would constitute probable cause. Even with probable cause, a merchant may delay a suspected shoplifter only for a reasonable time, however.
3. B. Trespass to land occurs when a person, without permission, enters onto another's land, or remains on the land. An owner does not need to be aware of an act before it can constitute trespass, and harm to the land is not required. A trespasser may have a complete defense, however, if he or she enters onto the land to help someone in danger.
4. A. The basis of the tort of defamation is publication of a statement that holds an individual up to contempt, ridicule, or hatred. Publication means that statements are made to or within the hearing of persons other than the defamed party, or that a third party reads the statements. A secretary reading a letter, for example, meets this requirement. But the statements do not have to be read or heard by a specific third party. (Whether someone is a public figure is important only because a public figure cannot recover damages for defamation without proof of actual malice.)
5. B. The standard of a business that invites persons onto its premises is a duty to exercise reasonable care. Whether conduct is unreasonable depends on a number of factors, including how easily the injury could have been guarded against. A landowner has a duty to discover and remove hidden dangers, but obvious dangers do not need warnings.
6. C. To commit negligence, a breach of a duty of care must cause harm. If an injury was foreseeable, there is causation in fact. This can usually be determined by the but-for test: but for the wrongful act, the injury would not have occurred. Thus, an actor is not necessarily liable to all who are injured. Insurance coverage and business dealings are not factors.
7. B. Strict liability is liability without fault. This is imposed on dangerous activities when they (1) involve potentially serious harm to persons or property, (2) involve a high degree of risk that cannot be completely guarded against by the exercise of reasonable care, and (3) are activities not commonly performed in the area. The other choices represent irrelevant factors.
8. D. Advertising is bona fide competitive behavior, which is not a tort even if it results in the breaking of a contract. Obtaining more customers is one of the goals of effective advertising. Taking unethical steps to interfere with others' contracts or business relations could constitute a tort, however.

9.   D. Under the Communications Decency Act, an Internet service provider (ISP) may not be held liable for defamatory statements made by its customers on-line. Congress provided this immunity as an incentive to ISPs to "self-police" the Internet for offensive material.

10.   C. Trespass to personal property is intentional physical contact with another's personal property that causes damage. Sending spam through an Internet service provider (ISP) is intentional contact with the ISP's computer systems. A negative impact on the value of the ISP's equipment, by using its processing power to transmit e-mail, constitutes damage (the resources are not available for the ISP's customers). Also, service cancellations harm an ISP's business reputation and goodwill.

Issue Spotters

1.   Yes. The person committing the act is guilty of battery—an unexcused, harmful, or offensive physical contact intentionally performed. A battery may involve contact with any part of the body and anything (a blouse, in this problem) attached to it.

2.   Yes. Trespass to personal property occurs when an individual unlawfully harms another's personal property or otherwise interferes with the owner's right to exclusive possession and enjoyment.

3.   No. As long as competitive behavior is bona fide, it is not tortious even if it results in the breaking of a contract. The public policy that favors free competition in advertising outweighs any instability that bona fide competitive activity causes in contractual or business relations. To constitute wrongful interference with a contractual relationship, there must be (1) a valid, enforceable contract between two parties; (2) the knowledge of a third party that this contract exists; and (3) the third party's intentionally causing the breach of the contract (and damages) to advance the third party's interest.

Chapter 5

True-False Questions

1.   T

2.   F. A copyright is granted automatically when a qualifying work is created, although a work can be registered with the U.S. Copyright Office.

3.   T

4.   T

5.   F. Anything that makes an individual company unique and would have value to a competitor is a trade secret. This includes a list of customers, a formula for a chemical compound, and other confidential data.

6.   F. Trade names cannot be registered with the federal government. They are protected, however, under the common law (when used as trademarks or service marks) by the same principles that protect trademarks.

7.   F. A copy does not have to be the same as an original to constitute copyright infringement. A copyright is infringed if a substantial part of a work is copied without the copyright holder's permission.

8.   F. A trademark may be infringed by an intentional or unintentional use of a mark in its entirety, or a copy of the mark to a substantial degree. In other words, a mark can be infringed if its use is intended or not, and whether the copy is identical or similar. Also, the owner of the mark and its unauthorized user need not be in direct competition.

9.   T

10.   F. Proof of a likelihood of confusion is not required in a trademark dilution action. The products involved do not even have to be similar, and the owner and the unauthorized user of a mark do not have to be competitors. Proof of likely confusion is required in a suit for trademark *infringement*, however.

Fill-in Questions

70; 95; 120; 70

Multiple-Choice Questions

1.   B. A firm that makes, uses, or sells another's patented design, product, or process without the owner's permission commits patent infringement. It is not required that an invention be copied in its entirety. Also, the object that is copied does not need to be trademarked or copyrighted, in addition to being patented.

2.   A. The user of a trademark can register it with the U.S. Patent and Trademark Office, but registration is not necessary to obtain protection from trademark infringement. A trademark receives protection to the degree that it is distinctive. A fanciful symbol is the most distinctive mark.

3.   B. Ten years is the period for later renewals of a trademark's registration. The life of a creator plus seventy years is a period for copyright protection. No intellectual work is protected forever, at least not without renewal. To obtain a patent, an applicant must satisfy the U.S. Patent and Trademark Office that the invention or design is genuine, novel, useful, and not obvious in light of contemporary technology. A patent is granted to the first person to create whatever is to be patented, rather than the first person to file for a patent.

4.   A. Copyright protects a specific list of creative works, including literary works, musical works, sound recordings, and pictorial, graphic, and sculptural works. Although there are exceptions for "fair use," a work need not be copied in its entirety to be infringed. Also, to make a case for infringement, proof of con-

sumers' confusion is not required, and the owner and unauthorized user need not be direct competitors.

5.   D. A process used to conduct business on the Web may be patented in some circumstances. Other business processes and information that cannot be patented, copyrighted, or trademarked are protected against appropriation as trade secrets. These processes and information include production techniques, as well as a product's idea and its expression.

6.   C. Trademark law protects a distinctive symbol that its owner stamps, prints, or otherwise affixes to goods to distinguish them from the goods of others. Use of this mark by another party without the owner's permission is trademark infringement.

7.   B. A certification mark certifies the region, materials, method of manufacture, quality, or accuracy of goods or services. A collective mark is a certification mark used by members of a cooperative, association, or other organization (a union, in this problem). A service mark distinguishes the services of one person or company from those of another. A trade name indicates all or part of a business's name.

8.   D. This is not copyright infringement or patent infringement because no copyright or patent is involved. Trademark dilution occurs when a trademark is used, without the owner's permission, in a way that diminishes the distinctive quality of the mark. That has not happened here. Also, this is not cybersquatting because no one is offering to sell a domain name to a trademark owner. It is further unlikely that this violates the Anticybersquatting Consumer Protection Act because there is no indication of "bad faith intent."

9.   C. The Berne Convention provides some copyright protection, but its coverage and enforcement were not as complete or as universal as that of the TRIPS (Trade-Related Aspects of Intellectual Property Rights) Agreement. The Paris Convention allows parties in one signatory country to file for patent and trademark protection in other signatory countries.

10.   A. Publishers cannot put the contents of their periodicals into online databases and other electronic resources, including CD-ROMs, without securing the permission of the writers whose contributions are included.

Issue Spotters

1.   The owner of the customer list can sue its competitor for the theft of trade secrets. Trade secrets include customer lists. Liability extends to those who misappropriate trade secrets by any means, including modems.

2.   This is patent infringement. A software maker in this situation might best protect its product, save litigation costs, and profit from its patent by the use of a license. In the context of this problem, a license would grant permission to sell a patented item. (A license can be limited to certain purposes and to the licensee only.)

3.   Yes. This may be an instance of trademark dilution. Dilution occurs when a trademark is used, without permission, in a way that diminishes the distinctive quality of the mark. Dilution does not require proof that consumers are likely to be confused by a connection between the unauthorized use and the mark. The products involved do not have to be similar. Dilution does require, however, that a mark be famous when the dilution occurs.

Chapter 6

True-False Questions

1.   T

2.   F. Felonies are crimes punishable by imprisonment of a year or more (in a state or federal prison). Crimes punishable by imprisonment for lesser periods (in a local facility) are classified as misdemeanors.

3.   F. These are elements of the crime of robbery. (Robbery also involves the use of force or fear.) Burglary requires breaking and entering a building with the intent to commit a crime. (At one time, burglary was defined to cover only breaking and entering the dwelling of another at night to commit a crime.)

4.   F. This is an element of larceny. The crime of embezzlement occurs when a person entrusted with another's property fraudulently appropriates it. Also, unlike robbery, embezzlement does not require the use of force or fear.

5.   T

6.   F. The crime of bribery occurs when a bribe is offered. Accepting a bribe is a separate crime. In either case, the recipient does not need to perform the act for which the bribe is offered for the crime to exist. Note, too, that a bribe can consist of something other then money.

7.   F. The recipient of the goods only needs to know that the goods are stolen. The recipient does not need to know the identity of the thief or of the true owner to commit this crime. Thus, not knowing these individuals' identities is not a defense.

8.   T

9.   T

10.   T

Fill-in Questions

unreasonable; probable; due process of law; jeopardy; trial; trial by; witnesses; bail and fines

Multiple-Choice Questions

1.   D. A person who wrongfully or fraudulently takes and carries away another's personal property commits larceny. Unlike burglary, larceny does not

involve breaking and entering. Unlike embezzlement, larceny requires that property be taken and carried away from the owner's possession. Unlike forgery, larceny does not require the making or altering of a writing. Unlike robbery, larceny does not involve force or fear.

2. A. The elements of most crimes include the performance of a prohibited act and a specified state of mind or intent on the part of the actor.

3. C. Fraudulently making or altering a writing in a way that changes another's legal rights is forgery. Forgery also includes changing trademarks, counterfeiting, falsifying public documents, and altering other legal documents.

4. B. Embezzlement involves the fraudulent appropriation of another's property, including money, by a person entrusted with it. Unlike larceny, embezzlement does not require that property be taken from its owner.

5. C. The standard to find a criminal defendant guilty is beyond a reasonable doubt. This means that each juror must be convinced, beyond a reasonable doubt, of the defendant's guilt. The standard of proof in most civil cases is a preponderance of the evidence.

6. A. The federal crime of mail fraud has two elements: a scheme to defraud by false pretenses, and mailing, or causing someone else to mail, a writing for the purpose of executing the scheme. It would also be a crime to execute the scheme by wire, radio, or television transmissions.

7. B. In considering the defense of entrapment, the important question is whether a person who committed a crime was pressured by the police to do so. Entrapment occurs when a government agent suggests that a crime be committed and pressure an individual, who is not predisposed to its commitment, to do it.

8. C. A person in police custody who is to be interrogated must be informed that he or she has the right to remain silent; anything said can and will be used against him or her in court; and he or she has the right to consult with an attorney. The person also must be told that if he or she is indigent, a lawyer will be appointed. These rights may be waived if the waiver is knowing and voluntary.

9. C. If, for example, a confession is obtained after an illegal arrest, the confession is normally excluded. Under the exclusionary rule, all evidence obtained in violation of the constitutional rights spelled out in the Fourth, Fifth, and Sixth Amendments normally is excluded, as well as all evidence derived from the illegally obtained evidence. The purpose of the rule is to deter police misconduct.

10. B. A formal charge issued by a grand jury is an indictment. A charge issued by a government prosecutor is called an information. In either case, there must be sufficient evidence to justify bringing a suspect to trial. The arraignment occurs when the suspect is brought before the trial court, informed of the charges, and asked to enter a plea.

Issue Spotters

1. No. A mistake of fact, as opposed to a mistake of law, will constitute a defense if it negates the mental state required for the crime. The mental state required for theft involves the knowledge that the property is another's and the intent to deprive the owner of it.

2. Yes. With respect to the gas station, she has obtained goods by false pretenses. She might also be charged with larceny and forgery, and most states have special statutes covering illegal use of credit cards.

3. Yes. The National Information Infrastructure Protection Act of 1996 amended the Counterfeit Access Device and Computer Fraud and Abuse Act of 1984. The statute provides that a person who accesses a computer online, without permission, to obtain classified data (such as consumer credit files in a credit agency's database) is subject to criminal prosecution. The crime has two elements: accessing the computer without permission and taking data. It is a felony if done for private financial gain. Penalties include fines and imprisonment for up to twenty years. The victim of the theft can also bring a civil suit against the criminal to obtain damages and other relief.

Chapter 7

True-False Questions

1. F. A bilateral contract is accepted by a promise to perform. A unilateral contract is formed when the offeree (the party who receives the offer) completes the requested act or other performance.

2. F. An oral contract is an express contract, which may be written or oral. In an express contract, the terms are fully stated in words. In an implied contract, it is the conduct of the parties that creates and defines the terms.

3. F. An unenforceable contract is a valid contract that cannot be enforced due to certain defenses. A voidable contract is a valid contract in which one or both of the parties has the option of avoiding his or her legal obligations.

4. T

5. F. A court imposes a quasi contract to avoid the unjust enrichment of one party at the expense of another. Quasi contracts are not true contracts.

6. F. One of the elements for a valid offer is that the terms be definite enough to be enforced by a court. This is so that a court can determine if a breach occurred and, if so, what the appropriate remedy would be. An offer might invite a specifically worded acceptance, which could constitute sufficiently definite terms.

7. T

8. F. Irrevocable offers (offers that must be kept open for a period of time) include option contracts. Other irrevocable offers include a merchant's firm offer and, under the doctrine of promissory estoppel, an offer on which an offeree has changed position in reliance.

9. F. The mirror image rule requires that the terms of an offeree's acceptance must exactly match the terms of the offeror's offer to form a valid contract. Any other response effectively rejects the offer, terminating it. An offeree may, of course, include a counteroffer with his or her rejection.

10. T

Fill-in Questions

serious; offeror; reasonably definite; offeree

Multiple-Choice Questions

1. B. One party has performed; the other has not. The contract is executed on the one side and executory on the other, and classified as executory. Once the delivered goods are paid for, the contract will be fully executed.

2. A. In considering an implied-in-fact contract, a court looks at the parties' actions leading up to what happened. If, for example, a plaintiff furnished services, expecting to be paid, which the defendant should have known, and the defendant had a chance to reject the services and did not, the court would hold that the parties had an enforceable implied-in-fact contract.

3. A. An obligation to pay will be imposed by law to prevent one party from being unjustly enriched at another's expense. This is the doctrine of quasi contract. The doctrine will not be applied, however, if there is a contract covering the matter in dispute. Also, there are some circumstances in which parties will not be forced to pay for benefits "thrust" on them, particularly if this is done over their protest.

4. A. An express contract is a contract in which the terms are fully expressed in words, but those words do not necessarily have to be in writing. A contract that is implied from conduct is an implied-in-fact contract. Implied-in-law, or quasi, contracts are not actual contracts but are imposed on parties by courts.

5. A. A voidable contract is a valid contract that can be avoided at the option of one or both of the parties. If a party with the option chooses to avoid the contract, both parties are released from their obligations under it. If a party with the option elects to ratify the contract, both parties must perform.

6. C. When an acceptance is made conditional, it constitutes a rejection, but the conditions state a counteroffer. A counteroffer is both a rejection of an original offer and a simultaneous making of a new offer.

7. A. Generally, an offer may be revoked any time before acceptance. Most offers are revocable, even if they say that they are not, as long as the revocation is communicated to the offeree before acceptance. This may be done by express repudiation or by acts that are inconsistent with the offer and that are made known to the offeree (such as a sale to someone else about which the offeree learns).

8. C. An acceptance is effective if it is timely. Under the mailbox rule, using a mode of communication expressly or impliedly authorized by the offeror makes an acceptance effective when sent. If no mode is expressly stated, the mail is acceptable. Here, the offeror did not specify a certain mode, so the mode that the offeree used to accept was a reasonable means.

9. D. The promisee was not legally obligated to undertake the act, and the promisor was not legally obligated to pay the promisee until the performance was completed. Also, consideration must be bargained for. Performance or a promise is bargained for if, as in this problem, the promisor seeks it in exchange for his or her promise and the promisee gives it in exchange for that promise.

10. D. Generally, a promise to do what one already has a legal duty to do is not legally sufficient consideration, because no legal detriment or benefit has been incurred or received. This is the preexisting duty rule. Unforeseen difficulties may qualify as an exception to this rule, but an increase in ordinary business expenses, which is a type of risk usually assumed in doing business, does not qualify as an unforeseen difficulty.

Issue Spotters

1. Yes. A person who is unjustly enriched at the expense of another can be required to account for the benefit under the theory of quasi contract. The parties here did not have a contract, but the law will impose one to avoid the unjust enrichment.

2. No. Taking into consideration the owner's frustration and the obvious difference between the value of the car and the "stated" price, a reasonable person would realize that the offer was not made with serious intent and that the party who "paid" the price did not have an agreement.

3. Yes. Under the doctrine of detrimental reliance, or promissory estoppel, the promisee is entitled to payment of $5,000 from the promisor on graduation. There was a promise, on which the promisee relied, the reliance was substantial and definite (the promisee went to college for the full term, incurring considerable expenses, and will likely graduate), and it would only be fair to enforce the promise.

Chapter 8

True-False Questions

1. T
2. T
3. F. An illegal contract is void. A court will not enforce it on behalf of any party to it.
4. F. A contract with an unlicensed practitioner may be enforceable if the purpose of the statute is to raise government revenues, but not if the statute's purpose is to protect the public from unlicensed practitioners.
5. F. A covenant not to compete may be upheld if the length of time and the size of the geographic area in which the party agrees not to compete are reasonable. A court may in fact reform these terms to make them reasonable and then enforce them as reformed.
6. T
7. F. If the parties to both sides of a contract are mistaken as to the same material fact, either party can rescind the contract at any time. This is a bilateral, or mutual, mistake. Either party can enforce a contract, however, if the mistake relates to the later market value or quality of the object of the contract.
8. T
9. F. Proof of injury is not needed to rescind a contract for fraud. Proof of injury is required, however, to recover damages on the basis of fraud.
10. F. The UCC's Statute of Frauds requires that contracts for sales of goods priced at $500 or more ($5,000 or more under the 2003 amendments to the UCC) must be in writing to be enforceable. Of course, there are exceptions. Oral contracts for customized goods, for example, may be enforced in some circumstances, as may oral contracts between merchants that have been confirmed in writing.

Fill-in Questions

ratification; disaffirm; indicates; ratification

Multiple-Choice Questions

1. C. Ratification is the act of accepting and giving legal force to an obligation that was previously not enforceable. A minor may disaffirm a contract within a reasonable time after attaining majority, however, particularly if the minor returns the consideration received, does not take possession of the subject matter of the contract, or otherwise takes steps that would be inconsistent with ratification.
2. C. To disaffirm a contract, a minor must return whatever he or she received under it. In a state in which there is also an obligation to return the other party to the position he or she was in before the contract, the minor must also pay for any damage to the goods.
3. D. This promise (a covenant not to compete) is enforceable, because it is no broader than necessary for the other party's protection. Such promises may be considered contracts in restraint of trade, illegal on grounds of public policy, when they are broader than necessary (particularly in terms of geographic area and time), or are not accompanied by a sale of a business.
4. D. A contract with an unlicensed party is illegal and not enforceable by either party to it if the purpose of the licensing statute is to protect the public from unauthorized practitioners. If the purpose of the statute is to raise government revenues, however, the contract is enforceable.
5. B. The reasonableness of a covenant not to compete, accompanied by the sale of a business or included in an employment contract, is determined by the length of time and the size of the area in which the party agrees not to compete. In some cases, a court might even reform overly restrictive terms to prevent any undue burdens or hardships.
6. C. This statement is none of the other choices because it is a statement of opinion, and thus is not generally subject to a claim of fraud or any of the other causes of action listed here. A fact is objective and verifiable. Puffery often involves vague assertions of quality. Affirmatively concealing a material fact, failing to respond when asked, and in some cases failing to volunteer pertinent facts may constitute fraud, however. Taking advantage of a party with whom one is in a confidential relationship to influence their entering into a "good deal" might constitute undue influence. Threats of physical harm may amount to duress.
7. D. When parties contract, their agreement establishes the value of the object of their transaction for the moment. Each party is considered to assume the risk that the value will change or prove to be different from what he or she thought. In this case, the buyer assumed the risk of a drop in the price. If instead the mistake had involved a material fact and had been mutual, the buyer may have been able to avoid the contract (or enforce it).
8. C. Either party can enforce this oral contract. A contract that cannot be performed within one year must be in writing to be enforceable. Because the employee was hired to work for six months, the contract can be performed within a year and does not need to be in writing to be enforced.
9. D. A collateral promise must be in writing to be enforceable unless the main purpose of the party making the promise is to secure a benefit for himself or herself. Here, the problem does not include such a purpose. (A collateral promise is a secondary, or ancillary, promise to a primary, or principal, contractual relationship—a third party's promise to assume the debt of a primary party to a contract, for example.)

10. C. Under the UCC, an oral contract for goods priced at $500 or more ($5,000 under the 2003 amendments to the UCC) is enforceable to the extent that the buyer accepts delivery of the goods (or the seller accepts payment). Note that there must be delivery or payment for this exception to the Statute of Frauds to apply.

Issue Spotters

1. No. Generally, An exculpatory clause (a clause attempting to absolve parties of negligence or other wrongs) is not enforced if the party seeking its enforcement is involved in a business that is important to the public as a matter of practical necessity, such as an airline. Because of the essential nature of these services, they have an advantage in bargaining strength and could insist that anyone contracting for their services agree not to hold them liable.

2. Yes. Rescission may be granted on the basis of fraudulent misrepresentation. The elements of fraud include an intent to deceive, or *scienter*. *Scienter* exists if a party makes a statement recklessly, without regard to whether it is true or false, or if a party says or implies that a statement is made on some basis such as personal knowledge or personal investigation when it is not. An action for fraud can be maintained when a party who unknowingly misstates a material fact later learns of the misstatement but does not reveal it.

3. A court might conclude that under the doctrine of promissory estoppel, the employer is estopped from claiming the lack of a written contract as a defense. This oral contract may be enforced because the employer made a promise on which the employee justifiably relied in moving, the reliance was foreseeable, and injustice can be avoided only by enforcing the promise. If the court strictly enforces the Statute of Frauds, however, the employee may be without a remedy because a contract that cannot be performed within one year from the day after its making must be in writing to be enforceable.

Chapter 9

True-False Questions

1. F. Intended beneficiaries have legal rights in contracts under which they benefit. An intended beneficiary is a party whom the contracting parties intended to benefit. Third parties who benefit from a contract only incidentally (incidental beneficiaries) normally do not have rights under the contract.
2. T
3. T
4. F. A material breach of contract (which occurs when performance is not at least substantial) excuses the nonbreaching party from performance of his or her

contractual duties and gives the party a cause of action to sue for damages caused by the breach. A *minor* breach of contract does not excuse the nonbreaching party's duty to perform, however, although it may affect the extent of his or her performance and, like any contract breach, allows the nonbreaching party to sue for damages.
5. T
6. F. Liquidated damages are certain amounts of money estimated in advance of, and payable on, a breach of contract. *Liquidated* means determined, settled, or fixed.
7. T
8. T
9. F. There can be no enforceable contract if the doctrine of quasi contract is to be applied. Under this doctrine, to prevent unjust enrichment, the law implies a promise to pay the reasonable value for benefits received in the absence of an enforceable contract. This recovery is useful when one party has partially performed under a contract that is unenforceable.
10. T

Fill-in Questions

the contract price and the market price; specific performance; the contract price and the market price

Multiple-Choice Questions

1. A. The rights of an intended third party beneficiary to a contract vest when the original parties cannot rescind or change the contract without the third party's consent. This occurs when the beneficiary learns of the contract and manifests assent to it. This also occurs when the beneficiary changes position in reliance on the contract.
2. A. An accord is an executory contract to perform an act to satisfy a contractual duty that has not been discharged (that is, to provide and accept performance different from what was originally promised). An accord suspends the original obligation. A satisfaction is the performance of the accord. If a party does not perform under an accord, the nonbreaching party can bring an action based on either the accord or the original contract.
3. C. A novation substitutes a new party for an original party, by agreement of all the parties. The requirements are a previous valid obligation, an agreement of all the parties to a new contract, extinguishment of the old obligation, and a new contract (which must meet the requirements for a valid contract, including consideration).
4. D. Accord and satisfaction, agreement, and operation of law are valid bases on which contracts are discharged, but most contracts are discharged by the parties' doing what they promised to do. A contract is fully discharged by performance when the contracting

parties have fully performed what they agreed to do (exchange services for payment, for example).

5. C. This contract is discharged by objective impossibility of performance. On this basis, a contract may be discharged if, after it is made, performance becomes objectively impossible because, as in this problem, a change in the law renders performance illegal. This is also the result if one of the parties dies or becomes incapacitated, or the subject matter of the contract is destroyed. Circumstances that would not qualify include nonpayment because a certain bank is closed, a labor strike, and bad weather (which would more likely only temporarily suspend performance).

6. A. The failure of one party to perform under a contract entitles the other party to rescind the contract. Both parties, however, must make restitution (return goods, property, or money previously conveyed). Here, on breaching the contract, which entitled the employer to rescind the deal, the contractor did not return the amount of the employer's payment.

7. C. A breach of contract by failing to perform entitles the nonbreaching party to rescind the contract, and the parties must make restitution by returning whatever benefit they conferred on each other, particularly when the breaching party would otherwise be unjustly enriched.

8. C. Under a contract for a sale of goods, the usual measure of compensatory damages is the difference between the contract price and the market price, plus incidental damages. On a seller's breach, the measure includes the difference between what the seller would have been owed if he or she had performed and what the buyer paid elsewhere for the goods.

9. B. The measure of damages on breach of a construction contract depends on which party breaches and when the breach occurs. If, as in this problem, the owner (buyer) breaches during construction, normally the contractor (seller) may recover its profit plus the costs incurred up to the time of the breach.

10. B. On the seller's breach of a contract, the buyer is entitled to be compensated for the loss of the bargain. Here, the buyer will receive what was contracted for, but it will be late. When, as in this problem, a seller knew that the buyer would lose business if the goods were not delivered on time, the loss of the bargain is the consequential damages (the amount lost as a foreseeable consequence of the breach).

Issue Spotters

1. No. The builder has substantially performed its duties under the contract. Assuming this performance was in good faith, the builder could thus successfully sue for the value of the work performed. For the sake of justice and fairness, the buyer will be held to the duty to pay, less damages for the deviation from the contract deadline.

2. A nonbreaching party is entitled to his or her benefit of the bargain under the contract. Here, the innocent party is entitled to be put in the position she would have been in if the contract had been fully performed. The measure of the benefit is the cost to complete the work ($500). These are compensatory damages.

3. This clause is known as an exculpatory clause. In many cases, such clauses are not enforced, but to be effective in any case, all contracting parties must have consented to it. A clause excluding liability for negligence may be enforced if the contract was made by parties in roughly equal bargaining positions, as two large corporations would be.

Chapter 10

True-False Questions

1. F. Courts usually do enforce shrink-wrap agreements. The reasoning is that the shrink-wrap terms constitute an offer, proposed by a seller and accepted by a buyer after the buyer had an opportunity to review the terms.

2. T

3. T

4. F. Under the Electronic Signatures in Global and National Commerce (E-SIGN) Act, which Congress passed in 2000, no contract, record, or signature can be denied legal effect simply because it is in an electronic form (although some documents are specifically excluded).

5. F. The UETA, like the Uniform Computer Information Transactions Act (UCITA), was drafted by the National Conference of Commissioners on Uniform State Laws and the American Law Institute as a proposal of legislation for the states to enact individually. Most states have enacted the UETA. (Only a couple of states have enacted the UCITA.)

6. F. Parties to a transaction can waive or vary any or all of the provisions of the UETA (that is, they can opt out or choose not to have it apply), but the UETA applies in the absence of an agreement to the contrary. The parties must have agreed to conduct their transaction electronically, however.

7. T

8. T

9. F. Under the UETA, an e-record is considered received when it enters the recipient's processing system in a readable form, even if no person is aware of its receipt.

10. T

Fill-in Questions

need not; E-SIGN Act and the UETA; but does not create; does not apply

Multiple-Choice Questions

1. B. The terms of a shrink-wrap agreement typically concern warranties, remedies, and other issues. The other answer choices in this question represent locations of the terms in click-on agreements, in "fine print," and in computer code that may not be readable by humans. A shrink-wrap agreement is typically between the manufacturer of hardware or software and its user.

2. A. Shrink-wrap agreements have not always been enforced. The most important consideration is the time at which the manufacturer communicated the terms to the end-user. If they are proposed after a contract is entered into, they can be construed as proposals for additional terms, to which the consumer must expressly agree.

3. C. A binding contract can be created by clicking on, for example, an "I agree" button if an opportunity is provided to read the terms before the button is clicked. If the terms are not revealed until after an agreement is made, however, it is unlikely that, as in cases involving shrink-wrap agreements, they would be considered part of the deal. Here, the problem states that the button referred to the terms, meaning the buyer knew, or should have known, what was being agreed to.

4. B. Under the E-SIGN Act, no contract, record, or signature may be denied legal effect solely because it is in electronic form. An e-signature is as valid as a signature on paper, and an e-document is as valid as a paper document. One possible complication is that state laws on e-signatures are not uniform. Most state have enacted the Uniform Electronic Transactions Act (UETA) but with individual modifications.

5. A. The UETA does not apply unless the parties agree to use e-commerce in their transaction. The UETA does support all electronic transactions, but it does not provide rules for them.

6. D. To fall under the UETA, the parties to a contract must agree to conduct their transaction electronically. The UETA then applies in the absence of an agreement between the parties to the contrary, although they can waive or vary any or all of its provisions. Whether the contract involves computer information is irrelevant under the UETA.

7. C. To be "sent," an e-record must be properly directed from the sender's place of business to the intended recipient, in a form readable by the recipient's computer, at the recipient's place of business. This location is the recipient's place of business with the closest relation to the transaction. If a party does not have a place of business, the party's residence is used. An e-record is received when it enters the recipient's processing system in a readable form, even if no person is aware of the receipt

8. B. If the parties to a deal subject to the UETA agree to a security procedure and one party fails to detect an error because the party does not follow the procedure, the conforming party may be able to avoid the effect of the error. To do so, the conforming party must (1) promptly notify the non-conforming party of the error and of his or her intent not to be bound by it and (2) take reasonable steps to return any benefit or consideration received. If there can be no restitution, the transaction may not be avoidable. (If the parties do not agree on a security procedure, other state laws determine the effect of the mistake.)

9. D. The UETA applies only to e-records and e-signatures in a transaction (an interaction between two or more people relating to business, commercial, or government activities). The UETA does not apply to laws governing wills or testamentary trusts, the UCC (except Articles 2 and 2A), the Uniform Computer Information Transactions Act, and other laws excluded by the states that adopt the UETA.

10. D. The UETA is like most other uniform acts that apply in the business context. For contracts that fall within its scope, it applies in the absence of an agreement to the contrary. Parties who would otherwise be covered by the UETA can agree to opt out of all or part of the act and agree not to be covered by it, however, or vary any or all of its provisions. The parties must have agreed to conduct their transaction electronically, however.

Issue Spotters

1. The effect of an e-record is determined from its context and circumstances. Any relevant evidence can prove that an e-record is, or is not, the act of a party to a deal. A party's name or "signature" on an e-record is not necessary to give effect to it, although a party's name typed on, for example, an e-mail purchase order, qualifies as a "signature" and is attributable to the party.

2. If a state enacts the UETA without modifying it, the E-SIGN Act does not preempt it. The E-SIGN Act preempts modified versions of the UETA to the extent that they are inconsistent with the E-SIGN Act. Under the E-SIGN Act, states may enact alternative procedures or requirements for the use or acceptance of e-records or e-signatures if the procedures or requirements are consistent with the E-SIGN Act, the procedures do not give greater legal effect to any specific type of technology, and the state law refers to the E-SIGN Act if the state adopts the alternative after the enactment of the E-SIGN Act.

3. First, it might be noted that the UETA does not apply unless the parties to a contract agree to use e-commerce in their transaction. In this deal, of course, the parties used e-commerce. The UETA removes barriers to e-commerce by giving the same legal effect to e-records and e-signatures as to paper documents and signatures. The UETA it does not include rules for those transactions, however.

Chapter 11

True-False Questions

1. T
2. T
3. F. Unlike the common law rule that a contract modification must be supported by new consideration, the UCC requires no consideration for an agreement modifying a contract.
4. F. A contract will be enforceable, and a writing will be sufficient under the UCC's Statute of Frauds, if it indicates that a contract was intended, if it includes a quantity term, and—except for transactions between merchants—if it is signed by the party against whom enforcement is sought. Most terms can be proved by oral testimony or be supplied by the UCC's open term provisions (for example, price, delivery, and payment terms). A contract is not enforceable beyond the quantity of goods shown in the writing, however, except for output and requirements contracts.
5. T
6. T
7. F. Title passes at the time and place at which the seller delivers the goods—unless the parties agree otherwise, which is always an option under the UCC.
8. T
9. F. Under a *shipment* contract, the risk of loss (and title) passes from seller to buyer at time and place of shipment. Under a destination contract, risk of loss (and title) passes when the goods are tendered at a certain destination.
10. T

Fill-in Questions

F.O.B.; F.O.B.; F.O.B.; F.A.S.

Multiple-Choice Questions

1. C. A merchant is a person who acts in a mercantile capacity, possessing or using expertise specifically related to the goods being sold. A merchant for one type of goods is not necessarily a merchant for another type, however. The test is whether the merchant holds himself or herself out by occupation as having knowledge or skill unique to the goods in the transaction.
2. A. Under the UCC, a sales contract will not fail for indefiniteness even if one or more terms are left open, as long as the parties intended to make a contract and there is a reasonably certain basis for the court to grant an appropriate remedy. If the price term is left open, for example, and the parties cannot later agree on a price, a court will set the price according to what is reasonable at the time for delivery. If one of the parties is to set the price, it must be set in good faith. If it is not fixed, the other party can set the price or treat the contract as canceled.
3. D. In a transaction between merchants, additional terms in the acceptance of an offer become part of a contract *unless* they qualify as one of these exceptions.
4. A. The contract is subject to the Statute of Frauds, and thus should be in writing to be fully enforceable. (Initialed notes, among other things, may constitute a sufficient writing.) A contract that is subject to the Statute of Frauds but is not in writing will be enforceable, however, under the partial performance exception when payment is made and accepted (at least to the extent of the payment actually made). Other enforceable exceptions include admissions in court and contracts for specially made goods (if they are not suitable for sale to others and if substantial steps have been taken toward their manufacture).
5. A. An unconscionable clause is one that is so unfair and one-sided that it would be unreasonable to enforce it. When considering such a clause, a court can choose among the answers choices in this problem. To assess unconscionability, a court may weigh such factors as a high price, a consumer's level of education, and his or her capacity to compare prices.
6. B. This agreement (F.O.B. Alpha) is a shipment contract under which the seller is not required to deliver the goods to the buyer's location, but only to place them into the possession of a carrier. Under this shipment contract, the risk of loss passes when the seller gives the goods to the carrier.
7. A. When goods are to be picked up by a buyer, if a seller is not a merchant, risk passes on the seller's tender of delivery (unless the parties agree otherwise). The goods were tendered before the theft, so the buyer suffers the loss. If the seller is a merchant, the risk of loss passes when the buyer takes possession of the goods.
8. A. If a bailee holds goods for a seller and the goods are delivered without being moved, under a negotiable document of title, the risk of loss passes when the buyer receives the document. If the document is nonnegotiable, however, more is required to transfer the risk: the buyer must also have had a reasonable time to present the document and demand the goods. In either case, the risk can also pass on the bailee's acknowledgment of the buyer's right to possess the goods. In any case, if the bailee refuses to recognize the buyer's right, the loss stays with the seller.
9. B. Under a destination contract, the risk of loss passes when the seller tenders delivery at the specified destination. Here, the destination was the buyer, and the goods were destroyed before they reached that location. Also, note that "F.O.B." indicates the seller bears the cost of the transport to the specified destination.
10. A. Generally, the party who breaches a contract bears the risk of loss. Here, the seller breached by shipping defective goods. The risk would have passed to the buyer if the buyer accepted the goods in spite of their defects. (If the buyer had accepted the goods and

then discovered the defects, the buyer could have revoked its acceptance, which would have transferred the risk back to the seller.)

Issue Spotters

1.   A shipment of nonconforming goods constitutes an acceptance and a breach, unless the seller seasonably notifies the buyer that the nonconforming shipment does not constitute an acceptance and is offered only as an accommodation. Without the notification, the shipment is an acceptance and a breach. Thus, here, the shipment was both an acceptance and a breach.

2.   The seller suffers the loss. If goods are so nonconforming that a buyer has the right to reject them, the risk of loss will not pass from the seller to the buyer until the defects are cured or the buyer accepts the defective goods. Here, the defects had not been cured and the buyer had not yet accepted the goods. Note that if the goods were shipped and arrived at the buyer's location, the risk would remain with the seller because the goods were defective.

3.   No. A seller has voidable title if the goods that he or she is selling were paid for with a bad check (a check that is later dishonored). Normally, a buyer acquires only the title that the seller had, or had the power to transfer, but a seller with voidable title can transfer good title to a good faith purchaser (one who buys in good faith without knowledge that the seller did not have the right to sell the goods). Under those circumstances, an original owner cannot recover goods from a good faith purchaser. Here, the ultimate buyer is a good faith purchaser.

Chapter 12

True-False Questions

1.   T
2.   T
3.   T
4.   F. If the parties do not agree otherwise, the buyer or lessee must pay for the goods at the time and place of their receipt (subject, in most cases, to the buyer or lessee's right to inspect). When a sale is on credit, a buyer must pay according to credit terms, not when the goods are received. Credit terms may provide for payment within thirty days, for example. A credit period usually begins on the date of shipment.
5.   F. If a contract does not state where goods are to be delivered, and the buyer is to pick them up, the place for delivery is the seller's place of business (unless the parties know that the goods are elsewhere, in which case the place of their delivery is their location).

Shipment and destination contracts are subject to different rules that depend on their terms.

6.   F. A buyer or lessee who accepts nonconforming goods can revoke the acceptance, but only notifying the seller or lessor, which must occur within a reasonable time and before goods have, for example, spoiled. If the goods are perishable, the buyer or lessee must follow any reasonable instructions of the seller or lessor regarding the goods. (This is also the case when the buyer or lessee rejects the goods.)

7.   F. Before the time for performance, if a buyer or lessee clearly communicates his or her intent not to perform, the seller or lessor can suspend performance and wait to see if the other will perform, or the seller or lessor can treat the anticipatory repudiation as a breach, suspend performance, and pursue a remedy.

8.   F. A buyer can reject an installment only if its nonconformity *substantially impairs* the value of the installment and it cannot be cured (in which case, the seller has breached the contract).

9.   T
10.   T

Fill-in Questions

conforming; and; buyer; receipt; even if

Multiple-Choice Questions

1.   C. The parties to a contract can stipulate the time, place, and manner of delivery. In the absence of specific details, however, the seller or lessor's obligation is to tender delivery at a reasonable hour and in a reasonable manner. The buyer must be notified, and the goods must be kept available for a reasonable time.

2.   B. Replevin is an action to recover specific goods in the possession of a party who is wrongfully withholding them. When a seller (or lessor) refuses to deliver (or repudiates the contract), the buyer or lessee may maintain an action to replevy the goods. The buyer or lessee must show, however, an inability to cover.

3.   C. It is the seller's obligation to tender delivery of goods. Under a shipment contract, a seller must make a reasonable contract for the transportation of goods, tender to the buyer whatever documents are necessary to obtain possession of goods from the carrier, and notify the buyer that shipment has been made.

4.   C. If a buyer repudiates a contract or wrongfully refuses to accept goods, a seller can sue for damages equal to the difference between the contract price and the market price at the time and place of tender. The seller can also recover incidental damages, which include the cost of transporting the goods. If the market price is less than the contract price, damages include the seller's lost profits.

5.   B. Under the circumstances in this problem, the buyer's best course is to attempt to obtain substitute

goods for those that were due under the contract. When a buyer is forced to obtain cover, the buyer can recover from the seller the difference between the cost of the cover and the contract price, plus incidental and consequential damages, less whatever expenses (such as delivery costs) were saved as a result of the seller's breach.

6. C. Depending on the circumstances, when a seller or lessor delivers nonconforming goods, the buyer or lessee can reject the part of the goods that does not conform (and rescind the contract or obtain cover). The buyer or lessee may instead revoke acceptance, or he or she may recover damages, for accepted goods.

7. C. A buyer (or lessee) can sue for damages when a seller (or lessor) repudiates the contract or fails to deliver the goods, or when the buyer has rightfully rejected or revoked acceptance of the goods. The place for determining the price is the place at which the seller was to deliver the goods. The buyer may also recover incidental and consequential damages, less expenses saved due to the breach.

8. C. In an installment contract, a buyer can reject an installment only if a nonconformity substantially impairs the value of the installment and cannot be cured. Thus, among the answer possibilities here, the rejection of the first installment is the best choice. This deviation might be curable, however, by an adjustment in price or by a shipment of conforming goods, so an answer that suggested these alternatives might represent an even better choice.

9. B. Unless the contract provides otherwise, a buyer (or lessee) has an absolute right to inspect tendered goods before making payment, to verify that they are as ordered. If they are not as ordered, the buyer has no duty to pay, and the seller cannot enforce any right to payment.

10. A. If, before the time of performance, a party to a contract informs the other party that he or she will not perform, the nonbreaching party can treat the repudiation as a final breach and seek a remedy or wait, for a commercially reasonable time, hoping that the breaching party will decide to honor the contract. In either case, the nonbreaching party can suspend his or her performance.

Issue Spotters

1. Yes. A seller is obligated to deliver goods in conformity with a contract in every detail. This is the perfect tender rule. The exception of the seller's right to cure does not apply here, because the seller delivered too little too late to take advantage of this exception.

2. Yes. In a case of anticipatory repudiation, a buyer (or lessee) can resort to any remedy for breach even if the buyer tells the seller (the repudiating party in this problem) that the buyer will wait for the seller's performance.

3. If a buyer wrongfully refuses to accept conforming goods, the seller can recover damages. The measure is the difference between the contract price and the market price (at the time and place of tender), plus incidental damages. If the market price is less than the contract price, the seller gets lost profits.

Chapter 13

True-False Questions

1. T

2. F. Warranties are not exclusive. A contract can include an implied warranty of merchantability, an implied warranty of fitness for a particular purpose, and any number of express warranties.

3. T

4. F. An action based on negligence does not require privity of contract. At one time, there was a requirement of privity in product liability actions based on negligence, but this requirement began to be eliminated decades ago. Privity of contract is also not a requirement to bring a suit based on strict product liability.

5. F. In an action based on strict liability, a plaintiff does not have to prove that there was a failure to exercise due care. That distinguishes an action based on strict liability from an action based on negligence, which requires proof of a lack of due care. A plaintiff must show, however, that (1) a product was defective, (2) the defendant was in the business of distributing the product, (3) the product was unreasonably dangerous due to the defect, (4) the plaintiff suffered harm, (5) the defect was the proximate cause of the harm, and (6) the goods were not substantially changed from the time they were sold.

6. T

7. T

8. T

9. F. Under certain circumstances, consumers have a right to rescind their contracts. This is particularly true when a creditor has not made all required disclosures. A contract entered into as part of a door-to-door sale may be rescinded within three days, regardless of the reason.

10. T

Fill-in Questions

can; can; can; need not; must

Multiple-Choice Questions

1. C. An implied warranty of merchantability arises in every sale of goods by a merchant who deals in goods of the kind. It makes no difference whether the

merchant knew of or could have discovered a defect that makes a product unsafe. The warranty is that the goods are "reasonably fit for the ordinary purposes for which such goods are used." The efficiency and the quality of their manufacture, and the manufacturer's compliance with government regulations, are not factors that directly influence this determination.

2. A. To disclaim an implied warranty of fitness for a particular purpose, a warranty must be conspicuous, but the word *fitness* does not have to be used. A disclaimer of the implied warranty of merchantability must mention *merchantability*. Warranties of title, however, can be disclaimed only by specific language (for example, a seller states that it is transferring only such rights as it has in the goods), or by circumstances that indicate no warranties of title are made.

3. D. This is a statement of opinion (puffing). Puffing creates no warranty. If the salesperson had said something factual about the vehicle (its miles per gallon, its total mileage, whether it had been in an accident, etc.), it would be more than puffing and could qualify as an express warranty.

4. D. In a product liability action based on strict liability, the plaintiff does not need to prove that anyone was at fault. Privity of contract is also not an element of an action in strict liability. A plaintiff does have to show, however, in a suit against a seller, that the seller was a merchant engaged in the business of selling the product on which the suit is based. Note that recovery is possible against sellers who are processors, assemblers, packagers, bottlers, wholesalers, distributors, retailers, or lessors, as well as against manufacturers.

5. C. If a manufacturer fails to use due care to make a product safe, the manufacturer may be liable for product liability based on negligence. This care must be used in designing the product, selecting the materials, producing the product, inspecting and testing any components, assembling the product, and placing warnings on the product.

6. D. The FTC has the power to issue a cease-and-desist order, but in some cases, such an order is not enough to stop the harm. With counteradvertising (also known as corrective advertising), an advertiser attempts to correct earlier misinformation by admitting that prior claims about a product were untrue.

7. B. A regular-size box of laundry soap, for example, cannot be labeled "super-size" to exaggerate the amount of product in the box. Labels on consumer goods must identify the product, the manufacturer, the distributor, the net quantity of the contents, and the quantity of each serving (if the number of servings is given). Other information may also be required.

8. D. In a door-to-door sale, a consumer generally has at least a three-day cooling-off period within which to rescind the transaction. Salespersons are required to give consumers written notice of this right. If a sales presentation is to a consumer who speaks only Spanish, the notice must be in Spanish, too.

9. C. Under the Fair Debt Collection Practices Act, once a debtor has refused to pay a debt, a collection agency can contact the debtor *only* to advise him or her of further action to be taken.

10. B. This is required under Regulation Z (which was issued by the Federal Reserve Board under the Truth in Lending Act) and applies to any creditor who, in the ordinary course of business, lends money or sells goods on credit to consumers, or arranges for credit for consumers. The information that must be disclosed includes: the specific dollar amount being financed; the annual percentage rate of interest; any financing charges, premiums or points; the number, amounts, and due dates of payments; and any penalties imposed on delinquent payments or prepayment.

Issue Spotters

1. Yes. The manufacturer is liable for the injuries to the user of the product. A manufacturer is liable for its failure to exercise due care to any person who sustains an injury proximately caused by a negligently made (defective) product. In this problem, the failure to inspect is a failure to use due care. Of course, the maker of the component part may also be liable.

2. Yes. Under the doctrine of strict liability, persons may be liable for the results of their acts regardless of their intentions or their exercise of reasonable care (that is, regardless of fault). There is no requirement of privity.

3. Yes. The FTC has issued rules to govern advertising techniques, including rules designed to prevent bait-and-switch advertising. Under the FTC guidelines, bait-and-switch advertising occurs if the seller refuses to show the advertised item, fails to have in stock a reasonable quantity of the item, fails to promise to deliver the advertised item within a reasonable time, or discourages employees from selling the item.

Chapter 14

True-False Questions

1. F. A negotiable instrument can be transferred by assignment or negotiation. When a transfer fails to qualify as a negotiation, it becomes an assignment and is governed by the rules of assignment under contract law.

2. T

3. F. To be negotiable, an instrument must be payable on demand or at a definite time. Instruments that say nothing about when payment is due are payable on demand.

4. F. This is an order instrument. Order instruments that meet the requirements for negotiability are negotiable. An instrument that contains any indication that does not purport to designate a specific payee (for example, "payable to bearer") is a bearer instrument. A bearer instrument that meets the requirements for negotiability is also negotiable. When an instrument is not negotiable, it may be transferred by assignment.

5. F. This promise would support a contract but would not satisfy the value requirement for HDC status. Value sufficient to make a holder an HDC includes taking an instrument in payment of, or as security for, a preexisting debt; giving a check in payment for the instrument; and performing the promise for which the instrument was issued.

6. F. Personal defenses (such as breach of contact or breach of warranty) can be used to avoid payment to an ordinary holder, but only universal defenses are good against an HDC.

7. T

8. T

9. F. All transferors of negotiable instruments, including those who present instruments for payment, make certain implied warranties regarding the instruments. For example, a person who transfers an instrument for payment warrants to any other person who in good faith accepts or pays the instrument, with some exceptions, that the instrument has not been altered.

10. F. An unauthorized signature can be binding, however, if the person whose name is signed ratifies it. The person's negligence may also prevent him or her from denying liability. Usually, when there is a forged or unauthorized indorsement, the burden of loss falls on the first party to take the instrument with the forged indorsement.

Fill-in Questions

payee; an indorsement in blank; bearer; delivery; order

Multiple-Choice Questions

1. A. Before the payee indorsed the back of the check, it was an order instrument. It could be negotiated further only with the payee's signature (and with delivery). After the check was indorsed, it became a bearer instrument and could be negotiated by delivery alone. If a bearer instrument is lost, it can be negotiated by whoever finds it.

2. D. A draft is created when the party creating it orders another party to pay money, usually to a third party. The drawee (the party on whom the draft is drawn) must be obligated to the drawer, either by an agreement or through a debtor-creditor relationship, for the drawee to be obligated to the drawer to honor the draft. A trade acceptance is a draft; a check is a draft.

3. C. A restrictive indorsement requires the indorsee to comply with certain instructions regarding the funds involved (but it does not restrict the negotiation of the instrument). A blank indorsement specifies no particular indorsee and can be a simple signature. A qualified indorsement disclaims contract liability on the instrument (for example, an indorser adding "without recourse" to his or her signature is a qualified indorsement). A special indorsement names the indorsee ("pay to Adam") with the signature of the indorser.

4. C. A holder of a time instrument who takes it after its due date is "on notice" that it is overdue. Such a holder cannot become an HDC. Nonpayment by the due date should indicate to any purchaser who is obligated to pay that there is a defense to payment on the instrument.

5. B. If a drawer believes an imposter to be the named payee at the time the drawer issues an instrument, the imposter's indorsement is effective (not considered a forgery) as for as the drawer is concerned. This is also true when there are other parties between the drawer, the imposter, and the drawee (for example, when the imposter negotiates the check to a third person who presents it to the drawee for payment).

6. D. If a person is deceived into signing a negotiable instrument, believing that he or she is signing something other than a negotiable instrument, fraud in the execution is committed against the signer, who has a valid defense against payment even if the instrument is negotiated to an HDC.

7. B. Makers of notes and acceptors of negotiable instruments are primarily liable. (Drawers—and indorsers—have secondary liability.) A drawee (the bank in this problem) becomes primarily liable becomes an acceptor, which occurs when, as here, it accepts a check for payment.

8. B. Based on their signatures on an instrument, a drawer and a payee-indorser have secondary liability. Parties who are secondarily liable promise to pay only if the following events occur: (1) the instrument is properly and timely presented; (2) the instrument is dishonored; and (3) notice of dishonor is given in a timely manner to the secondarily liable party.

9. A. When a drawee fails to accept or pay a draft, including a check, the drawer's (secondary) liability arises. The party holding the draft can then attempt to obtain payment from the drawer.

10. B. A holder takes an instrument for value when he or she pays cash for it, gives a negotiable instrument for it, or makes an irrevocable commitment to a third person. The holder is an HDC to the extent that he or she gives value for the instrument (and meets the other requirements for HDC status). Here, the value given for the instrument does *not* include the unperformed part of the agreement. Thus, the seller is an HDC only to the extent for which value has been given at the time that the note is sold.

Issue Spotters

1. This party is an HDC to the full extent of the note. One of the requirements for becoming an HDC is taking an instrument for value. A party may attain HDC status to the extent that he or she gives value for the instrument. Paying with cash or with a check is giving value.

2. Yes. As in cases of forgery, in which the person whose name is used is not liable, this firm can assert the defense of the unauthorized signature against any HDC, because the employee exceeded authority in signing the check on behalf of the firm.

3. No. When a drawer's employee provides the drawer with the name of a fictitious payee (a payee whom the drawer does not actually intend to have any interest in an instrument), a forgery of the payee's name is effective to pass good title to subsequent transferees.

Chapter 15

True-False Questions

1. T

2. F. If a bank pays a check over a customer's proper stop-payment order, the bank is obligated to recredit the customer's account, but only for the amount of the actual loss suffered by the drawer because of the wrongful payment.

3. F. A bank's duty to honor its customer's checks is not absolute (although when a bank receives an item payable from a customer's account, but there are insufficient funds in the account to cover the amount, the bank can choose to pay it and charge the customer's account). Failing to pay an overdraft will not subject the bank to criminal prosecution, though a person who writes a bad check may be prosecuted (and sued).

4. T

5. T

6. T

7. T

8. F. Under the Expedited Funds Availability Act of 1987, there are different availability schedules for different funds, depending on such factors as the location of the bank on which an item is drawn, what type of item it is, the age and activity of an account, and the amount of the item.

9. T

10. F. A forged drawer's signature on a check has no legal effect as the signature of the party whose name is signed. If the bank pays the check, the bank must recredit the customer's account (unless the customer's negligence contributed substantially to the forgery).

Fill-in Questions

drawer; creditor; principal; drawee; debtor; agent

Multiple-Choice Questions

1. D. When a bank pays a check on a drawer's forged signature, generally the bank is liable. This is particularly true when the bank's negligence substantially contributes to the forgery. If the customer's negligence contributed to the forgery, however, the bank may not be liable. The amount of the check does not affect liability.

2. C. Each bank in the collection chain, including the depositary bank, must pass the check on before midnight of the next banking day following receipt. Under the deferred posting rule, a check received after a bank's cutoff hour, can be considered received the next day.

3. D. This is assuming the drawer's state allows oral stop-payment orders. If a drawee bank pays a check over a customer's stop-payment order, the bank is obligated to recredit the account of the customer, but the bank is liable for no more than the actual loss suffered by the drawer.

4. A. A bank that pays a customer's check bearing a forged indorsement must recredit the customer's account or be liable to the drawer customer for breach of contract. A customer has a duty to examine returned checks and corresponding bank statements, however, and must report any forged indorsements within three years.

5. B. A drawee bank's contract is with its customer, not with those who present its customers' checks for payment. Thus, a drawee bank is not liable to a holder who presents a check for payment, even if the drawer has sufficient funds on deposit to pay the check. The holder's recourse is against the drawer, who may subsequently hold the bank liable for a wrongful refusal to pay.

6. A. A bank is not obligated to pay a stale, uncertified check. If the bank decides to pay it, however, the bank might consult the customer first or simply pay it an d charge the customer's account of the amount.

7. C. If a drawee bank cashes a customer's check over a forged indorsement, or fails to detect an alteration on a check of its customer-drawer and cashes the check, the bank is liable for the loss. (The customer's negligence can shift the loss, however.) The bank may be able to recover some of the loss from the forger, if he or she can be found.

8. C. If a drawee bank cashes a customer's check over the customer's (drawer's) forged signature, the bank is liable for the loss. (Of course, this is assuming that the customer's negligence did not cause the loss—the customer's negligence can shift the loss, as noted above.) The bank may be able to recover at least some of the loss from the forger, however.

9. C. The customer is liable for this amount because the bank was not notified that the card was missing until after the withdrawal. If a customer does not inform the institution within less than two business days after learning of a card's loss or theft, the customer's liability for unauthorized transactions is up to $500.

10. D. An issuer of e-money may be subject to the Right to Financial Privacy Act if the issuer is deemed to be (1) a bank by virtue of its holding customer funds or (2) an entity that issues a physical card similar to a credit or debit card. In other words, accepting customer deposits would be enough, but investigating credit backgrounds would not. (As its name implies, the Right to Financial Privacy Act provides legal safeguards for the privacy of a user of e-money against its issuer.) An entity that does not accept deposits may be subject to other laws, including the Uniform Money Services Act.

Issue Spotters

1. Yes, to both questions. In a civil suit, a drawer is liable to a payee or to a holder of a check that is not honored. If intent to defraud can be proved, the drawer can also be subject to criminal prosecution for writing a bad check.

2. Yes, to both questions. The general rule is that a bank must re-credit a customer's account when it pays on a forged signature. The bank has no right to recover from a holder who, without knowledge, cashes a check bearing a forged drawer's signature, however. Thus, the bank in this problem cannot collect from its customer or from the party who cashed the check. The bank's recourse is to look for the thief.

3. The drawer is entitled to $6,300—the amount to which the check was altered ($7,000) less the amount that the drawer ordered the bank to pay ($700). The bank may recover this amount from the party who presented the altered check for payment.

Chapter 16

True-False Questions

1. T

2. F. The financing statement must include the names of the debtor and creditor, and describe the collateral. Also, to avoid problems arising from different descriptions, a secured party can repeat the security agreement's description in the financing statement or file the two together.

3. F. A debtor who has defaulted has redemption rights. Before the secured party decides to retain the collateral or before it is disposed of, the debtor can take back the collateral by tendering performance of all secured obligations and paying the secured party's expenses. (Other secured parties have this same right.)

4. F. When more than one creditor claims a security interest in the same collateral, the first interest to be filed takes priority. The first to attach has priority if none of the interests has been perfected.

5. T

6. T

7. F. This is the most important concept in suretyship: a surety can use any defenses available to a debtor (except personal defenses) to avoid liability on the obligation to the creditor. Note, though, that a debtor does need not to have defaulted on the underlying obligation before a surety can be required to answer for the debt. Before a *guarantor* can be required to answer for the debt of a debtor, the debtor must have defaulted on the underlying obligation, however.

8. F. Any individual can be a debtor under Chapter 7, and any debtor who is liable on a claim held by a creditor may file for bankruptcy under Chapter 7.

9. F. The filing of a bankruptcy petition, voluntary or involuntary, automatically stays most litigation and other actions by creditors against the debtor and his or her property. A creditor may ask for relief from the stay, but a creditor who willfully violates the stay may be liable for actual damages, costs, and fees, as well as punitive damages.

10. F. Under Chapter 11, the creditors and the debtor formulate a plan under which the debtor pays some of the debts, the other debts are discharged, and the debtor is then allowed to continue in business.

Fill-in Questions

7; 11; 13; 7; 11; 13; 7; 11; 13

Multiple-Choice Questions

1. C. A *financing statement* must provide the names of the debtor and the creditor and describe the collateral covered by the security agreement. Filing a financing statement (which is the most common means of perfecting a security interest) gives notice to other creditors of the secured party's interest.

2. C. The first security interest to be filed or to be perfected has priority over other filed or perfected security interests. Although the first lender was not the first to provide funds to the debtor, it was the first to file its financing statement. Priority between perfected security interests is nearly always determined by the time of perfection (which is usually by filing). Note, though, that perfection may not protect a secured party's interest against the claim of a buyer in the ordinary course of business, and some others.

3. D. In most states, filing is in a central office (of the state in which the debtor is located). When collateral consists of timber to be cut, fixtures, or collateral to be extracted, a filing in the county in which the col-

lateral is located is typically required. Of course, if perfection is by a pledge (possession), no filing is necessary.

4. B. Garnishment is a collection remedy directed at a debtor's property or rights held by a third party. A garnishment order can be served on a judgment debtor's employer (or bank, or other third party) so that part of the debtor's paycheck (or bank account, or other property) will be paid (or otherwise delivered) to the creditor.

5. C. The debt is $200,000. The amount of the homestead exemption ($50,000) is subtracted from the sale price of the house ($150,000), and the remainder ($100,000) is applied against the debt. Proceeds from the sale of any nonexempt personal property could also be applied against the debt. The debtor gets the amount of the homestead exemption, of course.

6. A. A guarantor is secondarily liable (that is, the principal must first default). Also, in this problem, if the officer were, for example, the borrower's only salaried employee, the guaranty would not have to be in writing under the main-purpose exception to the Statute of Frauds. A surety is primarily liable (that is, the creditor can look to the surety for payment as soon as the debt is due, whether or not the principal debtor has defaulted). Usually, also, in the case of a guarantor, a creditor must have attempted to collect from the principal, because usually a debtor would not otherwise be declared in default.

7. C. Under Chapter 11, creditors and debtor plan for the debtor to pay some debts, be discharged of the rest, and continue in business. Under Chapter 13, with an appropriate plan, a small business debtor can also pay some (or all) debts, be discharged of the rest, and continue in business. A petition for a discharge in bankruptcy under Chapter 11 may be filed by a sole proprietor, a partnership, or a corporation; a petition for a discharge under Chapter 13, however, may be filed only by a sole proprietor, among these business entities.

8. D. Under Chapter 13, a debtor can submit a plan under which he or she continues in possession of his or her assets, but turns over disposable income for a three-year period, after which most debts are discharged. When applicable, a Chapter 13 plan must provide for the surrender of all collateral to the creditors. Note that a court will not refuse to approve a Chapter 13 plan on the objection of a creditor or a trustee if the property to be distributed under the plan is ore than the amount of the creditors' claims.

9. B. Under Chapter 7 or Chapter 11, a corporate debtor (or an individual debtor or a partnership, but not a farmer or a charitable institution) who has twelve or more creditors can be forced into bankruptcy by three or more of them, who collectively have unsecured claims for at least a certain amount. (The amount is periodically increased.) A debtor with less than twelve creditors can be involuntarily petitioned into bankruptcy by one or more of them, if the petitioner (or petitioners) has a claim for at least a certain amount.

10. D. Claims that are not dischargeable in bankruptcy include the claims listed in the other answer choices: claims for back taxes accruing within three years before the bankruptcy, claims for alimony and child support, and claims for certain student loans. There are many others.

Issue Spotters

1. A creditor can put other creditors on notice by perfecting its interest—filing a financing statement in the appropriate public office, or taking possession of the collateral until the debtor repays the loan.

2. Yes. In this problem, the party who assured the lender of payment on behalf of the debtor is a surety. A surety has a right of reimbursement from the debtor for all outlays the surety makes, as here, on behalf of the suretyship arrangement.

3. The order of their priority is the party with the mechanic's lien, the party with the perfected security interest, and, lastly, the party with the unperfected security interest. Mechanic's liens (and artisan's liens) have priority over perfected security interests. Secured parties have the next highest priority. Unsecured creditors are generally paid last, if at all.

Chapter 17

True-False Questions

1. T

2. T

3. T

4. T

5. F. An agent is liable for his or her own torts, but a principal may also be liable under the doctrine of *respondeat superior*. The key is whether the tort is committed within the scope of employment. One of the important factors is whether the principal authorized the act that constituted the tort.

6. T

7. F. The parties to an agency may always have the *power* to terminate the agency at any time, but they may not always have the *right*. If a party who terminates an agency does not have the right to do so, he or she may be liable for breach of contract.

8. T

9. F. An e-agent is a semi-autonomous computer program that is capable of executing specific tasks, including responding to e-messages or other e-actions without review by a human being.

10. F. One of the main attributes of an agency relationship is that the agent can enter into binding contracts on behalf of the principal. When an agent acts within the scope of his or her authority in entering a contract, the principal is bound, whether the principal's identity was disclosed, partially disclosed, or undisclosed to the other party to the contact.

Fill-in Questions

performance; notification; loyalty; obedience; accounting

Multiple-Choice Questions

1.   A. Agency law is essential to the existence of most business entities, including corporations, because without agents, most firms could not do business. A corporate officer who serves in a representative capacity, as in this problem, is an agent. The corporation is the principal. For a contract to be binding on the firm, it needs only to be signed by the agent and to be within the scope of the officer's authority.

2.   A. There is a long list of factors that courts can consider in determining whether an individual is an employee or an independent contractor, and all of the choices in this question are among those factors. The most important factor, however, is the degree of control that the employer has over the details of the work.

3.   B. In performing an agency, an agent is expected to use reasonable diligence and skill, which is the degree of skill of a reasonable person under similar circumstances. If an agent claims special skills, such as those of in this problem, he or she is expected to use those skills.

4.   A. An agent's duties to a principal include a duty to act solely in the principal's interest in matters concerning the principal's business. This is the duty of loyalty. The agent must act solely in the principal's interest and not in the interest of the agent, or some other party. It is also a breach of the duty of loyalty to use a principal's trade secrets or other confidential information (but not acquired skills) even after the agency has terminated.

5.   D. Implied authority can be conferred by custom, inferred from the agent's position, or inferred as reasonably necessary to carry out express authority. In determining whether an agent has the implied authority to do a specific act, the question is whether it is reasonable for the agent to believe that he or she has the authority.

6.   A. Until an agent is notified of the principal's decision to terminate the agency relationship, the agent's authority continues.   Similarly, third parties with whom the agent deals must be informed of the termination to end the agent's apparent authority, as regards those third parties. Unless an agency is in writing, in which case it must be terminated in writing, an agent can learn of a termination through any means.

7.   B. When an agent enters into a contract within the scope of his or her authority, the principal is liable, whether or not the principal's identity was disclosed. The agent is also liable as a party to the contract when neither the identity of the principal nor the fact of the agency is disclosed.

8.   A. Apparent authority exists when a principal causes a third party reasonably to believe that an agent has the authority to act, even if the agent does not otherwise have the authority to do so. If the third party changes positions in reliance on the principal's representation, the principal may be estopped from denying the authority. Thus, here, the principal could not hold the customers liable for failing to pay.

9.   C. An agent (or employee) is liable for his or her own torts, whether or not they were committed within the scope of a principal's employment. The principal is also liable under the doctrine of *respondeat superior* when a tort is within the scope of the employment. One of the important factors in determining liability is whether the agent was on the principal's business or on a "frolic of his or her own."

10.   D. An agency relationship can be created only for a legal purpose. An agency relationship created for an illegal purpose, such as a scheme to defraud, is unenforceable. Also, it should be kept in mind that although a principal must have contractual capacity, an agent does not need it. Even a person who is legally incompetent can be an agent.

Issue Spotters

1.   When a person enters into a contract on another's behalf without the authority to do so, the other may be liable on the contract if he or she approves or affirms that contract. In other words, the employer-principal would be liable on the note in this problem on ratifying it. Whether the employer-principal ratifies the note or not, the unauthorized agent is most likely also liable on it.

2.   Yes. A principal has a duty to indemnify an agent for liabilities incurred because of authorized and lawful acts and transactions and for losses suffered because of the principal's failure to perform his or her duties.

3.   Most likely, yes. A principal is liable for a loss due to an agent's knowing misrepresentation if the representation was made within the scope of the agency and the agent's scope of authority.

Chapter 18

True-False Questions

1.   T

2.   F. Employers are free to offer employees no benefits. Federal and state governments participate in insurance programs designed to protect employees and their families by covering some of the financial impact of retirement, disability, death, and hospitalization.

3.   T

4. F. A "whistleblower" is one who reports wrongdoing. These statutes protect employees who report their employers' wrongdoing from retaliation on the part of those employers.

5. F. The Electronic Communications Privacy Act prohibits the interception of telephone (and other electronic) communications. Some courts recognize an exception for employers monitoring employee business-related calls, but monitoring personal conversations is not permitted.

6. F. An employer may be liable even though an employee did the harassing, if the employer knew, or should have known, and failed to take corrective action, or if the employee was in a supervisory position. Similarly, the employer may be liable for harassment by a non-employee, if the employer knew, or should have known, and failed to take corrective action.

7. T

8. T

9. F. Title VII covers only employers with fifteen or more employees, labor unions with fifteen or more members, labor unions that operate hiring halls, employment agencies, and federal, state, and local agencies.

10. T

Fill-in Questions

either; unless; may; Some; A few states; may not

Multiple-Choice Questions

1. A. Investigating theft is the only circumstance in which an employer may require polygraph tests. Drug tests are prohibited by some states, and restricted by others or by collective bargaining agreements. Their use may also be subject to tort actions for invasion of privacy. An employer may monitor employees' *business* phone conversations but not their *private* ones.

2. B. Intentionally inflicted injuries are not covered by workers' compensation. Many states cover problems arising out of preexisting conditions, but that is not part of the test for coverage. To collect benefits, an employee must notify the employer of an injury and file a claim with the appropriate state agency.

3. B. Under the Family and Medical Leave Act (FMLA) of 1993, employees can take up to twelve weeks of family or medical leave during any twelve-month period and are entitled to continued health insurance coverage during the leave. Employees are also guaranteed the same, or a comparable, job on returning to work.

4. C. Under the Consolidated Omnibus Budget Reconciliation Act (COBRA) of 1985, most workers' medical, optical, or dental insurance is not automatically eliminated on termination of employment. The workers can choose to continue the coverage at the em-

ployer's group rate, if they are willing to pay the premiums (and a 2 percent administrative fee).

5. A. Before filing a lawsuit, the best step for a person who believes that he or she may be a victim of discrimination is to contact a state or federal agency to see whether their claim is justified. The appropriate federal agency is the Equal Employment Opportunity Commission. Most states have similar agencies that evaluate claims under state law.

6. A. Sexual harassment occurs when, in a workplace, an employee is subject to comments or contact that is perceived as sexually offensive. An employer may be liable even though an employee did the harassing. If the employee was in a supervisory position, as in this problem, for an employer to be held liable, a tangible employment action may need to be proved. Here, the employee's pay was cut.

7. C. An employer who is subject to the Americans with Disabilities Act cannot exclude arbitrarily a person who, with reasonable accommodation, could do what is required of a job. A disabled individual is not required to reasonably accommodate an employer. Also, the standard is not "significant additional costs," to either the employer or the disabled individual.

8. C. Title VII prohibits showing a preference for members of one minority over members of another. Title VII also prohibits making distinctions according to the race of a person's spouse, friends, or other contacts. The other laws mentioned in the answer choices prohibit discrimination on the basis of age and disability, respectively, as suggested by their titles.

9. A. The Age Discrimination in Employment Act (ADEA) of 1967 requires, for the establishment of a *prima facie* case, that at the time of the alleged discrimination, the plaintiff was forty or older, was qualified for the job, and was discharged or otherwise rejected in circumstances that imply discrimination. The difference between a *prima facie* case under the ADEA and under Title VII is that the ADEA does not require a plaintiff to show that someone who is not a member of a protected class filled the position at the center of the claim.

10. C. The employer's best defense in this problem would be that being able to pass the tests is a business necessity—it is a necessary requirement for the job. Discrimination may be illegal even if it is not intentional, and whether or not all men pass the tests is not relevant to whether there is discrimination against women. If the employer hires some women for the job, it could not argue successfully that gender is a BFOQ for the job.

Issue Spotters

1. Yes. Some courts have held that an implied employment contract exists between employer and employee under an employee handbook that states employees will be dismissed only for good cause. An employer who fires a worker contrary to this promise can be held liable for breach of contract.

2. No. Generally, the right to recover under workers' compensation laws is determined without regard to negligence or fault. Unlike the potential for recovery in a lawsuit based on negligence or fault, however, recovery under a workers' compensation statute is limited to the specific amount designated in the statute for the employee's injury.

3. Yes, if she can show that she was not hired solely because of her disability. The other elements for a discrimination suit based on a disability are that the plaintiff (1) has a disability and (2) is otherwise qualified for the job. Both of these elements appear to be satisfied in this problem.

Chapter 19

True-False Questions

1. F. In a sole proprietorship, the owner and the business are the same. The owner receives all of the profits, and the income of the business is taxed as the owner's personal income. If the owner dies, the business is automatically dissolved.

2. T

3. F. General partners are subject to personal liability for the debts and obligations of a partnership. This is true whether or not they have participated in its management. On the firm's dissolution, its creditors (partners and non-partners) have the highest priority in the distribution of the firm's assets. If those assets are not sufficient to pay the creditors, the general partners are liable for the difference.

4. F. State law applies. Like the formation of a corporation and other forms of limited liability organizations, the formation of a limited liability company (LLC) requires that articles of organization be filed in the state of formation. Otherwise, an LLC will not be held to exist, and its members will not enjoy the features that they wanted.

5. F. One of the chief advantages of a limited liability company (LLC) is that it offers the limited liability of a corporation. Because an LLC also offers the tax advantages of a partnership, many businesses are using this form of organization.

6. F. A feature that makes a limited liability partnership attractive is that its partners can avoid liability for any partnership obligation, whether in contract, tort, or otherwise. Of course, each partner is liable for his or her own wrongful acts.

7. F. The liability of the *limited* partners in a limited partnership is limited to the amount of their investment in the firm, but the liability of the *general* partners is the same as that of the partners in a general partnership (unlimited).

8. F. The members of a joint venture may be sued individually, but the joint venture cannot be sued as an entity.

9. T

10. F. A franchisor can exercise greater control in this area, because the *franchisor* has a legitimate interest in maintaining the quality of the product or service to protect its name and reputation.

Fill-in Questions

members; limited liability company; limited partners; limited partnership

Multiple-Choice Questions

1. D. There are no limits on the liability of the owner of a sole proprietorship for the debts and obligations of the firm. A sole proprietorship has greater organizational flexibility, however, than other forms of business organization.

2. A. This arrangement for the payment of an employee (a base wage and a sales commission) does not make the employee a partner in the employer's business. There are three attributes of a partnership: sharing profits, joint ownership of a business, and an equal right in the management of the business. None of these are present here.

3. C. Ordinarily, limited partners are liable for the debts of their limited partnerships only to the extent of their capital contributions to the firms. A general partner, in contrast, may be held personally liable for the full amount of the firm's obligations.

4. B. A limited liability company (LLC) can be taxed as a partnership, a sole proprietorship (if there is only one member), or a corporation, but electing to be taxed as a partnership is often preferable. The income can be passed through to its members without being taxed at the company level. Generally, there is no particular advantage to being taxed as a corporation. In fact, avoiding the double corporate tax is one reason for forming an LLC.

5. C. One of the advantages of the limited liability company (LLC) form of business organization is that its members are not personally liable for the debts of their firm regardless of the extent of their participation in management (unlike a limited partnership). In fact, unless agreed otherwise, an LLC's management will be considered to include all members. Another advantage is that there is generally no limit on the number of members that a firm can have.

6. C. Professionals, and others, who organize as a limited liability partnership can avoid personal liability for the wrongdoing of other partners. In that circumstance, they may have only the same liability as a limited partner in a limited partnership.

7. B. A joint venture is similar to a partnership, and is generally subject to partnership law, but unlike a partnership, a joint venture is created in contemplation of a limited activity.

8. B. Antitrust laws are most likely to be violated if the franchisor requires the franchisee to purchase exclusively from the franchisor. A franchisor's setting of prices at which products may be sold may also violate antitrust laws.

9. A. In this type of franchise, a franchisor typically requires a franchisee to pay it a fee for the right to sell its products. The franchisor also usually requires that the franchisee pay the franchisor a percentage of the receipts from the sales of the products.

10. C. Franchise agreements typically provide that the franchisor can terminate a franchise for cause. If no set time for termination is provided, a reasonable time will be implied. A franchisor cannot usually terminate a franchise without notice.

Issue Spotters

1. When a business is relatively small and is not diversified, employs relatively few people, has modest profits, and is not likely to expand significantly or require extensive financing in the immediate future, the most appropriate form for doing business may be a sole proprietorship.

2. Although there are differences, all of these forms of business organizations resemble corporations. A joint stock company, for example, features ownership by shares of stock, management by directors and officers, and perpetual existence. A business trust, like a corporation, distributes profits to persons who are not personally responsible for the debts of the organization, and management of the business is in the hands of trustees, just as the management of a corporation is in the hands of directors and officers. An incorporated cooperative, which is subject to state laws covering nonprofit corporations, distributes profits to its owners.

3. Too much control may result in the franchisor's liability for torts of a franchisee's employees. For example, if the employee performs in a manner that is attributed to the control of the franchisor, and this performance results in an injury to another, the franchisor may be held liable.

Chapter 20

True-False Questions

1. T

2. F. A corporation formed in a country other than the United States, but that does business in the United States, is an alien corporation. A foreign corporation is a corporation formed in one state, but doing business in another state.

3. F. Each state has its own body of corporate law, and these laws are not identical. Most states have adopted, at least in part or at least in principle, the Model Business Corporation Act or its revision, the Revised Model Business Corporation Act. There is still variation among the states, however, some of which do not follow either act.

4. F. Any damages recovered in a shareholder's derivative suit are normally paid to the corporation on whose behalf the shareholder or shareholders exercised the derivative right.

5. T

6. F. Officers and directors owe the same fiduciary duties to the corporations for which they work. They both owe a duty of loyalty. This duty requires them to subordinate their personal interests to the welfare of the corporation.

7. F. The business judgment rule immunizes directors (and officers) from liability for poor business decisions and other honest mistakes that cause a corporation to suffer a loss. Directors are not immunized from losses that do not fit this category, however.

8. T

9. F. Dissolution can occur by this means, but there are many other ways to bring about the dissolution of a corporation. Also, liquidation, which is the other step in the termination of a corporation, can be performed without court supervision.

10. T

Fill-in Questions

but ownership is not; can; recorded as the owner in the corporation's books

Multiple-Choice Questions

1. D. State incorporation laws vary, so looking for the state that offers the most favorable provisions for a particular firm is important. There are some principles that states commonly observe, however. For example, in all states a firm can have perpetual existence, but cannot do business under the same, or even a similar, name as an existing firm.

2. D. Implied powers attach when a corporation is created. These powers include the power to borrow money, to lend money, to extend credit, and to make charitable contributions. The other powers listed here are typically expressed in state statutes.

3. A. Corporate directors manage the business of a corporation. The directors normally employ officers, who oversee the daily operations. The directors may be initially designated by the incorporators or promoters, but are later elected by the shareholders (the owners of the corporation).

4. A. Directors must exercise care in their duties. For example, they are expected to use a reasonable amount of supervision over corporate officers and employees when they delegate work. Their liability for breach of this duty could be grounded in negligence or mismanagement of corporate personnel. They are also expected to be loyal: faithful to their obligations and duties.

5. A. A shareholder's derivative suit is a claim filed on behalf of the corporation. Such a suit may allege, for example, that officers or directors misused corporate assets. Of course, any damages that are awarded must be paid to the corporation. Preemptive rights, rights of first refusal, and proxies relate to the sale, purchase, and voting of shares of stock.

6. B. Unless a state statute provides to the contrary, a quorum of directors must be present to conduct corporate business, such as the declaration of a dividend. A quorum is a majority of the number of directors authorized in the firm's articles or bylaws. The rule is one vote per director.

7. A. The board of directors hires the company's officers and other managerial employees, and determines their compensation. Ultimate responsibility for all policy decisions necessary to the management of corporate affairs also rests with the directors.

8. A. In either a merger or consolidation, the surviving corporation acquires all of the assets and assumes all of the debts of its predecessors (the corporations that formed it).

9. D. A corporation's failure to comply with administrative requirements could also result in a court-ordered dissolution. Filing an annual report is an administrative requirement. Dissolution may be ordered if a corporation fails to commence business operations after forming. Other reasons include obtaining a corporate charter through fraud and abuse of corporate powers. Failure to declare a dividend and failure to earn a profit are not grounds for which a court would order a dissolution, if the directors are otherwise complying with their fiduciary duties

10. C. In a merger, the surviving corporation assumes all of the debts and liabilities of the disappearing corporation. Of course, the surviving corporation also inherits all of the disappearing corporation's rights. These rights and liabilities include those arising from litigation. (When one firm "absorbs" another, the firm doing the "absorbing" will be the survivor.)

Issue Spotters

1. Under these circumstances, a minority shareholder can petition a court to appoint and receiver and liquidate the assets of the corporation.

2. Yes. A shareholder can bring a derivative suit on behalf of a corporation, if some wrong is done to the corporation. Normally, any damages recovered go into the corporate treasury.

3. Yes. A single shareholder—or a few shareholders acting together—who owns enough stock to exercise *de facto* control over a corporation owes the corporation and minority shareholders a fiduciary duty when transferring those shares.

Chapter 21

True-False Questions

1. T
2. T
3. T
4. T
5. F. Rule 506, issued under the Securities Act of 1933, provides an exemption for these offerings, if certain other requirements are met. This is an important exemption, applying to private offerings to a limited number of sophisticated investors.
6. T
7. T
8. F. *Scienter* is not a requirement for liability under Section 16(b) of the Securities Exchange Act of 1934, but it is required for liability under Section 10(b) and under Rule 10b-5.
9. F. Anyone who receives inside information as a result of an insider's breach of his or her fiduciary duty can be liable under Rule 10b-5, which applies in virtually all cases involving the trading of securities. The key to liability is whether the otherwise undisclosed information is *material*.
10. F. Most securities can be resold without registration. Also, under Rule 144 and 144A ("Safe harbor" provisions), there are specific exemptions for securities that might otherwise require registration with the SEC.

Fill-in Questions

prosecution; triple; ten; may

Multiple-Choice Questions

1. A. This purchase and sale is a violation of Section 16(b) of the Securities Exchange Act of 1934. When a purchase and sale is within a six-month period, as in this problem, the corporation can recover all of the profit. Proof of *scienter* is not required.
2. D. Under the Securities Act of 1933, a security exists when a person invests in a common enterprise with the reasonable expectation of profits derived primarily or substantially from the managerial or entrepreneurial efforts of others (not from the investor's own efforts).
3. A. Because of the low amount of the issue, it qualifies as an exemption from registration under Rule 504. No specific disclosure document is required, and there is no prohibition on solicitation. If the amount had been higher than $1 million but lower than $5

million, this offer might have qualified for an exemption under Regulation A, which requires notice to the SEC and an offering circular for investors.

4. D. The amount of this offering is too high to exempt it from the registration requirements except possibly under Rule 506 or Section 4(6). This issuer advertised the offering, however, and Rule 506 prohibits general solicitation. Thus, without filing a registration statement, the issuer could not legally solicit *any* investors (whatever it may have believed about the unaccredited investors). This offering does not qualify under Section 4(6), because unaccredited investors participated.

5. A. A corporate officer is a traditional inside trader. The outsider in this problem is a tippee who is liable because the tippee knew of the officer's misconduct. Liability here is based on the fact that the information was not public. Liability might be avoided if those who know the information wait for a reasonable time after its public disclosure before trading their stock.

6. D. The chief problem with this offering is that the issuer advertised it. Under Rule 506, private offerings in unlimited amounts may qualify for an exemption from registration, but no general solicitation is permitted without registration. Even if this issuer complied with all other SEC requirements, however, it should have given the required information to *all* investors, not only the unaccredited investors. (This offering does not qualify under Section 4(6), because unaccredited investors participated.)

7. D. This issue might qualify under Rule 505 or Section 4(6), except that again, the issuer advertised the offering, which it cannot do and remain exempt from registration. In other words, the amount of this offering disqualified the issuer from advertising it without filing a registration statement.

8. B. A registration statement must supply enough information so that an unsophisticated investor can evaluate the financial risk involved. The statement must explain how the registrant intends to use the proceeds from the sale of the issue. Also, besides the description of management, there must be a disclosure of any of their material transactions with the firm. A certified financial statement must be included.

9. A. Of course, the offering must be registered with the SEC before it can be sold, and this requires a registration statement. Investors must be given a prospectus that describes the security, the issuing corporation, and the risk of the security. A tombstone ad tells an investor how and where to obtain the prospectus.

10. A. Most resales are exempt from registration if they are undertaken by persons other than issuers or underwriters. Resales of restricted securities acquired under Rule 504a, Rule 505, Rule 506, or Section 4(6) may trigger registration requirements, but the original sale in this problem came under Rule 504.

Issue Spotters

1. The average investor is not concerned with minor inaccuracies but with facts that if disclosed would tend to deter or encourage him or her to buy or sell the securities. This would include facts that have an important bearing on the condition of the issuer and its business (liabilities, loans to officers and directors, customer delinquencies, and pending lawsuits).

2. No. The Securities Exchange Act of 1934 extends liability to officers and directors in their personal transactions for taking advantage of inside information when they know it is unavailable to the persons with whom they are dealing.

3. Yes. All states have their own corporate securities laws ("blue sky" laws).

Chapter 22

True-False Questions

1. F. This is a vertical restraint.

2. F. This is a horizontal restraint.

3. T

4. F. Exclusive dealing contracts are those under which a seller forbids a buyer from purchasing products from the seller's competitors.

5. F. Price discrimination occurs when sellers charge competitive buyers different prices for identical goods.

6. F. This is a *vertical* merger. A horizontal merger is a merger between firms that compete with each other in the same market.

7. F. This is a *horizontal* merger. A vertical merger occurs when a company at one stage of production acquires another company at a higher or lower stage in the chain of production and distribution.

8. T

9. T

10. T

Fill-in Questions

A restraint of trade; Monopoly power; monopoly power

Multiple-Choice Questions

1. A. An agreement to set prices in the manner described in the problem is a price-fixing agreement, which is a restraint of trade and a *per se* violation of Section 1 of the Sherman Act.

2. C. Conduct that is blatantly anticompetitive is a *per se* violation of antitrust law. Such conduct typically includes price-fixing agreements, group boycotts, and horizontal market divisions.

3. D. Territorial or customer restrictions, like the restriction described in the problem, are judged under a rule of reason. The rule of reason involves a weighing of competitive benefits against anticompetitive harms. Here, the manufacturer's restriction on its dealers would likely be considered lawful because, although it reduces *intra*brand competition, it promotes *inter*brand competition.

4. D. In applying the rule of reason, courts consider the purpose of the conduct, the effect of the conduct on trade, the power of the parties to accomplish what they intend, and in some cases, whether there are less restrictive alternatives to achieve the same goals.

5. C. The elements of the offense of monopolization include monopoly power and its willful acquisition. Market domination that results from legitimate competitive behavior (such as foresight, innovation, skill, and good management) is not a violation.

6. D. Price discrimination occurs when a seller charges different buyers different prices for identical goods. To violate the Clayton Act, among other requirements, the effect of the price discrimination must be to substantially lessen competition or otherwise create a competitive injury.

7. C. Conduct evaluated under the rule of reason is unlawful if its anticompetitive harms outweigh its competitive benefits. Conduct typically subject to a rule of reason analysis includes trade association activities, joint ventures, territorial or customer restrictions, refusals to deal, price discrimination, and exclusive-dealing contracts.

8. B. Similar exemptions from the antitrust laws include cooperative research among small business firms, cooperation among U.S. exporters to compete with comparable foreign associations, and joint efforts by businesspersons to obtain legislative, judicial, or executive action.

9. D. The U.S. Department of Justice can prosecute violations of the Sherman Act as criminal or civil violations, but can enforce the Clayton Act only through civil proceedings. The Federal Trade Commission can also enforce the Clayton Act (and has sole authority to enforce the Federal Trade Commission Act). A private party can sue under the Clayton Act if he or she is injured by a violation of *any* antitrust law.

10. A. An important consideration in determining whether a merger substantially lessens competition and hence violates the Clayton Act is market concentration (the market chares among the firms in the market). If a merger creates an entity with more than a small percentage market share, it is presumed illegal.

Issue Spotters

1. A unilateral refusal to deal violates antitrust law if it involves offenses proscribed under Section 2 of the Sherman Act. This occurs if the firm refusing to deal has, or is likely to acquire, monopoly power and the refusal is likely to have an anticompetitive effect on a particular market.

2. Size alone does not determine whether a firm is a monopoly—size in relation to the market is what matters. A small store in a small, isolated town is a monopolist if it is the only store serving that market. Monopoly involves the power to affect prices and output. If a firm has sufficient market power to control prices and exclude competition, that firm has monopoly power. Monopoly power in itself is not a violation of Section 2 of the Sherman Act. The offense also requires an intent to acquire or maintain that power through anticompetitive means.

3. This agreement is a tying arrangement. The legality of a tying arrangement depends the purpose of the agreement, the agreement's likely effect on competition in the relevant markets (the market for the tying product and the market for the tied product), and other factors. Tying arrangements for commodities are subject to Section 3 of the Clayton Act. Tying arrangements for services can be agreements in restraint of trade in violation of Section 1 of the Sherman Act.

Chapter 23

True-False Questions

1. F. The essence of a gift is that it is a voluntary transfer without consideration. The elements of a gift are donative intent, delivery, and acceptance.

2. F. If an accession is performed in good faith, ownership depends on the change in the value of the property. The greater the increase, the more likely it is that the improver will own the property.

3. T

4. T

5. T

6. T

7. F. Insurance is classified according to the nature of the risk involved.

8. F. An insurance broker is the agent of the applicant. If the broker fails to obtain coverage and the applicant is damaged as a result, the broker is liable for the loss.

9. T

10. T

Fill-in Questions

inter vivos; *causa mortis*; *causa mortis*; *causa mortis*; *inter vivos*

Multiple-Choice Questions

1. B. A right of survivorship, in which a deceased joint tenant's interest passes to the surviving joint tenant, is the distinguishing feature of a joint tenancy. Generally, to acquire or own property as joint tenants, the owners must specify that as the form they want their ownership to take. If these buyers had not specified that form, they would own the property as tenants in common.

2. B. The three elements for an effective gift are donative intent, delivery, and acceptance. Here, the giver had the intent, and the recipient clearly accepted, if delivery was effective, which it was. Delivery of the key to the box was constructive delivery of the earrings. Thus, the gift would have been effective even if the giver had died before the recipient had taken them from the box.

3. C. When goods are commingled, and the goods are lost, the owners bear the loss in the same proportion that they contributed to the whole. This is assuming that they can prove how much they contributed to the whole. Thus, the parties take out the same proportions that they put in.

4. D. A bailee must be given exclusive possession and control of the property and knowingly accept it. Here, there is no delivery of possession. Regarding the other choices, money does not need to be involved for a transaction to be a bailment, a car is personal property, and a signed contract is not necessary for a bailment (the bailment agreement may be oral).

5. B. A common carrier is liable for damage caused by the willful acts of third persons or by an accident when the goods are in the carrier's possession. Thus, the carrier is liable for most of the losses among these answer choices. The other loss is caused by an act of the shipper, however, and thus must be borne by the shipper.

6. C. An insurance company evaluates risk factors based on the information in an insurance application. For this reason, misrepresentation can void a policy, especially if the company can show that it would not have extended insurance if it had known the facts.

7. A. The insurable interest in life insurance must exist at the time the policy is obtained. Under a key-person life insurance policy, it will not matter if the key person is no longer in the business's employ at the time of the loss (the person's death).

8. C. To recover for a loss under a property insurance policy, an insurable interest in the property must exist when the loss occurs. It does not make any difference whether the property is owned in fee simple, or whether it is owned by an individual, or when an insurance policy is issued.

9. C. Property insurance can be canceled for gross negligence that increases the hazard insured against. Other reasons for canceling insurance include nonpayment of premiums, fraud or misrepresentation, and conviction for a crime that, like gross negligence, increases the hazard insured against.

10. B. Liability insurance protects against liability imposed on a company resulting from injuries to the person or property of another. Coverage under a liability policy may also include expenses involved in recalling and replacing a product that has proved to be defective.

Issue Spotters

1. Yes. A bailee's right of possession, even though temporary, permits the bailee to recover damages from any third persons for damage or loss to the property.

2. No. An incorrect statement as to the age of an insured is a misrepresentation. Under an incontestability clause, however, after a policy has been in force for a certain time (usually two or three years), the insurer cannot cancel the policy or avoid a claim on the basis of statements made in the application.

3. No. To obtain insurance, one must have a sufficiently substantial interest in whatever is to be insured. One has an insurable interest in property if one would suffer a pecuniary loss from its destruction. This interest must exist *when the loss occurs*. To obtain insurance on another's life, one must have a reasonable expectation of benefit from the continued life of the other. The benefit may be founded on a relationship, but "ex-spouse" alone is not such a relationship. An interest in someone's life must exist *when the policy is obtained*.

Chapter 24

True-False Questions

1. T

2. F. The owner of a life estate has the same rights as a fee simple owner except that the value of the property must be kept intact for the holder of the future interest.

3. F. An easement merely allows a person to use land without taking anything from it, while a profit allows a person to take something from the land.

4. T

5. F. Under the Fifth Amendment to the U.S. Constitution, when taking private property, the government is required to pay the owner just compensation.

6. T

7. T

8. F. A landlord can sell, give away, or otherwise transfer his or her property without affecting a tenant's obligations under a lease, except that the tenant becomes the tenant of the new owner.

9. F. There are different standards for different pollutants and for different polluters. There are even different standards for the same pollutants and polluters in different locations. The standards cover the amount of emissions, the technology to control them,

the notice that must be given to the public, and the penalties that may be imposed for noncompliance.
10.   T

Fill-in Questions

warranty; special warranty; quitclaim

Multiple-Choice Questions

1.   C. A *profit* is the right to go onto land in possession of another and take away some part of the land itself or some product of the land. In contrast, an easement is a right to make limited use of another person's land without taking anything from the property. A license is a revocable right to come onto another person's land.

2.   D. A warranty deed warrants the most extensive protection against defects of title. A quitclaim deed conveys to the grantee only whatever interest the grantor had in the property. A special warranty deed warrants only that the grantor or seller held good title during his or her ownership of the property (the grantor is not warranting that there were no defects of title when the property was held by previous owners). Each of these deeds can have affect a different result if the title to the property is later disputed.

3.   C. An *easement* is a right to make limited use of another's real property without taking anything from it. In this problem, it is an easement by necessity—the owner needs access to his property. The right to take something from the property is a profit. A revocable right to come onto the property is a license.

4.   C. When a landlord transfers his or her interest in leased property, the tenant becomes the tenant of the new owner. It is to this new owner that the tenant owes rent. Both parties must continue to follow the terms of the lease.

5.   A. A lease that does not specify how long it is to last but does specify that rent is to be paid at certain intervals creates a periodic tenancy. The tenancy is automatically renewed for each rental period unless it has been properly terminated.

6.   A. An environmental impact statement (EIS) must be prepared when a major federal action significantly affects the quality of the environment. An action that affects the quality of the environment is "major" if it involves a substantial commitment of resources and "federal" if a federal agency has the power to control it.

7.   C. Under the 1990 amendments to the Clean Air Act, different standards apply to existing sources and major new sources. Major new sources must use the maximum achievable control technology (MACT) to reduce emissions from the combustion of fossil fuels. Other factories and businesses must reduce emissions of hazardous air pollutants with the best available technology.

8.   B. If new motor vehicles do not meet the emission standards of regulations issued under the Clean Air Act, the EPA can order a recall of the vehicles and a repair or replacement of pollution-control devices. Liability for clean-up costs may arise under CERCLA in the context of a leak at a hazardous waste disposal site.

9.   C. A polluter may be ordered to clean up the pollution or to pay for the clean-up costs, and other penalties may be imposed. For example, fines may be assessed and imprisonment ordered.

10.   B. Under the Resource Conservation and Recovery Act, producers of hazardous waste must properly label and package waste to be transported. Under the Comprehensive Environmental Response, Compensation, and Liability Act, the party who generated the waste disposed of at a site can be held liable for clean up costs.

Issue Spotters

1.   Yes. An owner of a fee simple has the most rights possible—he or she can give the property away, sell it, transfer it by will, use it for almost any purpose, possess it to the exclusion of all the world, or as in this case, transfer possession for any period of time. The party to whom possession is transferred can also transfer his or her interest (usually only with the owner's permission) for any lesser period of time.

2.   This is a breach of the warranty deed's covenant of quiet enjoyment. The buyer can sue the seller and recover the purchase price of the house, plus any damages.

3.   The Comprehensive Environmental Response, Compensation, and Liability Act of 1980 regulates the clean-up of hazardous waste disposal sites. Any potentially responsible party can be charged with the entire cost to clean up a hazardous waste disposal site. Potentially responsible parties include the person who generated the waste (ChemCorp) the person who transported the waste to the site (Central), the person who owned or operated the site at the time of the disposal (Intrastate Disposal), and the current owner or operator of the site (ABC). A party held responsible for the entire cost may be able to recoup some of it in a lawsuit against other potentially responsible parties.

Chapter 25

True-False Questions

1.   F. According to the principle of comity, a nation will give effect to the laws of another nation if those laws are consistent with the law and public policy of the accommodating nation.

2. F. The act of state doctrine tends to immunize foreign nations from the jurisdiction of U.S. courts—that is, foreign nations are often exempt from U.S. jurisdiction under this doctrine.

3. F. As with the act of state doctrine, the doctrine of sovereign immunity tends to immunize foreign nations from the jurisdiction of U.S. courts.

4. F. The Foreign Sovereign Immunities Act sets forth the major exceptions to the immunity of foreign nations to U.S. jurisdiction.

5. T

6. T

7. F. U.S. courts can exercise jurisdiction over a foreign entity under U.S. antitrust laws when a violation has a substantial effect on U.S. commerce or is a *per se* violation of those laws.

8. T

9. T

10. T

Fill-in Questions

An expropriation; A confiscation; an expropriation; a confiscation

Multiple-Choice Questions

1. A. Of course, a U.S. firm is subject to the jurisdiction of a U.S. court. For a U.S. court to hear a case against a foreign entity under U.S. antitrust laws, the entity's alleged violation of the law must have a substantial effect on U.S. commerce (or be a *per se* violation). In other words, foreign and domestic firms may be sued for violations of U.S. antitrust laws.

2. C. The Foreign Corrupt Practices Act (FCPA) prohibits any U.S. firm from bribing foreign officials to influence official acts. Congress enacted the FCPA in 1977.

3. C. Under certain conditions, the doctrine of sovereign immunity prohibits U.S. courts from exercising jurisdiction over foreign nations. Under the Foreign Sovereign Immunities Act, a foreign state is not immune when the action is based on a commercial activity carried on in the United States by the foreign state.

4. A. Under the act of state doctrine, the judicial branch of one country will not examine the validity of public acts committed by a recognized foreign government within its own territory. The awarding of a government contract under the circumstances described in the problem meets this criterion.

5. C. U.S. courts give effect to the judicial decrees of another country under the principle of comity, if those decrees are consistent with the laws and public policies of the United States.

6. B. The Civil Rights Act of 1964, and other U.S. discrimination laws, apply to U.S. firms employing U.S. citizens outside (and inside) the United States. U.S. employers everywhere must abide by U.S. employment discrimination laws, so long as those laws do not violate the laws of the countries in which their workplaces are located. But those laws protect only U.S. citizens, not citizens of foreign countries.

7. A. A choice-of-forum, or forum selection, clause can specify the forum in which the parties to a contract want their disputes to be heard and resolved. Choice-of-language clauses are often used in international contracts to declare an official language for the interpretation of a contract in the event of disagreement. Such a clause may also provide for translations in certain languages. A *force majeure* clause stipulates that acts of God and other events outside the parties' control may excuse liability for nonperformance under the contract. An arbitration clause can require the submission of a dispute to arbitration, according to certain procedures, before a suit is filed in a court.

8. A. A distribution agreement in this context is a contract between a seller and a distributor to distribute the seller's products in the distributor's country. Such an agreement sets out the terms and conditions of the distributorship—price, currency of payment, availability of supplies, method of payment, and so on.

9. C. The U.S. Congress cannot tax exports, but it may establish export quotas. In particular, under the Export Administration Act of 1979, restrictions can be imposed on the export of technologically advanced products.

10. D. Unlike exports, imports can be taxed. A tax on an import is a tariff (generally set as a percent of the value). Imports can also be subject to quotas, which limit how much can be imported.

Issue Spotters

1. Under the principle of comity, a U.S court would defer and give effect to foreign laws and judicial decrees that are consistent with U.S. law and public policy.

2. A U.S. firm (or any domestic firm) can license its formula, product, or process to a foreign concern to avoid its theft. The foreign firm obtains the right to make and market the product according to the formula (or the right to use the process) and agrees to keep the necessary information secret and to pay royalties to the licensor.

3. The practice described in this problem is known as dumping. Seen as an unfair international trade practice, dumping is the sale of imported goods at "less than fair value." Based on the price of those goods in the exporting country, an extra tariff can be imposed on the imports. This is known as an antidumping duty.

Notes

Notes

Notes